MW00354921

A BOOK OF WONDERS

Marvels, Mysteries, Myth & Magic

A BOOK
of
WONDERS

MARVELS, MYSTERIES, MYTH & MAGIC:

Wherein the brief history of
the modern world
is narrated
by

Dr. Kevin Dann

FORTUNATUS

SAN RAFAEL, CALIFORNIA

First published in the USA
by Fortunatus Press,
© Kevin Dann 2008

All rights reserved

No part of this book may be reproduced
or transmitted, in any form or by
any means, without permission

For information, address:
LogoSophia, P.O. Box 151011
San Rafael CA 94915
logosophia.com

Printed in the
United States of America

Library of Congress Cataloging-in-Publication Data

Dann, Kevin T., 1956–
A book of wonders: marvels, mysteries, myth & magic:
wherein the brief history of the modern world is narrated
by Kevin Dann.—1st American pbk. ed.
p. cm.
Includes bibliographical references.
ISBN 978-1-59731-165-6 (pbk. : alk. paper)
1. Occultism. 2. History—Miscellanea. 3. Magic. I. Title.
BF1439.D36 2008
909—dc22
2008038957

Cover design by W. David Powell
Cover image, "Universum," from Camille Flammarion's
L'atmosphère: météorologie populaire (Paris, 1888),
colored by Hugo Heikenwaelder, 1998
Crop Circle photo (p 209), courtesy of Frank Laumen
'World on a String' (p 5), courtesy of Ashley Arruda

CONTENTS

Study generates knowledge;

Knowledge bears love;

love likeness;

likeness communion;

communion virtue;

virtue dignity;

dignity power;

and power performs the miracle.

— Johannes Trithemius

Preface

Pakwanonzian!
"You look brand new to me!"

THIS IS THE GREETING (in the language of the *Wonbanakiak*, or "Abenaki," the people who lived in the region that now encompasses Vermont, New Hampshire, and southern Quebec) that I have taught to my Modern Global History students for the last three years, and which they have echoed back to me, at first with reserve and embarrassment, but slowly, as we have settled in to know each other better, with heartfelt enthusiasm. "Enthusiasm"—literally, "to be filled with god"—is not what I expect you are feeling right now. Freshman or senior; psych major or nursing student; whether you took the high school 'global' course or not, you are absolutely *dreading* this class. History is dull. History teachers are dreadfully boring. (My high school history teacher, Mr. Henry Van Dyke, surely was! After two years with him, I made sure that I didn't have to take a single history class in college).

And history textbooks… well, have you heard anyone—besides a history teacher—say that they actually *liked* their textbook?

I wrote this textbook for *you*, with the help of over 500 PSU (that's Plattsburgh State University for anyone else who is reading this) students who have been brave and generous enough to allow me to go "outside the box" with my teaching of this course. In fairy tales, all good things seem to come in threes, and so it seemed that after three years of asking my students to produce a "Book of Wonders," it was time to create my own. Wonder is our original gesture when we come into the world; it's true! Go visit a maternity ward, and observe the newborns.

I know that you are far from newborn. Indeed, I have been stunned and humbled by how much of life—with all of its tragedies as well as triumphs—my students have experienced when I meet them. I know that one of you reading this book right now has recently gone through a tragic loss, and that you will likely sit through 14 weeks of my class, without ever telling me anything about it.

Most of you will in these next 14 weeks hit a rough patch. You will have a blowout fight with your girlfriend or boyfriend. You will get *really* sick even though you tried your best to avoid your roommate when she first caught that nasty crud. You will get news from home that a friend has been in a bad accident. One or two of you will drop out of college altogether this semester, after a string of setbacks. But no matter what challenges you may face, your professors think that theirs is the only course you are taking, and demand that you read that chapter before Thursday, or turn in this research paper by Friday.

Why is it that we college professors—particularly history profs—so often forget what you know in your bones, that you will learn the most from studies that interest you? Every semester, dozens of students come up to me and ask about such topics as crystal skulls, the Illuminati, aliens, Champ. They do not come to me during my office hours to discuss the Enlightenment; the Thirty Years War; or even the hot topic that makes us world history teachers hip and relevant—globalization. Year after year, they bring me DVDs and books and URL addresses that point in a very different direction from their textbook—*V for Vendetta*; *The DaVinci Code*; *The Matrix*; *Pan's Labyrinth*; Neil Gaiman's *Sandman* and *The Books of Magic* graphic novels; Philip Pullman's *His Dark Materials* trilogy. What do all these stories have in common? MYSTERY. We all love a mystery, and we all love the chance to solve one. Yet when we study history, do we ever get to feel as curious, as impatient to know whodunit and how and why, as we do when we sit in the dark with a hundred strangers at the movie theater?

I rarely go to the movies—perhaps once or twice a year. I have not had a television for over 15 years. This means that when you come to me to recommend the latest film that has a historical dimension—*300* or *Apocalypto* or the new Indiana Jones adventure—I will likely just watch the trailer, and read a few reviews, and then annoyingly point out the historical errors in the film.[1] In fact, it was the prospect of a forthcoming film that finally inspired me to write this book. On Friday, May 10, 2008—the last day of classes here at PSU—I was sitting in my car listening to the radio, on the ferry from Vermont over to New York. It was a spectacular spring day, the Adirondacks wearing their newly emerging chartreuse leaves, and the buildings of Clinton Community College framed against Lyon Mountain, which still sported a streak of snow down its granite side. The sun sparkling off the lake turned the whole scene into the Villa Balbaniello on Lake Como in northern Italy…and this made a perfect circle, since the Villa Balbaniello was where scenes in the second *Star Wars* movie, *Return of the Clones*, was filmed. I was dreaming about how wonderful it would be to be there on Lake Como, when I heard from the radio:

"You're a teacher?"

"Part time," coolly replied Harrison Ford, *aka* Indiana Jones. I could see it coming: this fall, when we reached the section of the course on the Cold War, I would have to compete for your attention with the stars of *Indiana Jones and the Kingdom of the Crystal Skull* —Ford's Indiana Jones and Cate Blanchett's Irma Spalko—and tens of millions of dollars worth of special effects. *Star Wars* creator George Lucas had been the one fascinated by the crystal skulls—just as he had been by the Ark of the Covenant, and the Holy Grail. Along with all the other folklore—that aliens, Atlanteans, or dwarf men from a Hollow Earth had created the skulls—Lucas had heard that Joseph Stalin had been interested in the skulls, just as Adolf Hitler had reputedly pursued the Holy Grail in his unholy quest for world domination.

1. Please don't let this stop you from suggesting things, and by all means talk about these films in class! I count on you to keep me informed about pop culture. My bookshelves have graphic novels and CDs that I would never have known about if students had not brought them to my attention. You might be wondering why I put this in a footnote…I did so because I wanted to find out if you would follow me here. A common mistake of college history professors is to assume that their students read footnotes. I assume that you don't—so this book will have very few footnotes. If you *are* reading this, you get a gold doubloon!

For the past two semesters, my students had come to me asking whether I knew anything about the "crystal skulls," and if I believed in their "powers." A glance at the Wiki entry for "crystal skull" quickly eliminated any ancient provenience for the artifacts, and also suggested how my students had come to know about the skulls, long before the release of the new Indiana Jones movie. In 1980 the skulls had been the stars of *Zork I: The Underground Empire*, an interactive fiction computer game. Since then, crystal skulls had been featured in *The Phantom* comic strip; the *Stargate SG-1* and other TV series; an assortment of role-playing games; webcomics; collectible card games; video games. In 2001, Tokyo Disney Sea theme park opened its attraction, "Indiana Jones Adventure: Temple of the Crystal Skull." There is a Seattle pop band called "Crystal Skulls." By the time you read this, likely there will be a breakfast cereal; a new Saturday morning cartoon show; and an anthropological museum which offers groups of children the chance to spend the night in the South American wing, next to the display case of crystal skulls.

Most history teachers will rightly understand all this as an opportunity to explore the *real* history behind the original artifacts. *Indiana Jones and the Kingdom of the Crystal Skull* will provide opportunities for studying Edwardian era exoticism, archaeological huckstering, and the surprising credulity of scientific institutions. Your English professor may take up a discussion of the symbolic dimension of the human skull throughout world myth and literature. Believe it or not, the cool thing that history and English literature (and sociology, psychology, and a host of other disciplines) can do is to speak intelligently about the places, people, and events that Hollywood puts up on the screen.

That Indiana Jones flick? Your profs know that this slick, manipulative, audience-driven vehicle to make millions of dollars for its investors is also a rich invitation to study the *real* history behind the original crystal skulls. They can help you to find out where the actual ones are; where they were discovered; and even how they came to inspire that first *Zork* computer game back in 1980, long before George Lucas and Steven Spielberg took an interest. While your younger brothers and sisters can collect the Indy Jones action figures or beg for the video game version, you can take a journey to Paris in 1880 to visit the curio shop of Monsieur Eugène Boban; to Macchu Pichu with Yale University archaeologist Hiram Bingham; to Yale itself in 1957, and discover tales even odder than Hollywood told. That barbershop on Elm Street in the film's version of New Haven was just a freeze-dried façade. As a historian, you can go have a conversation with the barber and his regular customers, and find out why they were wearing their hair that way in 1957. Not exotic enough? Then off we go to the Andes, to look for stories about Hiram Bingham among contemporary Peruvians, stories passed down from the workers he hired to slash away the jungle from the crumbling ruins, and to cart out the ancient artifacts that have lain in Yale's Peabody Museum for nearly a century, and which now the Peruvian government is demanding be returned.

These are all fascinating topics, and though they will undoubtedly bring an entirely new dimension to your appreciation of last summer's blockbuster movie, I am greedy for something more...

A Word About the Title of this Book

In Europe during the Middle Ages, the most learned philosopher and the humblest peasant alike engaged in heated discussion and spectacular speculation on the subject of "Wonders." The sports of Nature—Unicorns, Sea Serpents, Dragons, and Odd Things Falling From the Sky; Signs in the Heavens; Human Prodigies; Dark Days; Auroras & Comets; the deep mysteries of Earth & Heaven—all drew forth peoples' astonishment and earnest questions. Are there not Wonders—and Mysteries, Myths, Marvels, and Magic—in our age as well? *Of course there are!* But we moderns tend not to be aware of them, and when they make headlines, we tend to dismiss them as fakes or hallucinations. (See Chapter 10's discussion of crop circles.)

The subtitle's claim to "A Brief History of the Modern World" pays homage to both medieval and modern "universal histories," which, no matter how ambitious, hardly lived up to their name. Whether composed in the 9th century or the 19th, these histories were bounded by gaps in geographical coverage and by the ethnocentrism of their authors. My "Brief History" will abound with blind spots too, but I believe my history *is* universal in that it follows a narrative thread that, though circumscribed in terms of the characters and events it describes, has implications for every person on earth, both now and in the future. It is a distinctly "Eurocentric" tale, because these past five centuries have been most dramatically shaped by European ideas and impulses. More importantly, there has been at work over this half millennium a distinct rhythm of world destiny that made this peninsular continent so prominent in world affairs. It was not always—and shall not always—be so, but *it is so now.*

As I write this, American presidential candidate Barack Obama has just returned from a European tour that garnered the attention—and approval—of the world expressly because of his commitment to global concerns. Coming as it does after eight years of bullying, unilateral United States foreign policy, Obama's message of nations working together is a welcome change. But the world is still in many ways on a hair trigger; two days ago, journalist Seymour Hersh spoke publicly about his discovery (from very reliable sources inside the Bush administration) that Vice-President Dick Cheney convened advisers at the White House to discuss how to provoke war with Iran.

In just two days, the Olympic Games are to begin in Beijing. Founded in 1894 by a French aristocrat and historian who, after the French defeat in the Franco-Prussian War, sought a way to bring nations together, the modern Olympic Games are perhaps the most widely recognized symbol of international cooperation, despite the persistent episodes of contentious politics associated with the Games. Almost as soon as the Beijing Games' slogan—"One World, One Dream"—was unveiled, its call for unity was shattered: the Olympic torch relay was met throughout its route by people protesting China's human rights record; recent violence in Tibet; China's role in the war in Darfur; its support of repressive regimes in Myanmar and Zimbabwe; and the political status of Taiwan. In the weeks leading up to the opening of the Games, two buses were bombed in the city of Kumming in southwestern China, and a Muslim Uighur independence group killed 16 police officers in an attack in the western city of Kashgar.

At no moment in my lifetime—nor in any previous lifetime—has the illustration below seemed a more accurate picture of humanity's situation. A former student of mine, Ashley Arruda, drew this as the cover for her Book of Wonders assignment a couple of years ago. Ashley's drawing suggests that each and every one of us is the hand holding that thread; the story inside this book suggests the same. That is why we must know the *real* story of these past 500 years. It is *our* world, *our* history. Let us approach it with wonder…

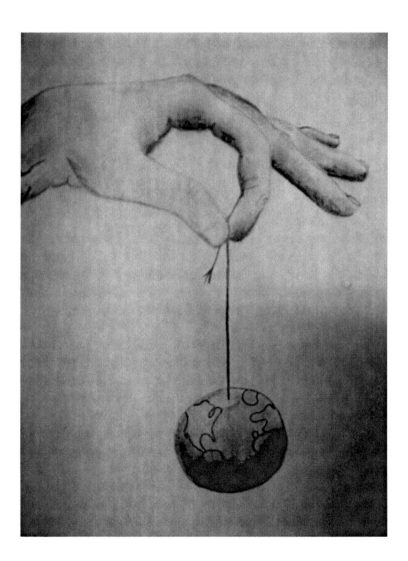

1: A Question of the Grail

Hear, then, what manner of tale this is, telling of things both pleasant and sad, with joy and trouble for company. Grant there were three of me, each with skill to match mine, there would still be need of unbridled inspiration to tell you what, single-handed, I have a mind to tell...As yet he is unborn to this story whom I have chosen for the part, the man of whom this tale is told and all the marvels in it.

—Prelude to Wolfram von Eschenbach's *Parzival*

Prelude: Following the Fire

On the morning of January 1, 2000, as the first rays of the rising sun struck the white sands on one of the central Pacific nation of Kirbati's 32 coral islands, a conch shell sounded, and then an old man began to paddle out into the sea. Standing in the prow of the big canoe stood a young boy, holding a torch that symbolized the journey westwards across the earth of the new millennium's first day. A crowd of local people gathered on the beach to sing and dance their hearts out while others beat furiously on great box drums.

Nearly twenty-four hours later, across the International Date Line in Tonga, the 81-year-old King Tafa'ahau Tupou IV led his people in prayer before a choir sang Handel's *Messiah*. During those 24 hours, a wave of celebration swept with the sun across the globe. In New Zealand, the new millennium's first baby—a boy—was born at one minute past midnight. In Australia, more than 20 tons of fireworks were exploded above Sydney harbor while the word "ETERNITY"—immortalized locally by a reformed thief who had for 40 years written the word in yellow chalk on Sydney sidewalks—lit up the side of Sydney Harbor Bridge. In Japan, Shinto monks rang temple bells to ward off evil spirits. In China, the country that gave the world fireworks, an immense display vied with Sydney's to be recognized as the world's largest. Across a stretch of the Great Wall, ten thousand Chinese men and women held torches outlining the shape of a dragon, the auspicious symbol of Chinese civilization. When the New Year's bell struck, 2,000 newly married Chinese couples embraced their spouses. In India, scores of people recited the *Gayatri* mantra while the sun rose over the Ganges. In Moscow, enormous crowds gathered in Red Square to drink champagne and vodka in the shadow of St. Basil's Cathedral, the emblem of Russian culture. In Jerusalem, Bethlehem, and Nazareth, Christian pilgrims gathered in prayer at the sites where their faith's story had begun. For Muslims and Jews, whose lunar calendars gave a different advent of the new year and millennium, celebrations were understated—or banned; Jerusalem's rabbis forbade hotels from throwing New Year's Eve parties, and Saudi Arabia's Sheik Abdullah bin Jabrain declared that "Celebrating the holidays of the infidels, even out of courtesy, is forbidden."

In London, astride the Greenwich meridian, the Archbishop of Canterbury led prayers and the Queen sang "Auld Lang Syne" with Prime Minister Tony Blair. Facing the New Year, century, and millennium, President Bill Clinton chose to speak of global interconnectedness: "It's clear that our fate in America increasingly will be tied to the fate of other nations and other people around the world."

America's City of Angels was the last metropolitan area to experience and celebrate the arrival of the new millennium, and by the time that Los Angeles mayor Richard Riordan and comedian Jay Leno had thrown the switch to light up the iconic "Hollywood" sign, it was clear that the world had escaped the digital doomsday that had been widely predicted—the millennium computer bug, or "Y2K." On the first day of the new millennium, the world looked very much the same as it had on the last day of the old millennium. Over the next week, Israel and Syria would hold inconclusive peace talks; on the 10th, America Online announced that it would be bought by Time-Warner for $162 billion, the largest corporate merger ever; four days later, the Dow Jones Industrial Average closed at 11,723, marking the peak of the Dot-com bubble. A couple of weeks later, director Michael Moore and the band Rage Against the Machine set up on the steps of Federal Hall on Wall Street, a couple of doors from the New York Stock Exchange, to film the video of "Sleep Now in the Fire." As the shoot was being broken up by police, the band members and about 200 fans rushed the Stock Exchange, making it through the building's first set of doors before Exchange security hit a button to bring down giant titanium bars and close the financial capital of the world at 3:15 PM. "We decided to shoot this video in the belly of the beast," said Moore, "and for a few minutes, Rage Against the Machine was able to shut down American capitalism—an act that I am sure tens of thousands of downsized citizens would cheer."

> *For it's the end of history*
> *It's caged and frozen still*
> *There is no other pill to take*
> *So swallow the one*
> *That made you ill*
> *The Nina The Pinta The Santa Maria*
> *The noose and the rapist*
> *The field's overseer*
> *The agents of orange*
> *The priests of Hiroshima*
> *The cost of my desire*
> *To Sleep now in the fire*

Songs of the Troubadours

As they so often did whenever reporting from Moscow, dozens of western TV news reporters stood in front of St. Basil's Cathedral, the New Year's Eve fireworks bursting in the sky above the onion-dome topped towers. Many mistakenly referred to the building as the Kremlin—the great, fortified complex immediately to the Cathedral's east that includes the Presidential palace. But on the eve of the new millennium, it was not just the slick young western journalists who were oblivious to the Cathedral's history. Few of the Russians reveling in Red Square could have narrated much of the building's history. Gone were the days when on Red Square and in every quarter of Moscow one found the *skomorokhi*, the minstrels whose *byliny*—epic songs loosely connected with actual people or events—told the Russian people the real news. *Byliny* literally translates to "what happened."

Commissioned by Ivan the Terrible in 1555, the church was built to commemorate Ivan's successful military campaign against the Tartar Mongols of the city of Kazan in 1552. Since his victory had come on the feast day of the Intercession of the Virgin, the Tsar chose to name his new church the Cathedral of the Intercession of the Virgin.

The Cathedral was intended to be an architectural representation of the New Jerusalem—the Heavenly Kingdom described in the *Book of Revelation* of St. John the Divine. The eight onion-dome-topped towers surrounded a central, ninth spire, creating an eight-pointed star. For the Christians of Moscow in the 16th century, the number eight symbolized the day of Christ's Resurrection and the promised Heavenly Kingdom that would begin after the Second Coming of Christ. The Cathedral's star-like plan also represented the four corners of the earth, the four Evangelists and the four equal-sided walls of the Heavenly City. At the time when the Cathedral was built, both the Tsar and the peasants were well acquainted with a *bylina* about a Heavenly City, the City of Great Kitezh.

According to the legend, Georgy II, the Grand Prince of Vladimir, founded the town of Little Kitezh on the Volga River in the year 1163. Then the Prince continued along the Volga, fording four rivers before reaching a beautiful spot on the shores of Lake Svetloyar (which means the "radiant shore") where he decided to build the town of Great Kitezh. Prince Georgy then ordered ditches to be dug, a wall to be erected around the city and three stone churches to be built within it, two of which were dedicated to the Assumption and one to the Annunciation of the Virgin. According to the legend, the city was built in the form of a square with a side of one hundred fathoms, but the Prince decided that this was too small, and gave orders to double its length.

The legend also said that in the year 1239, after Batu Khan—Genghis Khan's grandson—invaded Russia with his Mongol army, Prince Georgy gathered his forces to resist the Mongol invaders, but were defeated and pushed back to Little Kitezh on the banks of the Volga. Batu Khan besieged the town, driving the Prince and his remaining forces to Great Kitezh. After storming Little Kitezh and ordering everyone, from the youngest to the oldest, to be killed, Batu Khan continued after the Prince, capturing him in Great Kitezh: "And so the godless one pursued the Prince. And when he came to the city, he fell upon it with his vast horde and took the City of Great Kitezh on the shores of Lake Svetloyar. He killed the good Prince Georgy on the fourth day of the month of February. Then the godless Tartar Batu left that city." The first part of the legend ends with the words: "And they laid waste the realm of Moscow and other monasteries and also the City of Great Kitezh in the year 1248."

Immediately after these words about the destruction of the towns, the legend continues as though Great Kitezh had not been burnt and destroyed by the Mongols, *but had become invisible*: "And Great Kitezh will be invisible until the Second Coming of Christ...And so it will be in future ages: towns and monasteries will become invisible, because the Antichrist will begin to reign in the world."

The Russian legend of the Invisible City of Kitezh, though first written down in the 17th century, had been told generation after generation since the 13th century, and clearly the story was only partly *historical*. Batu Khan did invade Russia in 1239. There was a Prince Georgy, who lived from 1187 to 1238, but he was not as noble as the legend makes him out to be. Still, his courageous battle with the Mongols and his martyr's death in 1238 caused him to be much venerated among the Russian folk. The battle that destroyed Little Kitezh is known to have occurred in 1238, a decade earlier than the legend says. But the real problem is with "Great Kitezh": although the Lake Svetloyar mentioned in the legend indeed exists to this day, there are no traces of a stone-built city with three churches, nor a ditch and walls—not even a single trace of any settlement on the shores or nearby. The legend's precise measurements clearly speak of a town that actually never existed physically anywhere in Russia.

When the legend says that the City of Great Kitezh "became invisible," "protected by the hand of God" and "guarded by the Virgin," it is clear that it is not a physical, earthly city, but a *supersensible* one. The legend's "Great Kitezh"—indestructible and inaccessible to all outward foes—is an ideal spiritual archetype of a future condition of the Russian people. In fact, the legend is more about the *future* than the past. The second part of the legend begins: "The story of the hidden City of Kitezh and the quest for it. Whosoever promises to walk this path truly and without falsehood and zealously begins to fast and sheds many tears as he embarks upon it, whosoever promises rather to die of hunger than to abandon it and to endure many other sorrows and even death itself, may be assured that God will save him, that his every step will be known to and inscribed by his Angel." There follow scenes from the 12th chapter of the Book of Revelation, where John speaks of the cunning serpent who will pursue the woman who is to give birth to the Holy Child. According to the legend of Kitezh, this serpent is even now pursuing every human soul that strives to give birth within itself to the higher human being and to follow not the "broad path" of destruction but the "narrow path" which leads to the invisible City.

In 1555, the people of Moscow knew plenty about the broad path of destruction, not just from the blood-curdling stories of the murderous deeds of the Mongol hordes, but from their own bloody tyrant—Ivan IV, whom they christened *Ivan Grozny*—"Ivan the Dread." Today we know him as Ivan the Terrible, and terrible he was. From earliest childhood, Ivan delighted in humiliating people and torturing animals. At thirteen he ordered a rival prince to be torn to pieces by hunting dogs. At sixteen, he proclaimed himself sole ruler and claimed the title of *Tsar*—from the Roman word *Caesar*. In Ivan's view, Moscow was the "third Rome," and he was God's representative on earth, the successor of Caesar Augustus.

After his victory over the Mongols at Kazan in 1552, Ivan began to systematically annihilate Moscow's aristocracy. In 1565, he established the *Oprichnina*, his personal guard that was soon transformed into a totalitarian terrorist organization whose members were required to swear an oath of blind obedience to the Tsar's will. Initially numbering one thousand, they grew to over ten thousand. Dressed in black, the head of a dog attached to their saddles, the *Oprichnina* methods of mass murder, robbery, and torture were seen by the Russian people as a continuation of the terror that they had experienced for over two centuries at the hands of the Mongol hordes.

Muscovites also had in their midst an example of one who was on the narrow path—St. Vasily (Basil), the man whose name became associated with the Cathedral of the Intercession of the Virgin. After spending his youth apprenticed to a shoemaker, Basil at age 16 dedicated himself to a life of asceticism, going about Moscow barefoot and naked. He talked to people in the street and in taverns, using the language of allegory and signs to influence the righteous and the unrighteous. Passing places of great debauchery, Basil would embrace the corners of the house and declare: "Angels are standing outside this home and grieving over human sins."

On many occasions, Basil was known to foretell with great precision events that befell both individuals and the wider community. The people of Moscow called him "Basil the Wonderworker," believing that his gifts of clairvoyance had been granted by God as a reward for his righteous service. In 1521, through Basil's prayers before the *Vladimirskaya Theotokos*—the most venerated Orthodox icon, the *Theotokos* (Virgin Mary) being regarded as the holy protectress of Russia—Moscow and all of Russia were saved from invasion by the Crimean Khan, who had already burned the villages on the outskirts of Moscow, but who was then frightened by a vision a great armed legion, and retreated. In 1547, during an audience with the Tsar, Basil three times poured wine out the window, declaring that there was a fire threatening the city of Novgorod. Later news arrived from Novgorod saying that on three occasions, a great sheet of water fell from out of the sky, extinguishing the fire and saving the city.

Called "Basil the Fool for Christ," he spoke the truth to all—even the Tsár—without fear. It was known that on many occasions Basil had rebuked Ivan the Terrible for his mistreatment of innocent subjects, and yet, when Basil died, Ivan himself carried the body to the Cathedral of the Intercession of the Virgin to be buried, and then in 1555, ordered a ninth chapel built above Basil's grave, its spire adding an eccentric but altogether fitting point to the Cathedral's celestial star.

* * *

"What is it? The phantom of a cup that comes and goes?"
"Nay, monk! what phantom?" answered Percivale.
"The cup, the cup itself, from which our Lord Drank at the last sad supper with his own. . . .
But then the times grew to such evil that the holy cup was caught away to Heaven, and disappeared."
                              —Alfred Lord Tennyson, "The Holy Grail" (1885)

The second part of the legend of the City of Great Kitezh concludes with the words: "And nothing shall be added to or taken from what we have promulgated, nor shall anything be altered in any way, not a single full-stop or comma. If, however, someone were to add or change anything, he would –according to the decree of the holy fathers, who knew of these things and have confirmed them—be cursed. If anyone should presume to disbelieve this, he should read the lives of former saints and he will see that there was much along these lines in former times." These stern, admonishing words are strongly reminiscent of the concluding verses of the *Revelation* of St. John (22:18–19):

> For I testify unto every man that heareth the words of the prophecy of this book, If any man shall add unto these things, God shall add unto him the plagues that are written in this book. And if any man shall take away from the words of the book of this prophecy, God shall take away his part out of the book of life, and out of the holy city, and from the things which are written in this book.

There is a great legend from further west that dates to about the same time as the Russian legend of the invisible Kitezh, which also claims to have been given through divine intuition, and which was not to be distorted by any human interpretation. In 1180, just twelve years after the legend says that the building of the City of Great Kitezh was completed, the French poet and *trouvère* (troubadour) Chrétien de Troyes published *Perceval, The Story of the Grail.* Twenty years later another French troubadour, Robert de Boron, added the story that Joseph of Arimathea had used the Grail to catch the last drops of blood from Jesus's body as he hung on the cross, and had brought the Grail to Avalon, where it was guarded until the coming of Perceval. Another twenty years further on, in 1220, the German *Minnesinger* (troubadour) and knight Wolfram von Eschenbach brought the legend to its culmination.

In Wolfram's *Parzival,* the tale begins with the death of his father, a knight. Parzival's mother Herzeloyde takes him to the Soltane Wood, where she raises him in isolation, so that he will not follow his father's vocation. Eventually, however, a group of knights passes through the forest, and Parzival, impressed by their heroic bearing, determines to become a knight himself. He travels to King Arthur's court, proves his worthiness as a warrior by slaying the dread Red Knight, and is invited to join the Knights of the Round Table. Then begins his chivalric quest, centered on *Munsalvaesch,* the Castle of the Grail, which, like the City of Great Kitezh, becomes lost for a time to all mortal eyes, including Parzival's.

> *When indecision's in the heart*
> *The soul is bound to grieve and smart.*
> *For scorned alike and fêted*
> *Is he who bold is rated*
> *But vacillates twixt dark and light*
> *Like magpies in their black and white.*
> *Yet such a one may well be glad,*

For both in him their part have had,
Twixt heaven and hell he's drifting.
The man whose faith is shifting
Is wholly black as darkest night
Inside and out, devoid of light.

What was happening in the mid-13th century that caused the troubadours all over Europe and western Russia to sing songs of a magical kingdom caught away from humanity, with the promise to be regained in the distant future? Wolfram's song of Parzival points in poetic, playful language to a time when humanity was plagued by "indecision." At this time there spread across Europe a great wave of doubt as to the spiritual reality of the transubstantiation of the bread and wine in the ceremony of the Eucharist. This prompted certain esoteric (secret) Christian orders to shape an exoteric (public) tradition that could communicate secrets from the Grail Mysteries, even as these mysteries were in the process of being forgotten. That French *trouvères*, German *Minnesingers*, and Russian *skomorokhi* were all bringing to their audiences tales of "a once and future Kingdom" speaks to a great and growing development in that part of the world. These minstrels—who in a few short centuries would no longer be seen as Holy Fools who told the truest tales, but as trivial, buffoonish entertainers—were spreading abroad stories that would be needed by future generations who would doubt far more than just the reality of the transubstantiation. Foreseeing a time when the real news would be very difficult to hear, these inspired troubadours sang... for *us*.

The mid 13th century was a time of great crisis upon the Earth: around the year 1250, the spiritual world, in order to allow humanity to develop in complete freedom, drew back. This cutting of the cosmic umbilical cord would be marked by the advent of the Renaissance, as the northern Italian mindset would spread like fire across Europe and then the world. Humanity was about to leave its Soltane Wood, say goodbye to Herzeloyde, and say hello to a new consciousness. And in the process, the Grail Castle and the City of Great Kitezh inevitably faded from view. They became "invisible."

When Parzival left his mother, immediately the world began to rush at him with all manner of confusing and dazzling force. So it was for humanity. The cutting of the umbilical cord to the world of God provided an opening for the Beings who are everywhere and always the enemies of God, and they rushed in with their lances pointed straight at the heart of Western Christendom, the bearer of the Grail. These enemies chose as their earthly representative the orphaned Mongol child Temujin, who would become Genghis Khan.

The opening chapter in most contemporary world history textbooks concludes with the story of the Mongol Empire in the 13th and 14th centuries. The popular textbook *Worlds Together, Worlds Apart*, for example, states that:

[In] establishing and extending channels of exchange, the Mongols unwittingly created conduits for the flow of microbes to follow the land trails and sea lanes of human voyagers. These germs devastated societies even more decisively than did the Mongols. They were the real 'murderous hordes' of world history, infecting people from every community, class, and culture they encountered. (*Worlds Together, Worlds Apart*, 2005; 43–44)

How strange this would sound to a student sitting in a Hawkins Hall classroom a century ago! If you had been in a history class at Plattsburgh Normal School in 1909, studying to become a teacher here in the city school system, you would have read about Genghis Khan as the "Scourge of God," or "Mighty Manslayer," and his people, the Mongols, as brutish savages who set the world standard for murderousness. In 1909, it would have been just as common to call Genghis Khan a "Tartar," a corruption of the Chinese term for one of their neighboring nomadic tribes. In Roman mythology, "Tartarus" was the name for the Underworld, and so it was easy for European peoples to take up this Chinese name, since the "Tartars" had been giving Europe hell for centuries!

Like most peoples throughout world history the Mongols are called by the name that *others* had for them. Though the Mongol Empire may have been the largest—and most feared—contiguous empire in world history, covering by the mid-13th century nearly 12 million square miles (22% of the Earth's total land area) and holding sway over a population of over 100 million people, their eventual demise meant that their name for themselves is lost from history. For at least a brief period in the 13th century, the Mongol rulers called themselves the *Altan Orda*—the "Golden Horde." *Altan* proclaimed their sense of themselves as the center of the world, for along with the cardinal directions—black designating north, blue the east, red the south, and white the west—gold or yellow marked the very center of the Universe. *Orda* in their language meant "tent" or "camp," and by extension, a group of people banded together under one chieftain.

A tent along the banks of the Onon River is where the great Khan took his first breaths, just after his father Yesugei had vanquished a rival chieftain and put him to flight. The rival's name was "Temujin," and so, determined to commemorate the memory of his victory, Yesugei named his new son Temujin. Among the people in Yesugei's *orda* was an old astrologer named Sujujin, who upon casting the child's horoscope, declared that he would grow up to be a great warrior, whose kingdom would extend over the entire earth.

Astrologers continued to play an important role in Temujin's destiny. In 1206, a venerated old astrologer and prophet named Kököchu declared that he had been borne up on a great white horse to heaven, where he had conversed face to face with *Tengri*, the supreme Sky God. *Tengri* told Kököchu that he had chosen Temujin to carry out the Divine will, and bring the entire earth under his dominion. Temujin would thus be henceforth called "Genghis Khan," meaning "All Powerful Lord." As one of Temujin's teachers, Kököchu had instilled in his pupil this same sense of personal and world destiny: that the time had come when *Tengri's* judgment was to be fulfilled on Earth, and that he, Temujin, had been chosen by *Tengri* to be its human instrument and fulfiller. Temujin saw that he would sweep over the entire Earth like a death-bearing sandstorm, shattering and destroying everything and everyone in his path.

Along with maintaining a staff of personal astrologers, Genghis Khan practiced the art himself. Before each military campaign, he divined the outcome using a sheep's shoulder blade; cast into the fire, the bone cracked and twisted into patterns that he would read in trance, aided by his personal oracular spirit. Scribes would record his words, and afterwards he would compare his soothsayers' proclamations with his own oracle. In 1215, Genghis Khan brought into his magical retinue Yeh-lu Chu'tsai, a Chinese astrologer of Mongol extraction, and Yeh-lu became his closest advisor.

All of these astrologers—including the Khan himself—were also magicians, and this was true too of Genghis Khan's descendants. Marco Polo, in his *Travels*, tells many stories of magic in the court of Genghis Khan's grandson, Kublai Khan:

> The astrologers whom he entertains in his service, and who are deeply versed in the art of magic . . . sometimes display their skill in a wonderful manner; for if it should happen that the sky becomes cloudy and threatens rain, they ascend the roof of the Palace where the Great Khan resides, and by the force of their magic, prevent the rain from falling. . . .

Marco Polo also describes the magic of the *Bacsi*, another group in the Khan's employ, who would attend Kublai Khan during his meals, and "cause the flagons of wine, milk, or any other beverage to fill the cups spontaneously, without being touched by the attendants, and the cups to move through the air the distance of ten paces until they reach the hand of the Great Khan!" Returning home to Venice in 1295, Marco Polo often told stories of his travels and the curious sights of far Cathay and Tartary. His neighbors mockingly nicknamed his stories *"Il Milione"*— the millions—but it was not the stories of magic they disbelieved. Venice was itself still home to plenty of magicians and astrologers. Their incredulity focused on the vast distances and the great numbers described by Marco Polo.

From Marco Polo's account of his many years spent in the Kublai Khan's court, it is difficult to get a sense of just how terrified Europe was of the Mongols. That terror had reached a climax in the middle of the 13th century, simultaneous with the spreading of the Grail and Kitezh legends. Beginning in the fall of 1237, Batu Khan swept across central Russia, destroying all of the principal towns, including Moscow, Vladimir, and Little Kitezh (Gorodets); in December of 1240, Batu led the sacking and burning of Kiev, and the destruction of much of southern Russia. The Tartar hordes then moved on to the northwest, and into eastern Europe.

In April 1241, Batu Khan led some 10,000 warriors into Poland, where, at Legnica ("Leignitz" in German), he met a similar number of forces from Poland and Germany and members of various Christian military orders, led by Henry the Pious, the Duke of Silesia. The Mongols routed the European alliance, killing Prince Henry and many other knights. Polish chronicler Jan Dlugosz gives a picture of the devastation:

> Having collected their booty, the Tatars, wishing to know the exact number of the dead, cut one ear off each corpse, filling nine huge sacks to the brim. Then, impaling Prince Henry's head on a long lance, they approach the castle at Legnica (for the town has already been burned for fear of the Tatars) and display it for those inside to see, calling upon them through an interpreter to open the gates. The defenders refuse. . . . The Tatars then move on to Olomouc, where they camp for a fortnight, burning and destroying

everything round about. Moving on again, they halt for a week at Bolesisko, and, after slaughtering many of the inhabitants, continue into Moravia.

In this same account, Dlugosz tells of another method of Mongol terror:

Among the Tatar standards is a huge one with a giant X painted on it. It is topped with an ugly black head with a chin covered with hair. As the Tatars withdraw some hundred paces, the bearer of this standard begins violently shaking the great head, from which there suddenly bursts a cloud with a foul smell that envelopes the Poles and makes them all but faint, so that they are incapable of fighting. We know that in their wars the Tatars have always used the arts of divination and witchcraft, and this is what they are doing now. Seeing that the all but victorious Poles are daunted by the cloud and its foul smell, the Tatars raise a great shout and return to the fray, scattering the Polish ranks that hitherto have held firm, and a huge slaughter ensues.

Dlugosz's account of the Battle of Legnica certainly gives us a picture of the devastation wrought by the Mongols, and even his championing of the heroism of the Polish Prince and Knights cannot change the fact that it is Prince Henry's head—not the Khan's– that is paraded about on a pole. The Mongols won this battle at the door to Europe hands down. And yet they did not press on. Miraculously, and to the great relief of all of Europe, the Mongols abruptly returned to Asia.

Historians have debated for centuries why the Mongols made this abrupt about face, settling on the consensus that Batu Khan and his brother Subutai decided to return home upon hearing of the death of the Grand Khan Ogodei. But this ignores that the central impulse for the Mongol rulers had been to essentially *take over the earth*, to carry out the divine will of the god *Tengri*.

In Silesia, where this extraordinary event occurred, the miraculous retreat of the Mongols is still attributed to the prayers of Jadwiga (Hedwig), the mother of Henry the Pious. On the day that Henry was killed, she told a companion: "He has gone from me like a bird in flight, and I shall never see him again in this life." When the news came from the battlefield that Henry had been beheaded, it was Hedwig who comforted others. During her own lifetime her peers and subjects regarded her as a saint, and there are many legends about miracles that occurred because of her devotion to the poor.

Could this be possible? Could it be that the prayers of a single pious woman saved all of Europe in 1241? To reach the City of Great Kitezh, or the Castle of the Grail, one practices the deepest inner purity; a strict life of prayer and fasting; remorse for one's many imperfections; unshakable faith; a strong and constant meditative life; and finally, a vow of faithfulness to the chosen path taken in full freedom, together with a readiness to "endure many sorrows and even to suffer death." In the Kitezh legend, this is the narrow path that everyone—prince or pauper— must trod to reach Great Kitezh; Prince Parzival needs exactly these faculties to reach the Grail Castle. This is not a question of outward "borrowing" by one tradition from another; a supersensible inspiration or revelation is responsible for this uncanny convergence.

In Chrétien de Troyes's story of Parzival's departure from the Grail Castle, and its sudden disappearance, the text says: "But if someone sets out and begins to doubt, or becomes too unreserved in his praises, God will shut the city to such a person; and before him will lie only the forest or a place of desolation. Such a one will receive nothing, and his labors will be in vain." Wolfram too begins with a warning about doubt: "If vacillation dwell within the heart, the soul is bound to grieve and smart." All of the world's great traditions tell the same thing: to reach the hidden City/Castle, one must overcome "dullness & doubt" in one's soul. On the very eve of the "closing" of the spiritual world from humanity in 1250, Saint Hedwig lacked all dullness and doubt, and her faith can be imagined as prodigious enough that—with the help she summoned from the spiritual world—it overcame the legion of Mongol warriors who had beheaded her son and sacked the city of Legnica.

When Parzival first comes upon the Grail Castle, he finds inside the wounded Grail King, Amfortas, moaning in great pain. Though he enjoys the hospitality of the Castle, he takes his leave without ever investigating Amfortas's wound, or offering help. As he rides off from the Castle, he is scolded by a page for being a "silly goose." This need for a question, which expresses an inner activity of the soul, appears too in the legend of Kitezh, where it speaks of those who "want, seek, and yearn" to find a path to the invisible City. Whenever a person calls for help on his wearisome path, according to the legend: "Such a man is especially favored by the blessing of God, who helps, instructs, and guides him. . . ."

* * *

It is quite likely that at this point, you feel a bit like Parzival, dazed, confused, and a bit of a goose for all the questions that are blocking up your thinking and speaking. But your questions do not make you a goose! Indeed, in the Parzival legend, Parzival, meets an old knight, Gurnemanz, who tutors him for a time. One of his counsels to Parzival is: "Do not ask too many questions." Upon this advice, Parzival fails to ask "What ails thee, sire?" of Amfortas when he finds him, wounded, in the Castle of the Grail. It is *not* asking the question that makes a goose of Parzival![1]

At that point on his quest, Parzival was quite literal-minded, swallowing Gurnemanz's advice without thinking. The tale taken as a whole—and this is absolutely true of our lives as well—shows that one must step out of old habits of thought and deed. Like Parzival, we will all make mistakes along the way, but it is the rich, well-considered harvest of errors that makes us worthy of the journey.

---

1. Throughout this book, I will occasionally refer to people, places, things, and ideas that are wholly unfamiliar to you. You have an open invitation to ask me the meaning (or pronunciation, or origin) of *anything*—that is Parzival's task, and our task too in the present age.

2: *Joan and John:*

The Destinies of a Maid and a Monk

She is the Wonder of the Ages. And when we consider her origin, her early circumstances, her sex, and that she did all the things upon which her renown rests while she was still a young girl, we recognize that while our race continues she will be also the Riddle of the Ages.... It is beyond us. All the rules fail in this girl's case. In the world's history she stands alone—quite alone...Joan was competent in a law case at sixteen without ever having seen a lawbook or a court-house before; she had no training in soldiership and no associations with it, yet she was a competent general in her first campaign; she was brave in her first battle, yet her courage had had no education—not even the education which a boy's courage gets from never-ceasing reminders that it is not permissible in a boy to be a coward, but only in a girl; friendless, alone, ignorant, in the blossom of her youth, she sat week after week, a prisoner in chains, before her assemblage of judges, enemies hunting her to her death, the ablest minds in France, and answered them out of an untaught wisdom which overmatched their learning, baffled their tricks and treacheries with a native sagacity which compelled their wonder, and scored every day a victory against these incredible odds and camped unchallenged on the field. In the history of the human intellect, untrained, inexperienced, and using only its birthright equipment of untried capacities, there is nothing which approaches this ... she is easily and by far the most extraordinary person the human race has ever produced.
—Mark Twain, *Saint Joan of Arc* (1895)

La Pucelle[1] and Her Voices

Readers of the serialized installments of the story "Personal Recollections of Joan of Arc, by the Sieur Louis de Conte," in *Harper's Monthly* in 1895 were shocked to find out that both the narrator "Sieur Louis de Conte" and translator "Jean Francois Alden" were actually the renowned satirist Mark Twain. There was not a word of satire directed at Joan of Arc in Twain's work, which was the product of twelve years of research and two years of writing, and was based on the most historically accurate sources available at the time.

Joan had not always been so celebrated. She was reviled by William Shakespeare in the 16th century; neglected in the 17th; ridiculed by Voltaire in the 18th. But in 1841, a French historian published for the first time the unabridged edition of the record of Joan's trial for heresy. The first English translation did not appear until 1932; Twain lived in Paris while he finished the tale, immersing himself in French culture and language. Despite its having received mostly negative reviews, Twain declared it his best and most important work.

There seemed in Twain's relationship to Joan something of the singularity of destiny that so marked her extraordinary life. One day in 1849, while the twelve-year-old Sam Clemens was working as a printer's devil (an apprentice who performed a number of tasks) in Hannibal, Missouri, a gust of wind blew a stray leaf from a book across his path. Picking it up, he discovered that it described the persecution in prison by rough English soldiers of a person called "Joan of Arc"; on this single page he read the story of how the soldiers had stolen her clothes. Sam hurried home and asked his mother and brother if Joan of Arc was a real person, and learned that she had been a young French peasant girl who had saved her nation from English tyranny. He would on occasion tell this story as the turning point of his life; indeed, from the moment of this incident, the worlds of both history and literature opened up to young Samuel Clemens, and, though history has largely neutralized his radicalism, he became a fiery crusader for justice. Twain seemed to be drawn to Joan's story because he saw it as the epitome of the age-old struggle of the common folk against political and religious oppression. Like Henry Adams' *Mont St. Michel and Chartres*, which also put a Virgin at the center of the tale, Twain's story of Joan of Arc affirmed the value of a spiritual life at a moment when his culture was madly pursuing a path of industrialism, imperialism, and materialism.

Mark Twain prefaced his story with the declaration: "The details of the life of Joan of Arc form a biography which is unique among the world's biographies in one respect: *It is the only story of a human life which comes to us under oath,* the only one which comes to us from the witness-stand." In fifteen sessions over a period of three weeks in 1431, Joan was questioned by one Cardinal; 6 Bishops; 32 Doctors of Theology; 7 Doctors of Medicine—62 of the ablest politicians and academicians in France. Most of these judges were graduates and members of the University

---

1. During her own lifetime, Joan always called herself "*Pucelle*"—"Maid" or "Virgin." The people of France called her "*La Pucelle,*" the capitalized "L" emphasizing her prestige. Her voices—the spiritual beings who guided and guarded her—addressed her as "*Jehanne la Pucelle, Fille de Dieu.*" The common usage "Joan of Arc" appeared only in the late 16th century.

of Paris, which Joan had threatened in her attack on Paris just months before. Many of them had served the King of England as ambassadors or councilors, and nearly all of them had been on the English payroll at one time or another. Joan's victories for France had driven many of them—including the lead inquisitor, Bishop Cauchon—out of their dioceses, away from their places of power and authority. The nineteen-year-old Joan perhaps faced as formidable a task in her judicial battle with them as she had in her military adventures against the English.

On the fourth day of the trial Maître Jean Beaupère, Doctor in Theology, the Canon of Rouen, persistently questioned a vexed Joan about her voices. Joan identified the first voice that she heard as that of Saint Michael. By February 1429, when he commanded her to leave Dom-remy and seek help to rescue France from English rule, Joan had been acquainted with Michael's voice for four years. Maître Beaupère and the other inquisitors knew well the character of the Archangel Michael, knew his identity as the "Captain of the Host of the Lord"; "Protector of Israel"; "Prince of Light"; "Viceroy of Heaven." They knew the stories of his appearing, sword in hand, over the mausoleum of Hadrian, in answer to the prayers of Pope Gregory I; of the appa-ritions at Monte Gargano and Mont-Saint-Michel. But these were centuries ago. None of the inquisitors had a real, living relationship with Michael or any other Archangel.

Decades after the trial and execution of the Maid, the Maître Beaupère was a witness, not a judge, in another trial—the Trial of Nullification (that cleared Joan of the false charges that led to her execution)—and it is remarkable to see displayed there both his unbelief and his cowardice. While most of his peer inquisitors had decided that Joan's voices were demonic rather than divine, Maître Beaupère still held that they were *natural* rather than *supernatural*. He describes how one day he went with two of the other judges to see Joan in prison, to convince her to keep to her promise of wearing women's dress, but upon reaching the prison, they could not find the keeper. While waiting for him to arrive, several English soldiers came by and threatened to throw them into the moat, "at which we were much frightened, and went away without speaking to Jeanne."

When one reads the transcript of the trial, it is the undisputable power and force of Joan's personality that holds our attention. And yet there are recorded there many of the "riddles"—the seemingly inexplicable miracles, wonders, and prophecies performed by Joan. In 1909, just before Mark Twain died, Joan was beatified by the church, a process that required the documen-tation of four miracles. Three French nuns had given evidence of cures that they attributed to Joan's intercession; the Pope was allowed to dispense one miracle if the candidate had founded a religious order, and this was granted because Joan had saved France. But, as Mark Twain's story and the historical records themselves show, Joan's entire life was a miracle, and comprised many more individual wonders, marvels, and mysteries than these three miraculous cures.

There is nothing vague or "mystical" in Joan's descriptions of her "voices." In reply to her inquisitors she declares that she was thirteen when she first heard God's voice speak to her— "towards noon, in summer, in her father's garden." She heard the voice "on her right, in the direction of the church." There was a light—"a great light"—that came from the same direction as the voice. Over the weeks of the trial, the voices still spoke to her and guided her, even though she said that sometimes the din in the courtroom was so great that she could not hear them. This only exercised the judges further.

The judges were fully briefed on all of the astounding feats that Joan had performed since bursting onto the stage of world history in February of 1429. They knew that her father dreamed prophetically of her leaving home and being in the company of an army (though her father worried that this meant that his daughter might become a camp follower!); that she had predicted a French defeat near Orléans to Robert de Baudricourt, captain at Vaucouleurs (the prediction which made the captain take her seriously enough to then give her arms and assistance); that she had gained her sword from a vision of its being hidden behind the altar of the church of Saint Catherine at Fierbois; that she had also a precognitive vision of being wounded "above the breast" in the siege of Orléans; of her leap from the tower of her prison at Beaurevoir; that she had restored to life at Lagny an infant who had been dead for three days. There were many other miracles; this is but a small sample. What unites them all is their specificity of *action*; all contribute to her mission of saving France, and all of them are indisputable, witnessed by many and often recorded at or near the time of their occurrence.

The judges never expend any of their sophistry upon questioning the veracity of the stories of the miracles and wonders. They are in many ways as matter-of-fact in their questions as Joan is in her answers. When the issue of the sword comes up, they want to know why there are five crosses inscribed in it. About her magical standard (flag), they do not inquire how it worked, but who persuaded her to adorn it with angels. They press her about the flags carried by her soldiers—"were they made of linen or cloth?" There is the suggestion behind all of their questions that she is working illicit magic of some kind, which she always denies.

Some historians have said that this was the first witchcraft trial in Europe; if it is not the first, it still provides an amazing window into the thinking of early 15th century French peasants and professors alike about the workings of magic. Just a generation earlier, it would have been clear to all that a girl—particularly a virgin—who led a life of devotion to God would be graced by aid from God and his allies, the angels.

Joan was not only the *source* of prophecy but the *subject* of it. By the time of her trial, the French people spoke of Merlin's prophecy of a healing virgin who would "dry up the sources of evil with her breath, cry rivers of tears from her eyes, fill the island with a terrible clamor, and be killed by a ten-antlered stag." At her trial Joan was asked if she had ever heard it said in her youth that a virgin would come from the *Bois Chenu* (the oak forest near Domremy), to perform admirable deeds; in her typical matter-of-fact manner, she said she had, but that she never placed any faith in it. Before February 1429, a local seeress named Marie Robine had had visions of a woman taking up arms for France. Joan's own contemporaries—aside from the English and their accomplices, the Burgundian judges, who both were her sworn enemies—believed that the prophetic indications about Joan were affirmations of a divine plan for the Maid.

The question that I hope you are asking about this wondrous but altogether true tale is *why was God so determined to save France?* Why was He not equally on the side of the English? Perhaps God felt the way Mary Gordon suggests in her recent biography of Joan:

> And lest we forget what the real implications of the dynastic claims were, we should try
> to imagine an English France. An extension of the island kingdom across the channel: a

Normandy, Brittany, Provence, all English-speaking, a cultural history in which there was only cheddar and no brie, only Congreve and no Molière, only Chippendale and no French Provincial, only Turner and no Monet. In our time we have seen the ravages of nationalism so clearly that it is easy to think of it only as a curse, but to imagine the flattening out of culture that could have occurred if the English had won the Hundred Years' War is a deeply dispiriting mental exercise.

There is something to this explanation—far more than the suggestion that God's epicurean taste for brie and champagne and French art and literature led Him to throw His support behind the French cause above the English... but we will have to wait a bit before bringing it more clearly into focus. For it is a matter of the stars you see...

And speaking of stars, there is a very simple hint about Joan's wondrous life that has escaped the notice of every one of her biographers, from Shakespeare to Mark Twain to Mary Gordon. *She was born on the 6th of January, the Feast of Epiphany.* For the minstrel Wolfram von Eschenbach and other initiates of his century, it was known that the Twelve Holy Nights, between December 25th and January 6th, were a special time in which spiritual beings of the Hierarchies (including the Archangels) could work right into a mother's womb, if her child's karma facilitated this. At that time the individual soul meets both Christ and Michael, and is filled with the desire to imitate Christ. This is the ultimate white path, in which devotion and readiness to sacrifice are valued above all other things. Just before her birth, Joan received a form of natural initiation in which the impulse of Christ—an impulse that would inspire her to radiate its presence into her time and place on Earth—was made the deepest part of her soul.

* * *

A Life of Letters

At the trial of Joan of Arc, three notaries recorded the testimony in French, collating their notes at the end of each day. Four years later, their records were transcribed into Latin, and five copies were made... by hand! It would be another four years, in 1439, that Johannes Gutenberg of Mainz would invent mechanical printing with movable type. Certain prerequisites had to be met before this could happen: the letters needed to be of a particular hardness—which required the development of an alloy of lead, tin, and bismuth; these letters needed to be able to be mass-produced; an ink had to be found that would both stick to the letters and quickly dry on paper. Gutenberg made contributions to all of these technical processes and then wed them to a wooden press like the ones used for making olive oil and wine.

Like so many inventors, Gutenberg never reaped the rewards of his achievement. In 1462, the city of Mainz was sacked and Gutenberg was exiled. That same year, about 100 miles to the west in Trittenheim (and about the same distance east of Joan's village of Domremy), was born a boy whose life would be dedicated to the world of books that Gutenberg's invention had made possible. Johann Heidenberg was an only child of extremely poor parents; his father died before he was a year old. At age fifteen, he had "a marvelous vision"; one night he dreamed of a youth approaching him with two tablets, one inscribed with letters, the other with images. Asked to choose one, he chose "that tablet which seemed to be written," upon which the youth said, "Behold, God has heard your prayers and will grant you whatever you have asked, and indeed more than you have been able to petition." Despite arousing the anger of his cruel and unlettered stepfather, young John pursued this vision, sneaking out of the house at night to take lessons from a friend in the neighborhood.

By the age of eighteen, John left home and traveled to Heidelberg to study, and in 1482, traveling back home with a fellow student he encountered a blinding snowstorm, and took refuge in the Benedictine monastery at Sponheim. The next morning, they set out again, but as they reached a mountain pass the storm worsened. The friend suggested that they return to the monastery, but John was embarrassed to again seek the monks' hospitality. They continued on, but three times they were forced to seek shelter from the driving snow, and at last John acquiesced, and they returned to the abbey. When the storm passed, John declared that it must have been God's will that he remain there, and so he did.

Taking his vows at age 21, he dedicated himself to a life of letters—studying the Scriptures. Less than a year later, he was granted a third sign that his course was being guided by a higher force, when he was asked to become the Abbot of the Sponheim monastery. When John—now "Johannes Trithemius," the Latinized surname denoting the town of his birth—had arrived at Sponheim, the library consisted of 40 books; due to his collecting efforts, by the time he left in 1505 there were over 2000. Thanks to Gutenberg's invention, and John's passion for letters, we can say exactly when he turned from reading books to writing them: "In the year of our Lord 1484, on the day of the Holy Apostle and Evangelist St. Matthew, when I reached the age of 23, I first applied myself to the art of writing."

John chronicled this event, along with the rest of his boyhood biography, in 1507, in a work entitled *Nepiachus.* By that year, he had authored at least 19 of his own books—most notably the *cronica*, chronicles, or histories. A stream of visitors made their way to the Sponheim abbey to study with John, and to use his library, which was widely celebrated as unequal in all the world. One of his former Heidelberg teachers compared it to the famed library founded at Alexandria by Ptolemy.

John's passion for letters had led him into the literature of demonology and magic. In 1499, in a letter to a friend who was a Carmelite monk in Belgium, John had summarized the contents of a handbook he was writing on steganography, the art of writing secret messages. By the time that the letter arrived, the friend had died, and the letter fell into the hands of the Carmelite prior, who circulated it widely, accusing John of practicing black magic. This led to his becoming the most famous magician of his age; the Swiss alchemist and physician Paracelsus and German alchemist/magician Agrippa sought him out for instruction, and at least two princes made their way to Sponheim, eager to employ John's cryptic art in the service of transmitting state secrets.

His notoriety as a magician grew scandalous enough that he resigned as Abbot in 1505. In July he was summoned by the Holy Roman Emperor Maximilian to discuss "various questions of the Holy Scriptures." When the week of conversations was published as *Liber octo quaestionum ad Maximilian Caesarum defied et intellectu* (*The Book of Eight Questions from Emperor Maximilian, Regarding Faith and Intellect*), it was clear what was uppermost on the Emperor's mind—most of the questions dealt with the influence of sorcery, witchcraft, and miracles. Question Three, "On the miracles of the heathens," stated unequivocally that "magicians, having made implicit or explicit pacts with demons, are capable of performing miracles." John and Maximilian were essentially puzzling over the same dilemma as Joan's judges had 75 years before. But while Joan had no knowledge of demons, John knew plenty, speaking of their devilish antics in great detail:

> They behave like children who sometimes put on masks and hide, only to jump out and when they succeed in terrifying their shocked friends, they enjoy themselves enormously, as if they had achieved some great horror. . . . Sometimes they appear in visible form, at other times they are invisible; they upset the atmosphere, cause storms, hail and lightning; they ruin crops and ravage with their spells, whatever is produced by the earth. They cause illness in man and beast, and use every skill to carry out whatever plan they can think of to ruin man.

John's work shared with the examiners at Joan's trial a fundamental challenge—to devise a system for distinguishing between demons and angels, both of whom were universally known to share the environment with human beings. Since demons are tricksters, skilled in the art of appearing to be what they are not, it was imperative to have some way to tell them from one another. John occupied himself further with this, greatly expanding his classification of demons in *De Daemonibus*, a work he outlined in 1507–1508. The essential problem of the age was that the more exactly one classified and described these beings, the more likely one was to be accused of working with them. Clearly John worked with them; he wrote a short work on the ancient art of drawing spirits into crystals (ironically, it was a similar technique, undertaken as a commercial venture, that had led to Gutenberg's first financial setback as he was working on the printing press). In that work, precise instructions were given on how to communicate with the Archangels. Here too, John was pursuing his passion for *letters*, for above all it was the precision of the incantations that determined their efficacy. Again, the issue of identity was critical; the crystal gazer was instructed to ask the name of the spirit "in the name of the Trinity," followed by questions as to his office and true sign or character.

Still, the instructions hedged their bets, as unsure of these beings' "true sign or character" as Joan's inquisitors had been of hers: "Wilt thou swear by the blood and righteousness of our Lord Jesus Christ, that thou art truly Michael?" Here was a clear echo of the diagnosis expressed in Wolfram's prelude to *Parzival*—doubt had taken hold of humanity. Not long before this, the medieval mind knew the word "reality" as referring exclusively to spiritual, heavenly things. This was changing rapidly at the turn of the sixteenth century, and nowhere was it more dramatically expressed than in the debates about demonology.

The key for John was the moral nature of the practitioner. The magician must fundamentally be a pious person, one who ideally lived a life removed from worldly cares. The magician had to possess a pure and purified (of selfishness) will. John insisted that every external effect of magic should be accompanied by an internal effect in the magician himself. In John's philosophy knowledge—and magic was a very demanding form of knowledge—was not possible without love, nor love without knowledge. His personal motto began: "Study generates knowledge; knowledge bears love. . . ."

For John and for his contemporaries, both love and knowledge originated in, and returned to, God, who was the *intelligentiis primum*—the "First Intellect." Just as John's motto embodied a cascade of intermediate steps, God's intellect cascaded toward earthly realization down a chain of heavenly agents, beginning with the *intelligentiis secundeis*—the "Second Intellects," who were the Archangels. In 1508, the same year as he sketched the plan for *De Daemonibus* and published the *Book of Eight Questions,* John wrote a modest little work entitled: *A Treatise on the Seven Secondary Causes, i.e. Intelligences, or Causes, Who Move the Spheres According to God: A Little Book or MYSTICAL CHRONOLOGY, Containing within a Short Compass Marvelous Secrets Worthy of Interest.* Like the *Eight Questions,* he dedicated the book to Emperor Maximilian.

A "short compass" it certainly was in page length (less than 20), but not in its span of history, encompassing the successive epochs of time from the creation of the world until John's own era. In keeping with the sevenfold nature of the cosmos, each of the seven Archangels—who were associated with one of the seven planets (remember, the three outer planets would not be discovered for another three and a half centuries)—ruled those epochs for a period of 354 years and 4 months, during which time the Archangel gave his particular "stamp" to historical events.

Though John draws no attention to it, this 354⅓-year rhythm is exactly the period of twelve lunar synodic months. This is only some 10 months longer than the 353 years and 6 months that it takes for Saturn—known to the Greeks as *Kronos,* the planet of Time—to complete 12 circuits of the Zodiac. During these periods, humanity was thought to live within the spiritual atmosphere exuded by the seven Archangels, also known as "Spirits of Time." One may think of these 354-year periods as a kind of "month"; note the symmetry between the 354-day synodic year (12 months of 29½ days = 354 days) and the Saturn zodiacal circuit (12 revolutions through the zodiac in 353½ years). These Archangelic periods can be seen as an image of the transition from the eternal realm to the cyclic, time-bound realm that we know as "history."

Reading John's mystical chronology five centuries after he wrote it, we might be surprised how familiar we are with many of the events it mentions. He touches on the Tower of Babel; Moses delivering the Israelites from slavery; the destruction of Troy; Homer's poetry; the ancient Hebrew prophets; the Greek philosophers Pythagoras, Socrates, and Plato; Alexander the Great; Julius Caesar; Constantine; the birth of Merlin and King Arthur; Muhammad and the Saracens; the spread of the Mongol empire; the destruction of the Knights Templar; the "grievous wasting" of France by the English and Burgundians; the fall of Constantinople. The great turning point for all of this history was of course the birth of Christ, under the reign of Orifiel, the Archangel of Saturn. This was to John proof of "how faire and wonderfull the Ordination of Divine providence is," since the world had first been created under the rule of Saturn/Orifiel.

John's astrological logic is surprisingly sound as a general guide to the grand sweep of the world's cultural history over the previous dozen or so centuries. Reflecting on the various periods that had transpired under the reign of Samael, the "genius" of Mars, he pointed out how each one—particularly in the second half of the period—had seen "alterations of Monarchy, Religions and sects," with "Principalities and Kingdomes transferred to Strangers." The latest Samael period—from AD 1171 to AD 1525—was characteristic: "Many wars were all over the whole world, by which means infinite thousands of men perished, and sundry Kingdoms lost their former bounds." He went on to speak of how the Tartars "occasioned a very great plague in the World, nor yet do they cease"; how Jerusalem was taken by the "Saracens" (i.e., Muslims); Constantinople by the Germans; and the overall three and a half century tug-of-war within and against the Holy Roman Empire right up until his friend Maximilian's reign, during which "he brought the Switzers low by war, and even to this day makes war against the Rebellious Sicambrians."

John then turns from history to prophecy: "A strong sect of Religion shall arise, and be the overthrow of the Ancient Religion. It's to be feared least the fourth beast lose one head…This third Revolution of Mars shall not be consummated without Prophecie, and the institution of some new Religion, from this year of our Lord 1508." John died in 1516, the year in which *De Septum Secundeis* was published; the following October, another German monk, Martin Luther, nailed his 95 theses—his protests against the Catholic church's corruption—to the door of the Wittenberg Church, beginning the Protestant Reformation. Samael's earlier regencies had brought Noah's flood and the destruction of Troy; Luther's simple act would lead to tectonic change as well.

John concludes his chronology by pointing farther into the future, to November, 1879, when Gabriel's reign would end, and Michael would become the new *Zeitgeist* (literally, "spirit of the time"). This was Joan's Archangel, the liberator of France from England's greedy grasp. The Abbott of Trithemius said nothing about what one might expect in that era, nothing even about Michael's particular qualities. This would wait for other men of letters, other prophets.

* * *

L'arbre Fée de Bourlemont: Song of the Children (from Twain's Joan of Arc story)

> Arbre Fée de Bourlemont?
> The children's tears! They brought each grief,
> And you did comfort them and cheer
> Their bruised hearts, and steal a tear
> That healed rose a leaf.
>
> And what has built you up so strong,
> Arbre Fée de Bourlemont?
> The children's love! They've loved you long:
> Ten hundred years, in sooth,

They've nourished you with praise and song,
And warmed your heart and kept it young—
A thousand years of youth!

Bide alway green in our young hearts,
Arbre Fée de Bourlemont!
And we shall alway youthful be,
Not heeding Time his flight;
And when in exile wand'ring we
Shall fainting yearn for glimpse of thee,
O rise upon our sight.

In Mark Twain's story, *les fées*—translated as "fairies" in the 19th century edition of the trial transcript—leap forth as central characters, with their special tree at Bourlemont. They are, as the poem suggests, benevolent intermediaries between innocent children and the edenic world of Nature. Twain's fiction tells how a century before Joan's youth, the priest of Domremy had denounced *les fées* as "blood kin of the Fiend and barred out from redemption," and had banished them as punishment for their having appeared to an old woman of the village. The priest told them to never show themselves again, and so in Joan's youth they were only known from the old stories. But this did not stop the children from always hanging garlands at the tree "as a perpetual sign to the fairies that they were still loved and remembered, though lost to sight."

One night a woman passing the tree found the fairies at their revelry, "as many as three hundred of them, tearing around in a great ring . . . and leaning away back and spreading their mouths with laughter and song . . . and kicking their legs up . . . in perfect abandon and hilarity . . . the very maddest and witchingest dance the woman ever saw." When word spread in the village that the fairies had returned, the priest was sent to banish them once more. The alarmed children ran to fetch Joan to stop him, but she was laid low with a fever, and so the deed was done before France's yet-to-be heroine could save *les fées*. After this, the spring at the spot lost its freshness and coldness, snakes and insect pests appeared, and "the place was not quite the same afterward."

On the eve of the twentieth century, *les fées* had been so long banished from the western world that authors and artists could make of them any sort of symbol they wished—though most, like Mark Twain, chose to render them impotent and immature, like Peter Pan, stuck in a lost world. For the educated Victorian era readers of Joan's trial transcripts, the entire fuss made by Joan's inquisitors was a puzzle. But that fuss was the early warning of the same trouble that would plague the good Abbott John.

The "spirits" called up by the arcane formulas in the *Steganographia*; by the incantation given in the work on crystals; and noted by John in many of his other works, were hardly symbols, though symbols –including letters—were a powerful means of summoning them. They were *beings* whose "reality"—remember that in 15th century Europe this word still meant *spiritual realities*—was unquestioned. It was John's knowledge of those very beings that brought the

Renaissance's greatest magicians—including Paracelsus and Agrippa—and the Emperor himself to John's door for study of his occult philosophy.

These learned and powerful men —the most learned and powerful of their era, just as Genghis Khan and his retinue of shamans had been in theirs—were not trifling with magic out of idle curiosity. Indeed, "curiosity" was just what John feared most among his fellow men. The main purpose of his *De Daemonibus* was to "chase away and refute all the superstitious arts of the demons…especially in these times of ours in which men are excessively curious, and seek to know things which it is better not to know." The Latin root *cura*—care, diligence, fastidiousness—is a reminder that "curiosity" had from antiquity through the early 16th century been employed by philosophers to indicate the diligent desire for knowledge. With the rise of scientific knowledge, the word entered the vernacular, and philosophers like the Abbott Trithemius came to use it to denote the opposite—superficial, irresponsible searching after secrets. In the preface to his *Steganographia*, he declared that "ancient philosophers, masters in art as well as nature, when they discovered secrets, concealed them in various way and figures, to avoid that they might come to be known by the wicked."

Those who accused both Joan and John of black magic, sorcery, and witchcraft confused means and ends. The grimoires that John and his students studied and crafted were operating manuals to employ and direct *beings*—the beings that Paracelsus would soon classify as gnomes, undines, sylphs and salamanders. Conceived of by the ancient Greeks as ranging from benevolent to neutral to malevolent, their *"daemonae"* became "demons"—i.e., strictly harmful—as Europe experienced a process of profound disenchantment over the next few centuries. We moderns are altogether too thoroughly disenchanted to realize that at the heart of the word "enchant" is the magical process of song (*cantare*), by which the singer-bard originally called up the elemental beings of nature, for the mutual benefit of the community *and the beings.*

The great beauty of Joan's biography is that she did not see these beings—she knew of others who did, and said so at her trial—*but they still saw her, and came to her aid.* Her miraculous healings, her precognitive knowledge of events, even the delivery of her sword, were all manifested by the elemental beings. Though only some of her neighbors saw or heard *les fées,* they all knew that these creatures of the netherworld were capable of astounding feats, that they could see the future, penetrate the depths of the earth, travel great distances instantly. When the judges questioned Joan as to how she got her magic sword, they insist that she cast spells upon malevolent *fées*—demons—to help her to hide the sword in St. Catherine's church, so that she might then gain the confidence of the common folk of the region. The learned Burgundian judges are not so learned that they dismiss the reality of the elemental beings; they just mistake the beings' activity because of their own chauvinistic politics.

From reading her words at the trial, it seems quite clear that Joan herself was unaware that she was being aided by an invisible legion as well as the armored one lent to her by Charles VII. She did not know that the Archangel Michael employed gnomes, the elementals of the earth, to place the sword within the soil near the altar. Perhaps they fashioned it as well; for her part, she only knows that the sword serves her, she never pauses to ponder how it got there. She tells the judges simply that her voices told her it was there, and that she sent for it. "She had never seen the man who fetched it." Her faith is absolute, *and this is why the beings work so faithfully on her behalf.*

The judges insist on knowing what blessing she said over the sword; she answers that "she neither blessed it herself, nor had it blessed; she would not have known how to do it." *She would not have known how to do it.* John, the learned Abbott of Sponheim, collected every magical manual in existence, and wrote a few of his own, so that he—and not others!—might know how to bless a sword, or a ring, or perhaps his own pen. Joan had no need of a blessing. "She loved the sword, since it had been found in the church of St. Catherine, whom she loved." This John could understand.

Joan herself was unaware that she had been in conversation with the sword-wielding Archangel Michael years before he spoke to her in her father's garden, during those twelve holy nights leading up to her birth. And no doubt *les fées* were there as well, weaving the web of her future destiny, aware that she had dedicated herself to the Lord of the Elements, the Christ. The Italian *fata* preserves better than *fée* the origin of both in the Latin *fatum*—fate, or destiny. The destinies of Joan and John—one served by but not seeing *les fées*, the other seeking them with all his heart, and then keeping them hidden in plain sight, lest the curious come to know too much—hold keys to how *all* humanity must once again come to the Fairy Tree, to hang garlands there.

3: Out of the Labyrinth

The thirteenth chapter, wherein is recounted
how the Mexican king Montezuma
sends other sorcerers
who were to cast a spell on the Spanish
and what happened to them on the way.
And the second group of messengers—
the soothsayers, the magicians, and the high priests—
likewise went to receive the Spanish.
But it was to no avail;
they could not bewitch the people,
they could not reach their intent with the Spanish;
they simply failed to arrive.

> Bernardino de Sahagun,
> *General History of the Things of New Spain* (1569)

From Magic to Muggle

This past semester, after I had pantomimed the scene described by Marco Polo, where one of Kublai Khan's magicians floats a goblet of wine across the room to him, a student in my 8 AM class stopped me: "Do you mean to say that you believe that happened!? That there is such a thing as real, physical magic?" At this point, perhaps you are asking the same question. You should be, for the first two chapters have kept circling back to this thread of magic—from the court of the Khans in the 13th and 14th centuries, to France in the 15th century, and Germany in the early 16th. How can I justify making such an arcane topic central to my story?

Have you ever wondered how it is that you can barely find a single reference to magic in a typical global history textbook, and yet, today, in 2008, the bestselling books in the world—J. K. Rowling's *Harry Potter* series—are *entirely set within the world of magic and magicians*. In the *Harry Potter* books, all those who are incapable of performing magic are called "Muggles." How exactly is it that we now live in a Muggle world where almost all people think that magic is something that only appears in Harry Potter books, or David Copperfield and David Blaine stunts?[1] The repertoire of magic in Harry Potter's world neatly covers (with a playful Rowling twist) what was in the Renaissance grimoires or practiced by non-European magicians—Animagi Transformation; Metamorphmagi; Parselmouths; Flying; Divination; Legilimancy; Apparition & Disapparition; Teleportation; Veela Charms; Stunning Spells; Unbreakable Vows; Priori Incantatem; Dark Arts; Curses (including Unforgivable Curses); Magic Wands; Cloaks of Invisibility; Resurrection Stones.[2]

Before the 15th century, *the entire world ran on magic.* That we should find it occupied so central a place in the courts of both Asia, Europe, and Mesoamerica is no coincidence, and perhaps we can easily rationalize this: kings and emperors ruled by virtue of the amount of power they possessed, and magic was just one more arrow in their imperial quiver.

But there is more to it than this, for it is not just the kings and their magicians who believe in magic; *everyone in these societies believes in magic.* This belief lingers well into the modern era, finally diminishing at different times in different places. The disbelief starts in European cities of the 15th and 16th centuries, and spreads from there. Johannes Trithemius and the other Renaissance mages of Germany, England, France and Italy are busy codifying the knowledge in print—collecting old magical manuscripts and making their own grimoires—at just that time, because it has passed out of widespread popular practice among urban Europeans. Even at the margins, among the folk, magic becomes aberrant and arcane, rather than common and communal.

The easiest way to "track" that disbelief—or, as the scholars refer to it, "disenchantment"—is to examine the records of European contact with native peoples around the world during this time period. The epigraph above succinctly tells the tale: when the Spanish conquistadores led by Hernan Cortes arrive in Mexico, all of the Aztec emperor Montezuma's combined forces of magic fail to stop the advance of the Spanish. "They simply failed to arrive," says the chronicler Bernardino de Sahagun, meaning that the Mexican magicians failed to arrive at the result which had always been guaranteed them within their own society.

We shall read in much greater detail about the catastrophic failure of the old Aztec magic. Let us look at other such episodes of "disenchantment." In 1620, the great Penacook sachem/shaman Passaconnaway was summoned to a meeting of lesser sachems and shamans near Plymouth, to conjure against the Pilgrims. The Puritans spoke of how he was reputed to be able to make "water burn, rocks move, trees dance, and metamorphose himself into a flaming man."

1. J. K. Rowling has said that she created the word "Muggle" from "mug"—meaning someone who is easily fooled. In her own bit of word magic, she added the "-gle" suffix to make it sound "cuddly" and less harshly demeaning of the Muggles, who constitute 99% of her readership! In 2003, "muggle" was added to the Oxford English Dictionary; quite a remarkable sign of the times, given that it was only in 1976, after J.R. Tolkien had already died, that "hobbit" entered the OED lexicon.

2. It is perhaps of interest that the *Harry Potter* books share with some other early 21st century Western pop culture productions—e.g., *The DaVinci Code*; *The Secret*; widespread conspiracy theories about the Illuminati, Freemasons, etc.—a fascination for a secret elite society. And yet Hogwarts is just a plain old English boarding school! You might consider how it is that your state university pretends to be exclusive and arcane, but is hardly imparting any special, secret knowledge. The real mystery school is fully out in the open, available to us at every turn, and the only instrument or incantation necessary to master and manifest the magical is *our own mind.* And J.K. Rowling says she does not believe in magic!

And yet, his magic fell flat against the English settlers. Read the journals of Columbus in the Caribbean in 1492; Magellan in the Philippines in 1521; Jacques Cartier in the St. Lawrence Valley in 1534; Samuel de Champlain along the Atlantic coast in 1603; Henry Hudson at Manhattan in 1609; Captain James Cook in Hawaii in 1779. In each episode of contact, the old magic fails in the face of the decidedly un-magical consciousness of the European.

The European explorer, set free from the binding magical consciousness of his own past, typically mocks the native magician; here is Samuel de Champlain, describing the divination methods of a shaman (Algonquin, Montagnais, or Huron) in the war party that he accompanied in the summer of 1609 up the *Riviére des Iroquois* (the Richelieu):

> In all their encampments, they have their *Pilotois*, or *Ostemoy*, a class of persons who play the part of soothsayers, in whom these people have faith. One of these builds a cabin, surrounds it with small pieces of wood, and covers it with his robe: after it is built, he places himself inside, so as not to be seen at all, when he seizes and shakes one of the posts of his cabin, muttering some words between his teeth, by which he says he invokes the devil, who appears to him in the form of a stone, and tells him whether they will meet their enemies and kill many of them. This *Pilotois* lies prostrate on the ground, motionless, only speaking with the devil: on a sudden, he rises to his feet, talking, and tormenting himself in such a manner that, although naked, he is all of a perspiration. All the people surround the cabin, seated on their buttocks, like apes. They frequently told me that the shaking of the cabin, which I saw, proceeded from the devil, who made it move, and not the man inside, although I could see the contrary; for, as I have stated above, it was the *Pilotois* who took one of the supports of the cabin, and made it move in this manner. They told me also that I should see fire come out from the top, which I did not see at all. These rogues counterfeit also their voice, so that it is heavy and clear, and speak in a language unknown to the other savages. And, when they represent it as broken, the savages think that the devil is speaking, and telling them what is to happen in their war, and what they must do.
>
> But all these scapegraces, who play the soothsayer, out of a hundred words, do not speak two that are true, and impose upon these poor people. There are enough like them in the world, who take food from the mouths of the people by their impostures, as these worthies do. I often remonstrated with the people, telling them that all they did was sheer nonsense, and that they ought not to put confidence in them.

Champlain's dismissal is *our* dismissal; we assume that this performance is crude stage magic, sophomoric and deceitful sleight-of-hand. Champlain's skepticism is so complete that he even passes over the supposed attribution of the magic to *le Diable*. His opaqueness to the dimensions of timelessness and spacelessness is so pronounced that just a few days later, when he has a precognitive dream of a historic battle with the Iroquois, he makes no comment about it in his journal. For a brief instant, it seemed that the European consciousness had been folded into the native one, that Champlain had himself momentarily been caught up in his native allies' dream world. When he tells the Indians about his dream, they spring into action, mapping the coming battle in the dirt, confident of victory. Champlain, having stepped into the stream of Time, steps right back out, seemingly oblivious to his own role in the action.

Into the Labyrinth

Timelessness—magical feats of seeing the future are only possible if there is a way to enter the "stream of time," to escape the present moment for "timelessness." Spacelessness—similarly, when a soothsaying magician says that he has left his body to survey what the enemy is doing or where the game has gone, he enters a condition of "spacelessness."

Myths from all over the world describe the first human beings as fused with, or embedded in, Nature. For us, the most familiar description comes from the Bible. "Paradise" or "The Garden of Eden" is not a place, but a *condition of consciousness* where there is as yet no differentiation between the human being and his surround. The Hindu Vedas call this *Purusha*; in Mandean and Manichean myth it is personified as Adam Kadmon, akin to the "Old Adam" of Saint Paul. In the 4th century BC the great Chinese sage Chuang-Tzu characterized this earlier era: "Dreamlessly the true men of earlier times slept." "True men"—like similar phrases in all of these early myths—indicates that human history was seen as a process of the *contraction* of consciousness, a falling away from a Golden Age of complete merger with the environment. It is only our own modern creation myth—Darwinian evolution—which posits a period of "primitive men" who fight their way forward in time to become "true"—that is, *rational, scientific, free of any belief in magic and myth.*

Into the cave of that dreamless sleep came the first light of consciousness, and magic was born. The caves of the world—dark, enclosing; themselves a kind of picture of that early dreamless human being—are the best places to go to see this. On every continent, the earliest art depicts prey animals, often with indications of their capture or killing. The early hunters who made these drawings would then leave the cave to "enact" what they had just drawn. Their painstaking rituals, performed in the dark in silence, would bring the animal to them to be slain. Hunting peoples practiced similar rituals well into the 20th century.

Hunting is a *holy occupation*, each and every aspect of it shot through with precise ritual magical activity. In the myths of hunting peoples, the beginning of the world always was a time when animals and men talked to each other, and through their rituals, the hunters recreated this possibility. If an animal was to submit itself to be killed, the hunters had to win its favor, and they did so by intense spiritual preparation, which culminated in a "spirit hunt"—a non-physical, but altogether real, hunt. For the hunter who had successfully performed this inner, imaginal hunt, by the time he encountered his prey, the animal was already as good as dead.

This dream hunt, like the cave drawing hunt, is called "imitative" or "sympathetic" magic, where the symbolic images become equivalent to the creature itself. A vast array of magical techniques—other forms of picture-magic such as fetishes, totems, taboos, amulets; rain magic; magic of the seasons; word magic—oracles, forbidden names, incantations; touch magic based on the vital connections between things that were once linked (e.g., nails, hair, clothing, excrement);

sex magic, such as love sorcery and fertility rituals—all were predicated on this mysterious but universal "sympathy" between the symbol and its object.

The early cave art from around the world is marked by a lack of dimensionality; bodies of both animals and humans frequently blend into and over each other. When art moves out of the cave and onto the outer wall of vases and other vessels, the figures are similarly interwoven, like vining plants. Frescoes from 3000-year-old Egyptian graves, ancient Greek tile floor mosaics, and medieval tapestries are often marked by this magic interweaving, reflective of varying degrees of their makers' embeddedness in their environment.

There are cave and rock drawings from all over the world that give even more dramatic evidence of their makers' entirely different consciousness from our own. In these pictures, human beings appear with radiant haloes, auras, or nimbuses around their heads. To a lesser extent, one can consider also the widespread depiction of "horned" or "antlered" humans as contiguous with these haloed heads. They suggest that—as is also suggested today by individuals who can perceive the human aura—either the artists, or their entire societies, were able to see something that we no longer see. These depictions are *not* the same as the haloes that appear in Christian art, which are almost exclusively symbolic of the spiritual state of the individuals who bear them.[1] In the Australian rock art depicted here, these are not special individuals, for in some cases *all* of the human figures shown bear these same haloes. It is almost as if these pictures are a record of the moment when an ancient clairvoyance for the human aura was in the final stages of eclipse. It is fitting that the aura hovers above the human head—the seat of consciousness in modern, rational man.

It also seems fitting that almost all of these figures are lacking mouths. Though it seem incredible to us today, early human beings were able to communicate telepathically, and in a sense, *did not need to speak.*[2] Think too of the most powerful instrument of the shaman—and of the tribal group—for altering consciousness—the drum. When the Mongol magician wished to travel great distances to discover what was happening in another village, he mounted his imaginal "horse" and drove it with the beat of the drum. This capacity for magical rhythmic entrainment is not entirely lost; we can feel it pulling at us each time we listen to reggae or zydeco or rock 'n roll.

Have you ever stood near a waterfall and felt yourself go into trance? (You can also experience this under an apple tree when it is in full blossom in the spring; the buzzing of the honeybees can be so intense that it makes the hair on your arm stand up!) I used to live near a place where there

1. Saints and holy men of early Buddhist and Christian art have colored halos; the Buddhist saints bear colors symbolizing the direction with which they are associated—blue/North; yellow/South; red/West; green/East—while Christian saints also have nimbus colors symbolic of some aspect of their teaching or character.

2. Around the world, one can find survivals of this state of "mouthlessness," from the bearded masks of the Peking Opera to the masks worn by dancers in Papua New Guinea or used in the sacred mushroom ceremony in Mazatec mountain villages in Mexico. This latter example reminds us that drug use by moderns always leads to a lower level of consciousness. You can listen to a 1956 recording of this ceremony at: http://www.archive.org/details/mazatecmushroom. Dr. Gordon Wasson, who recorded the chant, showed that the words were from pre-contact times, and were equivalent to the Vedic chants of India.

had been a great waterfall on the Connecticut River, at Bellows Falls, Vermont. It is dammed up now, but before the first English settlers came to the valley in the late 18th century, the falls were visited by many native families, to spear salmon on their spring migration up the river. On one vertical face of rock near the falls, there are carved a series of haloed or antlered heads.

It is easy to stand there today and even with the much-diminished flow of water, imagine a Wonbanakiak *mdawlinno* (magician or shaman) entering into a trance, aided only by the thundering cataract below. One need not venture all the way to Australia to see such marvels; they are much closer at hand. On a slate pebble found in Maine is incised a man with his arms and fingers outspread in the universal symbol of astonishment, a halo hovering about his head and two spirit allies flanking him. To the north, scattered across the Canadian Shield, are dozens of similar figures, most notably at the spectacular petroglyph gallery at Peterborough, Ontario. Amongst the Onondaga Iroquois of New York, Thadodaho, the first name in the Roll Call of the Chiefs, is always depicted with antler-like projections from his head, showing his heightened state of participatory consciousness. Whether by projecting rays, encircling lines, or a corona of pecked dots, all these figures depicted the shaman with a halo, signifying the merger of his consciousness with nature. In Algonquian terminology, all of these beings were *mamagwashi*, "hairy spirits," the beings with light surrounding their bodies.

* * *

One of the capacities we have lost as moderns is to see the "sympathetic magic" that actually inheres in the structure of the created world. From the doubling over of the stream of water which can mesmerize us with its incessant, undifferentiated tone, leap to where it is received— the ear—and find in this exquisite organ an echo of that doubling in its labyrinthine, folded form. Just listening for a moment to the cascade of words from out of the Romance languages should alert us to the deeply magical character of the ear and that which it receives: Latin *carmen*; French *charme*; Spanish *encantado*—all signify "song" or "poem," but originally meant "a religious or magical incantation." Singing was originally, and still can surely be, a "charm" for spell-casting.

In ancient Greece and Rome, but even among folk cultures of early modern Europe, when oracles and mediums spoke, it was believed that the voices of disembodied spirits spoke forth from the *belly* of the oracle. That knowledge is preserved in our word "ventriloquism," *ventral* meaning the front/belly side. (Note that the ventriloquist, like the soothsayer, was understood as speaking not falsehoods, but *truth*; "sooth" is an Elizabethan word for "truth") And what lies within the belly? The *viscera*, whose labyrinthine structure echoes once again the form of the ear! Magicians the world over have used animal intestines to foretell events—the seemingly formless, non-directional entrails become in the diviner's hands a trail into the tangled forest of future events. The network of: cracks on a blackened sheep shoulder blade; delicate lines on the palm of the hand; rays in the eye's iris; tea leaves at the bottom of a cup—all become, in the soothsayer's vital, timeless and spaceless consciousness, equally pregnant tools for telling the future.

The next step in the intensification of consciousness we might call the Age of Myth. The mythic era *speaks*, and so art begins to show the mouth, which had been absent in the Age of Magic. In the 8th century BC, Homer invokes the Muse before beginning his epic poems, and the Muse has a rudimentary myth-uttering mouth. The simple slits on the Bellows Falls petroglyphs suggest that the people who made them had also stepped forth into the mythic consciousness. But the aura has diminished to two thin lines, indicating that where the mouth appears, the aura diminishes, eventually to be replaced entirely by the mouth. Once again, the words carry the history. "Mouth" and "myth" both stem from the Greek *mytheomai*, meaning "to discourse, talk, speak," and farther back *mu-*, "to sound." A related verb, *myein*, means "to close," as in to close the eyes or the mouth, and from this comes the Sanskrit *mukas* and Latin *mutus*, "mute, silent." The Greek *mystes* ("the consecrated") and *mysterion* ("mysterium") take us back to the time when in the early Christian monasteries, monks meditated with closed eyes.

The inward-turned eyes mean that the words spoken into the silence were aimed at the heart rather than the ear. The Bible is a rich source for seeing this relationship: "Thy words were unto me a joy and the rejoicing of my heart." (Jeremiah 15:16); "Now Hannah spake in her heart." (Samuel 1:13); "And these words…shall be upon thine heart." (Deuteronomy 6:6) "Out of the abundance of the heart the mouth speaketh." (Matthew 12:34); "Mary pondered these words in her heart." (Luke 2:19) The French saying *Savoir Coeur* and English "to know by heart" preserve this deep relationship from mouth to heart.

That the Elizabethan injunction "Take heart!" has yielded to "Look out!" and "Keep an eye on things" is no coincidence. Becoming "modern" meant first and foremost that the eye's empire triumphed over ear and mouth.

Perhaps you have been wondering how it is that a World History textbook has yet to include a timeline to help keep track of events. I was thinking that it would be more fun to have *you* make that timeline. Take five minutes now, and from your reading so far, make a timeline in the space below, noting events and individuals with dates:

Now, take a look at the timelines that you can find here: *http://www.cabinetmagazine.org/ issues/13/timelines.php*. Scan down the page to the illustration from the 1493 *Nuremberg Chronicle of the World* (so-called because it was published in that city), which depicts the history of the world as a set of seven concentric circles, representing seven ages, from the Creation until the Last Judgment. The *Chronicle's* concentric rings look more like a labyrinth than a timeline, reflecting the fact that even learned Europeans were only slowly emerging from the encircled round of the mythical mindset.

Despite its obviously flawed chronology, this labyrinthine pattern is a much truer approximation of the personal sense of felt time in 1500 than any straight line would ever be. When you walk —as did countless Europeans did in that era, in virtual pilgrimages to Jerusalem or other holy sites—the labyrinth at Chartres Cathedral (created around the year AD 1200), you constantly double back upon your path, almost touching places where you have previously walked. That is what time felt like to the early modern person. The labyrinth was actually a technology for time—and space—travel. Crossing the threshold into the labyrinth, the pilgrim truly escaped his time and place, and fully expected that if he remained keenly attentive as he walked, that when he reached the center, where the luminous light of the three massive stained glass rose windows shone, he would dwell for a moment within the Eternal.

It would be another 250 years before the first linear chart of world history appeared. In 1753, the French translator and disciple of Benjamin Franklin Jacques Barbeu-Dubourg created the *Carte chronologique*, a 54-foot-long scroll in a wooden case that included names (complete with symbols denoting martyrs, tyrants, etc.) and events grouped thematically. Like both the "Tree of Jesse" pictorial representations of Jesus' genealogy that frequently appeared in medieval stained glass windows and illuminated manuscripts, and the next real timeline—English chemist Joseph Priestley's *A Chart of Biography* (published in 1765, this chart showed the life spans of 2,000 famous men from 1200 BC to AD 1750), the *Carte chronologique* conceived of world history largely as a succession of individual biographies.

Ascending Mont Ventoux

Charting the path of the European consciousness out of its magical and mythical labyrinth is a bit like walking the labyrinth; as you read this section below, you might imagine that you are walking the 11 rings of the Chartres labyrinth, anticipating the moment when you reach the center. Imagine that as we enter the labyrinth, it is the year 1250. In Asia, Mongol hordes, though having retreated after the mysterious about face at Legnica, are still violently expanding their empire, the khans aided by the scapulimancy and entrail-divination of their shamans. Just a half a day's ride north from Chartres, at the University of Paris, Thomas Aquinas, following the lead of his teacher Albertus Magnus, is championing the world-embracing empiricism of Aristotle, thus ending the long reign of Platonic and Christian "interiority." Troubadours were writing the first personal poems, opening a small but significant gap between the human being and nature. In 1283, the first public clock in the world was erected in the courtyard of Westminster Palace.

To reach the year 1283, you have walked forward to the first bend in the path. Now you swing way out to the left, turn 180°, and return towards the entrance, to reach the year 1336. 450 miles south of Chartres, a young man named Francesco Petrarca has just ascended Mont Ventoux, northeast of Avignon. This is the heart of Troubadour country, and yet no nature-loving Troubadour had ever climbed the mountain; when Petrarch does so, he feels he has transgressed something, and writes a letter to his former theology professor:

> Yesterday I climbed the highest mountain of our region, motivated solely by the wish to experience its renowned height. For many years this has been in my soul and, as you well know, I have roamed this region since my childhood. The mountain, visible from far and wide, was nearly always present before me; my desire gradually increased until it became so intense that I resolved to yield to it. . . .

An old shepherd yelled at Petrarch to stop, but he pressed on. At the summit he is awe-struck:

> I look toward Italy, whither turned my soul even more than my gaze, and sigh at the sight of the Italian sky which appeared more to my spirit than to my eyes, and I was overcome by an inexpressible longing to return home. . . . Suddenly a new thought seized me, *transporting me from space into time.*

It is as if the shock sends him backwards in the labyrinth, but he recovers, and steps back into space, describing the ridge of the Pyrenees, the Mediterranean surf at Marseilles, the Rhône. And again he is overwhelmed, so he opens up a copy of Augustine's *Confessions* that he has carried with him to the mountain summit, and as "God and my companion are witnesses, my glance fell upon the passage: 'And men went forth to behold the high mountains and the mighty surge of the sea, and the broad stretches of the rivers and the inexhaustible ocean, and the paths of the stars, and so doing, lose themselves in wonderment.' So it was for Francesco Petrarca—from that day on Mont Ventoux until the end of his life, he would feel and express poetically this radically new expansion of his soul into space.

It would be another seven generations before Cristoforo Colombo, inspired by his reading of Marco Polo's *Travels*, would launch forth into that space. At nearly the same moment (in 1325) as Petrarch's day-long hike of Mont Ventoux, a young Moroccan Berber named Abu Abdullah Muhammad Ibn Abdullah Al Lawati Al Tanji Ibn Battuta (known as "Ibn Battuta") was making his first *hajj*—pilgrimage—to Mecca; he decided to continue traveling, eventually covering 75,000 miles over the entire Muslim world and beyond. In 1450, the Ming Emperor would send Admiral Zheng He and his treasure fleet on seven voyages to India, Arabia, and Africa. But there was no Muslim or Chinese Petrarch who climbed a high mountain for the view, and so these Argonauts returned, content with what they had seen, and explored no farther. They and the civilizations that fledged them rested content within the labyrinth of their ancestors' horizons.[1]

---

1. As I was finishing this section about Petrarch, I Googled "Mont Ventoux" to find out how long the hike was, and lo & behold! The Wikipedia entry "Ascent of Mont Ventoux" says: "Twentieth century historiography doubts that he

To track the European mind as it groped its way out of the labyrinth of past habits toward the new, we must look to the artists. At the turn of the 14th century, Giotto begins to bring into his paintings the first suggestions of shadow and depth. He allows space to enter the scene. In the work of his apprentices, Fra Angelico and Masolino, daylight shines ever more brightly, accentuating forms of hills and trees, and the sky stands out from the land. Masaccio paints the first clear contour of a man. Within the single architectural and artistic masterpiece of the Duomo, in Florence, constructed between 1296 and 1470, one finds the new consciousness of space displayed in Andrea Pisano's bronze reliefs on the doors of the Baptistery; in Paolo Vecello and Andrea de Castagno's frescoes; and in Brunelleschi's dome itself, which could not have been constructed without his having mastered perspective.

If we were to say when, after all the meandering within the labyrinth of the fifteenth century, the moment finally came when the European consciousness stepped into the transformative center circle, it would be the moment when Leonardo da Vinci wrote his *Trattato della Pittura* (*Treatise on Painting*), the first scientific and not merely theoretical description of all types of perspective. Leonardo too had tread the labyrinth to reach the apotheosis of perspective; among his thousands of notes and diary entries, there is one containing his earliest idea about perspective: "Perspective is a proof or test, confirmed by our experience, that all things project their images toward the eye in pyramidal lines." In this single sentence, the Aristotelian/ modern perspectival and Platonic/animist pre-perspectival outlooks do battle. "All things project their images toward the eye" relegates all of the activity to animate nature, which the human does not *perceive*, but receive. But in a later note Leonardo writes: "Perspective employs two counterposed pyramids. The one has its vertex in the eye and its base on the horizon. The second has its base resting against the eye and its vertex at the horizon…The second perspective results from the first." With this shift of emphasis to the eye of the subject, Leonardo moves from unconscious *participation* to conscious *relationship*; it is a realization that becomes the inheritance of all Europeans, and eventually, the entire world.

Casting our own inherited empirical eye upon the past, we can say that Leonardo gives the science and art of three-point perspective perfect expression. More so even than Christopher Columbus, Leonardo launches the human being into the world of Space, ending the painful pilgrimage through the labyrinth begun in 1336 by Petrarch. It is as if his incessant dreams and drawings of flying machines were the material expression of this epochal shift in the human relationship to Space. Space becomes the insistent concern of a whole array of disciplines. Coper-

---

even did climb Mont Ventoux," and says that medievalist Lynn Thorndike in 1943 disproved Petrarch's claim of having been the first to climb a mountain for pleasure. The original insight of Swiss historian Jakob Burckhardt, who told Petrarch's story as part of his brilliant *The Civilization of the Renaissance in Italy* (1878), has been totally lost in the literalistic rage for "facticity" that obsesses contemporary historians. A century of historical research and writing about this extraordinary period of human history has steadily stripped it of all wonder, majesty, and mystery. Indeed, the term "Renaissance" is fast disappearing from use, as textbook writers opt for "Early Modern" instead. It is important for you to know that professional historians—the very ones who brought acute self-awareness to the telling of stories about the modern world—are profoundly unconscious of their own cultural, historical, and ideological biases, and forget instantly the partialness, partiality, and ephemeralness of their own narratives.

nicus shatters the limits of the geocentric sky and discovers heliocentric space. Columbus goes beyond the encompassing Oceanus to discover Earth's space. Vesalius, the first major anatomist, discovers the body's space. William Harvey destroys the precepts of Hippocrates' humoral medicine and reveals the circulatory system. And there is Johannes Kepler, who by demonstrating the elliptical orbit of the planets, overthrows the ancient world's unperspectival image of circular and flat surfaces that dated back to Ptolemy's conception of the circular movement of the planets.

Leonardo's most famous demonstration of the perfected art of perspective is of course his *Ultima Cena—The Last Supper.* You have by now (thanks to the digital extension of perspective into virtual reality) walked around the refectory (dining hall) of the Santa Maria delle Grazie monastery in Milano, and discovered that the painted space of the fresco continues the actual space of the refectory. It is a *trompe l'oeil*, a trick of the eye that relies on all of Leonardo's knowledge of perspective and chiaroscuro (the arrangement of light and dark elements). The trick begins with Leonardo's having reproduced in the painting the actual lighting situation of the refectory for the afternoon and early evening of the most brightly lit seasons of the year, by making the right side brighter and putting the left side in the shade. Both the imaginary floor and ceiling of the painted chamber appear to carry through the actual room's floor and ceiling. All the lines of the imaginary room converge in the central vanishing point located just slightly left of center of Christ's temple. Leonardo filled the painting with artistic effects that balanced the mere mathematical perspective; he accentuates the length of the table to offset the exaggerated depth caused by the centralized perspective; he brings the whole table with Christ and the apostles forward and tilts the table to give the Dominican monks of Santa Maria delle Grazie the sense that they too were sitting at the Last Supper; he emphasizes the presence of each figure by painting them as if they were each directly in front of the viewer, no matter how far to Christ's left or right they might sit (or stand—and again Leonardo puts illusion to good effect by keeping all the apostles' heads lower than Christ's, even when they are standing and Christ is sitting).

Unlike most artists of his day, Leonardo knew in exquisite detail the arrangement and articulation of bones, muscles and tendons, and was able to reproduce bodily movements in a realistic way. Along with dissecting corpses for his anatomical studies, he was constantly making sketches of living people in all manner of activity. He would often follow a person for a whole day if they had some feature that interested him. From every corner of Milan he found models to whom he would tell amusing or frightening stories, so that he might catch their features in different modes of expression. When some structure or gesture caught his attention, he would go further and further into it, experimenting with its form in caricature. Studying the details of one aspect of a subject, his attention would invariably be caught by some other details, and off he would go in total pursuit of that. Commissioned to create an equestrian statue of his patron Ludovico's father, he went to the riding academy to study the horses, and ended up making countless sketches that took him far afield of his original task. All of this activity was an entirely new form of artistic expression, since it depended on exact observation of the physical world. Leonardo is himself a caricature, an extreme development of an entirely new kind of consciousness. It will take the rest of humanity centuries to catch up with realizing the creations that spring from his mind and hand.

* * *

"Symbols are a language that can help us understand the past."
—Robert Langdon, *The Da Vinci Code*

In the *Last Supper*, Leonardo brings together his facial and gestural studies to capture the drama of the moment when Christ reveals to his disciples which one of them will betray him. Christ is the focus of the painting, both architecturally and dramatically. Through the open window directly behind Christ's head we see an equal measure of Earth and Heaven, indicating Christ's position as both human and divine. His arms make the universal gesture of wonder—"AH!"—a gesture that we too make when we feel our own unity with the cosmos, and the inner gesture we make as we stand before Leonardo's masterpiece. Don't just take my word for this! Stand up, and let your arms sweep out away and down from each other to form the gesture that Christ makes in the painting. As you make the gesture, say the sound "AH." Now try the gesture and sound again, but opening your arms up toward the sky. Doesn't it feel like "AH"? There is nothing learned or studied about such a gesture; it comes straight out of a universal language.

In the figure of Christ, Leonardo also adhered to the traditional symbolic meaning of right and left. The left, as the passive hand, expresses self-sacrifice; the right is the shaping, active one, here active in its reaction toward Judas's act. Perhaps Leonardo was even portraying an internal drama taking place within Christ and expressing itself in two so very different and contrasting gestures—the drama of life and death. With this *mudra*-like (*mudras* are ritual hand movements in Hindu religious dancing) gesture of Christ, the left hand opened upwards and the right hand downwards, Leonardo was following an ancient archetypal pattern of meanings that had for thousands of years been present in the world's Mystery Schools. The up-turned hand signifies life, the down-turned one death. Both together, in their perpetual alternation and mutual quali- fication, encompass the whole of human existence. It is a gesture that is found in depictions of the dance of Shiva-Nataraja, the Hindu goddess who destroys the world and evermore recreates it. It exists in classical Indian dance; in the dance of the Sufis; and the ancient Greek "dance of the crane." In Leonardo's painting Christ points to his own death with his down-turned hand that almost touches that of Judas, while the upturned hand (directly above which Thomas ges- tures with a heavenward directed finger) can be seen as a promise of resurrection and ascension to heaven.

In the differentiated gestures of Christ's hands, and those of all the disciples, Leonardo depicted exactly what he had observed, all of which has since come to be recognized by modern anthropology as the exact expression of the meaning intended in each case. The open hand with the palm upwards, for example, is the gesture of giving. In the painting, Christ lays his gift—his deed of salvation, which is about to be ushered in by Judas's betrayal– at the feet of the apostles and of the observer, and indeed, at the feet of all humanity. By contrast, his right hand with its fingers spread and palm facing downward is clearly the sign that something is being held back or warded off.

Since the beginning of Christianity, it was widely understood that Christ encompassed the whole Zodiac, and that the twelve Apostles were an earthly reflection of the Zodiac's twelve-fold structure, but it was not until the twentieth century that students of the painting assigned specific correspondences to each apostle. Before you read of someone else's schema for what those zodiacal correspondences might be, spend a few minutes studying the hand gestures of the disciples. Mimic the gestures yourself and see how they feel. Can you guess what emotion Leonardo was seeking to convey with each gesture?

Beginning at the left side of the painting: (You may be wondering how we know the identity of the figures in the painting; Leonardo left many sketches in which the individual disciples are identified. Apart from all of Dan Brown's other distortions and inaccuracies, here is a fundamental one of which his Harvard "symbologist" Robert Langdon should have been aware: all he needed to do to find the identity of the figure on Christ's right was to look at the sketches and studies, which unambiguously identify this figure as John.)

BARTHOLOMEW: the circular, forward movement of the R-gesture that expresses the will forces of Taurus directed toward the future.

JAMES THE LESSER: gesture of Aquarius and the M-sound; with hands and arms sympathetically entering into another being.

ANDREW: gesture of Capricorn; hands and arms face forward in the "confrontation of thought with the world."

JUDAS: the strongly clenched right fist and the asymmetrical, warding-off rigid attitude represent the formative force of Scorpio—the dark power of the S-gesture.

PETER: gesture of Sagittarius; the limbs/upper arm are gripped in the will-gesture of decisiveness formed by the upper arms and thighs.

JOHN: gesture of Libra; the hands placed one upon the other express the establishment of balance, of weighing up or considering.

THOMAS: gesture of Aries; finger pointing straight upwards, signifying uprightness

JAMES THE GREAT: gesture of Leo; from the region of the heart with hands and arms opened out toward the circumference.

PHILIP: gesture of Cancer; hands and arms folded in to the chest, a gesture that leads inwards and is constricting, a shutting-off, internalizing gesture.[1]

---

1. Michael Ladwein, *Leonardo da Vinci: The Last Supper: A Cosmic Drama and An Act of Redemption*, (Temple Lodge: London, 2006), p. 81. Matthew, Judas Thaddeus, and Simon are unidentified.

Did Leonardo *know* that he was connecting the apostles' gestures with the cosmic zodiacal forces? No, not explicitly; as with much of this painting, Leonardo was clearly *inspired* by invisible spiritual beings acting through him. (This is of the original meaning of the word "inspire"—to *take in the spirit*.)

There is so much more that might be said about the extraordinarily precise and universally true (as opposed to the sloppy and entirely false "symbology" of Dan Brown's novel) symbolic gestural language depicted by Leonardo. Like nearly all of the great mythic texts and pictures of humanity, the real hidden message, the real objective lying behind Leonardo's depiction of the Biblical account of Christ's last supper with his disciples is the development of the human being along the path of his incarnations on the Earth, and the vision of the higher self. In this painting, which Leonardo struggled mightily to complete over 16 years, we have the first truly great work of art to be created in the age of the "Consciousness Soul." What is the Consciousness Soul? It is that aspect of the human soul which becomes conscious through its own efforts of its true spiritual and cosmic nature. Perhaps now we are a little closer to solving the mystery of why it took Leonardo so long to complete the painting: at the turning point of an entirely new age in human consciousness, a single man, laboring almost tragically, could artistically and intuitively sense the vastness of the themes and knowledge to be included in this work of art, but in some way it was almost too early, a premature grasping of something that would need—just as the very capacities that Leonardo brought into the world would also need—much more time to ripen and mature.

* * *

The Age of the Consciousness Soul: Why 1414?

The Western world today follows, as it has for over 1000 years, a "Christian" calendar—that is, the way we identify any event in history is by its timing in relation to the birth of Jesus Christ. We take it for granted that all years before that event we call "BC"—before Christ—and after Christ's death "AD"—*Anno Domini*, i.e., "in the year of our Lord."[1] At the time of Jesus's birth, the constellation Aries was rising on the eastern horizon at the vernal equinox, the beginning of the year. The symbol of Christ as the "lamb" is partly due to his having been born in the Age of the Ram.

But today this is no longer true; if you stand outside on March 21, you will see that the sun at that time is in Pisces. This is due to a phenomenon known as the precession of the equinoxes. Though an astronomical fact known for centuries, modern astrology ignores it. The Earth's rotation is not fixed in space, but wobbles like a rotating toy top, so that the axis falls backward (counter-clockwise) through the fixed stars, 1° every 72 years. (One degree is about twice the

---

1. Many academics now prefer "CE" (Common Era) and "bCE" (Before Common Era) since they are religiously neutral calendrical notations.

diameter of the Sun or Moon as viewed from Earth.) Since there are 30° in each zodiacal sign, it takes 2,160 years (30 x 72) to pass through each zodiacal constellation. A "zodiacal year" (also known as a Great Year or Platonic Year, since Plato was the first to describe it) thus lasts 25,920 (12 x 2160) years.

Astronomically, the Age of Aries ended in AD 215, when the position of the Sun at the spring equinox shifted backward into the constellation Pisces. Early Christians' use of two fishes going in opposite directions as the symbol for Christ refers to this astronomical/astrological fact. If you are a math whiz, perhaps something odd has already occurred to you: according to what I have just said about the length of an astrological age being 2,160 years, the Age of Pisces should last until AD 2375. Yet everyone knows that we live in the Age of Aquarius, right!? At least, that is what the famous song from the musical *Hair* says. And also, perhaps you were born on March 21; according to contemporary astrology, that means you are an Aries... and yet if you go out and look at the stars at that time, you will see that the Sun actually rises at about 6° Pisces—in other words, *you are really a Pisces!* (Yes, for about 80% of the rest of us, that means we are also not the astrological sign that we think we are, but *one sign back in the Zodiac.*)

Here then is what the Astrological Ages should look like, based on the precession of the equinoxes:

Age of Cancer	8426–6266 BC
Age of Gemini	6226–4106 BC
Age of Taurus	4106–1946 BC
Age of Aries	1946 BC–AD 215
Age of Pisces	AD 215–2375
Age of Aquarius	AD 2375–4535
Age of Capricorn	AD 4535–6695

Within certain mystery traditions, however, it has long been known that there is a time lag of approximately 1200 (1199) years between each Astrological Age and its respective Cultural Age, that is, the period in which the characteristics of the major events on Earth are shaped by that particular zodiacal sign. This of course is the intent of all of this complicated reckoning—to interpret history as a process that is influenced by the stars. Here are the dates of the associated Cultural Ages:

Age of Cancer	7227—5067 BC
Age of Gemini	5067—2907 BC
Age of Taurus	2907—747 BC
Age of Aries	747 BC—AD 1414
Age of Pisces	AD 215–2375
Age of Aquarius	AD 2375–4535
Age of Capricorn	AD 4535–6695

The time lag suggests that *transformation to a new state of consciousness is not affected instantly*. It proceeds subconsciously as various cultural impulses, then openly manifests on a wide scale only after a certain period of maturation. There is an ancient esoteric law that says that all new human impulses first manifest themselves in a single individual... AHA! Born in 1452, less than half a century after the new age began, Leonardo da Vinci seems an excellent candidate for just such an individual, bearing within himself the most important qualities that will unfold over the 2160-year Age of Pisces to follow. At any point in human history, the qualities and conditions of consciousness that exist around the planet will encompass both past, present and future; during the 16 years that Leonardo labored on the *Last Supper*, there were shamans in Siberia and Australia and all over the globe who were still drawing flat, un-perspectival representations of their prey animals on cave walls, and then killing that prey by magical means.

The 2,160- and 25,920-year rhythms in Time are astronomical facts, a consequence of actual rhythms in Space; is this also true of the 1199-year rhythm that marks the "time lag" in history? It is determined by a remarkable phenomenon in the heavens called the "Venus pentagram," which is created by the movement of the planet Venus around the sidereal (literally, "of the stars," meaning the *original, actual* zodiac, not the tropical zodiac of contemporary astrology, which ignores precession) zodiac, every 1199 years. In the length of time it takes for a complete cycle of the precession of the equinoxes through the sidereal zodiac (25,920 years), the Venus pentagram makes about 21½ rotations (21½ x 1,199 = 25,778½ years). The ratio of the Venus pentagram (1199) to the precessional cycle (25,920) is a little less than 1:24, i.e., one hour to one day. In other words, if the precessional cycle is likened to a "world day," then the rotation of the Venus pentagram is one "world hour." When a new Astrological Age begins, i.e., when the vernal point enters a new sign, a "world hour" still elapses before the new zodiacal impulse begins to register as a cultural phenomenon. This lapse of time is "measured"—or expressed—by the rotation of the Venus pentagram.

The synodic period of Venus is approximately 584 days. Plotting the greatest elongation west or east of this movement five successive times over a period of approximately 8 years and 5 days traces the figure of a Pentagram on the Zodiacal belt. The left "foot" of the pentagram precesses slightly with each turn, so that it "migrates" around the zodiacal circle, coming back to the same point in almost 25,920 years—the same time that it takes for the precession of the equinoxes to return to the same point.

What proof is there of such an exquisite world clock? Let us consider the transition from the Age of Aries to the Age of Pisces. On February 26, 747 BC, Babylonian King Nabonassar began his reign —on the first day of the Egyptian month of Thoth. In Egyptian and Babylonian thought, this was considered to begin the Age of Aries. And yet we know with mathematical precision that the vernal point entered Aries in 1946 BC, not 747 BC Here is the exact number of the Venus pentagram—1,199 years!

In other words, according to the Hermetic conception of parallel histories in Heaven and on Earth, a new age in cosmic history began in 1946 BC (Aries), and parallel to this, after a time lag of 1,199 years, the Cultural Age of Aries started in earthly history—in 747 BC What developments in 747 BC suggest a real change in human culture? Cuneiform texts show that records of dated astronomical observations began in the middle of the 8th century. Roman historian Quintus Fabius actually gives April 21, 747 BC as the date of the founding of Rome. This points to both the formation of a new culture—Rome—and the transformation of an old one—Babylon. It is also at this time that the great works of Homer—the Iliad and the Odyssey—were written, works that served as beacons of Greek culture life for centuries. Just after this, the great cultural impulse of Greek philosophy begins to blossom.

From 747 BC, the Cultural Age of Aries lasts 2,160 years, until AD 1414. What markers do we have of a significant shift in human cultural history at this date, the advent of the Cultural Age of Pisces? Leonardo's contemporary, Castiglione, wrote about the *Homo universalis*—the individual who is universally educated, who lives in harmony with Nature, and "is able to accomplish whatever he wills." Just as the Aries consciousness spread from its center in Greece and Rome, just as the Taurus consciousness before that spread out from its center in Egypt and Babylon, the Piscean consciousness spread from its geographical center in Europe throughout the "civilized"—and even "uncivilized"—world.

What more exquisite exemplar of the *Home universalis* is there than Leonardo da Vinci? Born just after the beginning of the Piscean Cultural Age, his life captures in miniature the accomplishments of an entire age yet to come.

The advent of new Cultural Ages are always marked by the birth of specific individuals who have critical missions for stewarding the unfolding of the zodiacal impulse. If we scan the time-line of world history for birthdates around 1414, we find that Joan of Arc was born in 1412! At her birth, in the little village of Rouens, who could have known that she alone would preserve France—and all of middle Europe—from the dry, materialist consciousness that was already developing so strongly across the English Channel?

4: A Little Linguistic Interlude

THE MOST DISTINCTIVE HALLMARK of the Consciousness Soul is that the human being becomes aware of all the environments, the "matrices," in which he was once unconsciously embedded. Along with stepping out of the labyrinth of space by way of developing three-point perspective, the modern human being does this through a new self-consciousness about language. Rather than solely being moved inwardly and motivated outwardly by words, he can say from where and when the words came.

As modern speakers of the English language, which becomes in the centuries after 1414 a particularly rich vehicle of expression for the Consciousness Soul, what phrase do we use to indicate that something—an idea, an event, a person—is important to us?

IT MATTERS!

When we ask "What is the matter?" we are asking what concern or circumstance is of primary importance at that moment. When we say, "It matters to me that…", we state that we regard a particular condition as central to our well-being. We know the word "matter" also as the term for "stuff"—all the physical components that make up our world. But where did this word come from? How and when and where was the word "matter" first used? In ancient Latin, the word *materia* came from an older word, *dmateria*, which was related to the even older Indo-Germanic root *dem-* or *dom*, as in *domus*, house. The primary sense of the word as relating to the immediate physical environment continued to be prominent in late popular Latin words like the Spanish *madera* and Portuguese *madeira*, meaning wood. (We can hear this connection in the Spanish word for the heath shrub so characteristic of the Mediterranean chaparral scrub forest, *madroño*.) The related word in French, *merrain*, means "timber." This connotation of a physical substance was extended in all the Romance languages, in the words *materia* (Spanish/Portuguese/Italian) and the Romanian *materie*.

Thanks to the Oxford English Dictionary, we can trace the history of this word and its correlated concepts in our own language. The OED reports that before the 14th century, *materie* and *matiere* meant a particular sort of oak timber used in building and ship construction. In 1386, when Geoffrey Chaucer used the word in *The Canterbury Tales*: "Lo, goode man, a flie and eek a frere wold falle in every dissche and matiere," he used it in the sense of "an event, circumstance, fact, question, state, or course of things which may be an object of consideration or practical concern." In 1384, Chaucer used the word to mean "the substance of a book, speech or the like": "Hard language and hard matere Is encombrous for to here." In 1498, William Tindale brought the word closer to our own idiomatic "It Matters" Phrase: "What mater maketh it if I speak words which I understand not?" In Shakespeare's *Two Gentlemen of Verona* (1591), we hear Valentine's servant Speede say "Item—she doth talk in her sleep," to which the other gentleman's (Proteus) servant Launce replies: "It's no matter for that, so she sleeps not in her talke." In 1599, in *Much Ado About Nothing*, a Shakespeare character says: "I was borne to speake all mirth, and no matter." Though there was great mirth—sheer frivolity—in Shakespeare's speech, there was also great matter—meaning, or import—in it as well, and his adoption of the word that once merely meant a particular sort of construction timber, as a way of saying that something was of weighty substance, is a bellwether of where the English consciousness had migrated in the early modern period. In Shakespeare's time, the alchemical arts of inner transformation were becoming the science of outer transformations in Nature, i.e., chemistry, and by the 18th century the word had also come to mean "the substance or substances of which an object is made."

The human being is made of words, and this word "matter" has literally become the stuff of which we believe we are made. In Joan of Arc and even Leonardo's day, it was more common to think of oneself as made of "starre stuff"—cosmic stellar substance, fashioned by God into a body. Even Leonardo, the most masterful observer and manipulator of matter in his day, conceived of all of those intricately woven sinews and tendons of the human body as fashioned by God, not some "blind watchmaker."

While the discipline of history in the West held out for a while before capitulating to the Darwinian model of the universe, both macrocosmic and microcosmic, contemporary historical practice is absolutely and totally MATERIALISTIC. Consider the opening sentence of the textbook *Origins of the Modern World*: "We are born and raised under circumstances neither of our own choosing nor of our own making." To all of the historic individuals we have met so far—Genghis Khan, Marco Polo, Joan of Arc, Johannes Trithemius, Leonardo—such an assertion would have been seen as a very serious sign of madness. To embrace such a bleak, purposeless, un-free view of human destiny has serious consequences. *Origins of the Modern World* author Robert Marks follows this mad remark with another one: "In fact, the world we confront is composed of economic, political, and cultural *structures*." This is what comes of playing with Tinker Toys and Lincoln Logs as a boy! The entire cosmos is reduced to prefab, synthetic parts, and the human being who lives amongst them is a cipher, a naught, destined merely by biology. This textbook's opening chapter is shot through with the triumph of a materialist biological outlook on history: its consideration of "The Material and Trading Worlds, circa 1400" (the title itself declaring its materialist bias) concludes with the cheery tale of the Black Death, which is seen as the product of a "conjuncture" of the Bubonic plague, increasing population and worsening climate, and the besieging of the Black Sea trading center of Caffa by a Mongol prince. The concept that *matters* most to Marks is the "biological old regime," the Darwinian struggle for existence within a world of material scarcity and life-threatening disease.

Let us not fall back off the golden path of the Consciousness Soul that leads to the Grail Castle and the City of the Heavenly Kitezh, into the labyrinth of merely suffering the magical action of our words. We can bring into our consciousness a wider view of history, and of human exist-ence, by asking how other languages at other times expressed what they felt was central and sig-nificant about existence. What word or words do you suppose have been used for 99.99% of human history, to express "an event, circumstance, fact, question, state, or course of things which may be an object of consideration or practical concern."

IT SPIRITS!

Speak the word "spirit" aloud. Now speak the word "matter." Close your eyes and feel inwardly the experience of the two words. Perhaps it begins to be clear to you now why such a word was applied to oak planks and that those 15th and 16th century English speakers extended it to express their newfound fascination with the material world. "Matter" sinks as you say it, into the dense dark earth; "Spirit" soars, springing from our lips, as if to return home to Heaven. When Joan's judges sought to impress some particularly critical point, or John of Sponheim stressed a significant operation of Angelic action, they wrote *spiritus* (They both—and this was true of most written texts until the late 16th century –wrote in Latin). Outside Europe, where the previous ages/stages of consciousness (Aries/Intellectual Soul & Taurus/Sentient Soul) lingered, every single human language signified "significance" with metaphors drawn from the spiritual realm. (Remember that the Latin *spiritus* "descended" from its heavenly source into the lexicon of the human body as the least physical of things—the breath).

The most gifted of linguists to come from England over to the Turtle Island continent of America was Roger Williams, the founder of the Rhode Island colony. In his *A Key into the Lan-guage of America* (1643), he says:

> There is a general Custome amongst them, at the apprehension of any Excellency in Men, Women, Birds, Beasts, Fish, etc. to cry out *Manitóo*—A God; & therefore when they talk amongst themselves of the English ships, & great buildings, of the plowing of their fields, & especially of Bookes & Letters, they will end thus: *Manitôwock*—They are Gods."

"*Manitôwock*—They are Gods." Not "they are made of superior stuff," "they have good genes" or "Sweet!" *Manitôwock*, what they do or think or are rises to such a level of "Excellency" that they are god-like, and God, even in 17th century new England, is invisible to all but a tiny handful of humans—be they the native Narragansett or the English colonists, even a Divine like Roger Williams.

Now perhaps we can understand why the spiritual world *conspired* (literally, to "breathe together") with La Pucelle to drive the English back from whence they came. Attacked with English longbows and cannon and consciousness and language which insistently materialized everything within its grasp, the delicate folk soul of La France would not have been able to with-stand the English assault. Meat pies and English ale; Newtonian mechanics and Darwinism; McDonald's and Disneyland would have penetrated French culture even earlier than they did, and the world would have been immeasurably poorer for it. In the Provencal tongue in which

Chrétien de Troyes sang the Parsifal tale, the Grail Castle was *Munsalvaesche*, the castle of the evil black magician Klingsor was the *Chasteil Merveil*. The lower register sounds of both Monsalvat and Castle of Marvels again remind us of the English language's talent and tendency to densify and concretize.

Having heard this dichotomous pair of declarations—"It Matters" vs. "It Spirits"—you may be feeling that it is necessary to ally yourself with one or the other. One of the dangers in the era of the Consciousness Soul is that of "one-sidedness"; given through the Renaissance's conquest of space the ability to step out of the labyrinth to see the world in an objective way that medieval people could not, we at the same time run the risk of identifying too strongly with one or the other outlook. Medieval man ran no such risk, for *perspective*—the condition of stepping out of the labyrinth—was not yet his. The true goal of the Age of the Consciousness Soul (remember, we have a full 2160 years to ripen this fruit!) is to reach a state where we can hold *multiple perspectives simultaneously*. Both "It Matters—using this phrase as shorthand for a materialist, Robert Marks-style explanation of history—and "It Spirits"—a spiritual explanation of events and characters—are true. Both are false, however, when fanatically held to in isolation from each other. Yes, there were plague-bearing fleas that bit the rats that bit the humans and so precipitated the catastrophic event known as the "Black Death." But is this then the sole significance of the Mongol invasion of Europe? Can such a biologically determinist reading of history tell us anything about the *why* of such an episode? Biologically determinist history, like modern biology itself, banishes freedom, and so is left mute about the reason for any chain of events. All of our modern concepts for describing the world are at best *proximal*, when the Age of the Consciousness Soul demands that our concepts strive for *ultimate* insight.

From an "It Spirits" perspective—one that acknowledges and celebrates the existence of spiritual *beings* that interact with another spiritual being, humans—the Mongol assault on Europe was an effort by certain powerful spiritual beings to crush the development of the Consciousness Soul, *which could only develop at first in central Europe.* In 1414, there was no other place on earth like Florence and Milan and Genoa; northern Italy ("Italy" was still 450 years in the future; the state of Italy was not created until 1861, before which it was a collection of warring city states) was as uniquely gifted in its combinations of season, light, cities, forests, mountains, and *fata* (fairies) as were Leonardo da Vinci or Lorenzo de Medici or Cristoforo Colombo in their individual talents.

Like Leonardo, we should seek to artfully balance Earth and Heaven, employing all of our senses' prodigious capacity for observation and description, never losing sight of higher, invisible principles, laws, and possibilities. Leonardo discovered the laws of perspective, then *went outside those laws* to create a masterpiece. If he had simply remained a slave to architectural law, the hungry monks of Santa Maria delle Grazie might have done more interior redecoration than the doorway they opened through the middle part of the fresco. During WW II, the monks might not have worked so hard to shore up the wall with sand bags to protect the wall from falling (an Allied bomb dropped in August 1943 destroyed much of the rest of the monastery). If we remain a slave to concepts like "biological old regime" and "contingency, conjuncture, and accident," we will end up inhabiting a very dismal story, a "tale full of sound and fury, signifying nothing."

I mentioned Robert Marks's opening assertion that the world is made of "structures"; he and other historians are also fond of explaining history in terms of *forces*. These are concepts diagnostic of the "It Matters" point of view, and valid enough for the material level of explanation. Note how insignificant, almost invisible, the human being becomes in such a narrative. Spectacularly variegated cultures of the past become mere variations on a few humdrum economic and social themes, and individual biographies—whether villainous (e.g., Genghis Khan) or heroic (Joan of Arc)—vanish. Spiritual beings are seen as mere hallucinations, conjured by historical actors out of childish fears and prejudices. Freudian interpretations of religion (humans invent God because they are afraid and full of unsatisfiable longings) give way to even more dreadfully pessimistic subsets of the "guns, germs, and steel" view of human history; the magnificent spiritual traditions become desperate life rafts thrown up as power-seeking humans inevitably crush each other in a long Darwinian drama.

You may seek long and hard, but you will find nowhere and at no time on Earth such a numbingly dreary story as this one. Instead, you will find myths of the crazy, cunning, chaotic, catastrophic, and creative deeds of *beings*. Literally hundreds of thousands of beings, some good, many very wicked. In between them all stands the human being, Parzival, dressed in rags (at first), a bit befuddled, but full of hopes and dreams. Like Parzival, we must learn to recognize the different sorts of beings (remember that upon meeting the knights in the Soltane Woods, he mistakes them for gods), or suffer the consequences of our errors in identification.

To master the world's taxonomy of the divine and demonic is an even more daunting task than the study of the past 500 years of world history, so we will attempt to understand just two— *Lucifer* and *Ahriman*. No doubt you have heard of the first—Light-Bringer; Morning Star; Satan; fallen angel of overweening pride. These days, it is more likely that you know Lucifer not from having read about him in the Book of Job or Revelations, but from the *Mortal Kombat* series, *Digimon Frontier,* or Neil Gaiman's *Sandman*. Ahriman might well be familiar to you as a cartoon character too; he has played a starring or supporting role in the *Warhammer 40,000*, *Dark Ages: Vampire*, and *Final Fantasy* video games; *Wonder Woman* comics; and the *Highlander* TV series.

Lucifer and Ahriman are not cartoon characters. They are beings, very powerful beings, which have had starring roles in all of human history. Lucifer's tale is told in various places in the Bible, and has been expanded upon in such canonical works of Western literature as Dante's *Inferno* and Milton's *Paradise Lost*. In the Book of Isaiah, Lucifer is heard to say: "I will ascend to heaven; I will raise my throne above the stars of God; I will sit on the mount of assembly on the heights of Zaphon; I will ascend to the tops of the clouds, I will make myself like the Most High." Lucifer seeks to encourage this sort of egotism in humans, approaching them from the will, so forcefully that the powers of thinking are cut off completely. Lucifer is a "cosmic fantasist," who preys upon pious people who strive after the spiritual world, and for the good, but only out of egotism, and without the light of hard won knowledge. His influence was especially strong in the past, and since the age of the Consciousness Soul, he has been eclipsed by Ahriman.

We know Ahriman from Zoroastrian thought, particularly from the great initiate Zarathustra. "Ahriman" is the English gloss on the Persian *Angra Mainyu,* literally "The Enemy Spirit." In Zoroastrian myth Ahriman is coeval with *Ahura Mazdao*, "The True God," and the two beings encompass the fundamental cosmic polarities—dark and light; death and life; evil and good. Ahura Mazdao, the omniscient *Asura* (Persian for "spirit") does not just embody Truth, Order, Wisdom; he *is* Truth, Order, Wisdom. Ahriman *is* the antithesis—falsehood, disorder, ignorance. In the *Rig Veda*, he is also *Druj*—the Lie; studying Ahriman's activity in the course of world history, one finds just how fitting this nickname is.

As Lucifer's aspiration is always upward, Ahriman's "direction" is down, into the material world, and his influence is felt especially in human thinking. He finds a very congenial home today not only in the realm of capitalist corporate culture, but in the university, where young people worship at the altar of disciplines whose directions –utilitarian economics; materialist physical and life sciences; dehumanized humanities; technologized arts—he has helped to inspire. Like Leonardo, the modern human being must overcome Ahriman by enlivening his thinking with the warmth of feeling; at the same time, we must temper the heat of our fantasy with the coolness of our hard-won reason. Like "It Matters" and "It Spirits," we must reach equilibrium between these cosmic antipodes.

If we think of the range of thinking, feeling and willing within our own character, or within our circle of friends and family, or beyond into what we know from our study of history, we can say that each activity falls within the spectrum of influence of these two beings. Consider someone you know who is an idealist. You admire his ideas, but he has a tendency in both his thinking and feeling to become too dreamy, too fantastic, too enthusiastic. All these characteristics suggest the influence of Lucifer. In his actions, he sometimes is authoritarian and tyrannical, suggesting his will life is Ahrimanic. Turning your attention to someone who is a "materialist"—that is, who places emphasis always on the material world—it is clear that his thought and feeling life tend toward dry, sober, bourgeois philistinism—i.e., Ahriman. His will however can easily become Luciferic—greedy, nervous, hypersensitive, animalistic. Writ large on the canvas of contemporary culture, we can see the catastrophic influence of both Lucifer and Ahriman.

LUCIFER

* Is more a being of soul and holds sway in man's inner being
* Is a haughty spirit
* Suppresses free will
* Robs man of the freedom to do evil
* Incites to transgressions of the will
* Fears conscious morality, but loves piety dictated by egoism
* Fluctuation; chaos
* He draws upwards, into the nebulous, mystical
* Has ascetic contempt for the earthly
* Promotes group-like emotions
* Is revolutionary
* Robs man of a genuine consciousness and harmony with the outer world
* Promotes hunger for knowledge

AHRIMAN

* Is more a spiritual being, the Lord of outer (material) nature
* Is a solitary spirit
* Strengthens the will, but only in order to achieve what is desired
* Inspires moral relativism
* Inspires error in thinking
* Fears the power of judgment, consequential thinking
* Emphasizes form and law
* Promotes pedantry and philistinism
* Furthers cold, inhuman science
* Loves routine and likes to work into the subconscious activity
* Is conservative and wants to remain in the present moment
* Promotes lies, clichés and ideologies
* Uses knowledge to achieve what is desired[1]

Sometimes when I have spoken of these two beings in class, certain sensitive students have been overwhelmed by a feeling of fear; one student even asked to leave the classroom! We must never forget that we all possess the one weapon that unfailingly vanquishes both of these spiritual beings—our *consciousness*. As long as our consciousness is clear and alert, unmuddied by lies, drugs, violence, fanaticism, depression, or fear, neither Lucifer nor Ahriman can harm us. Indeed, we strengthen ourselves through our confrontations with them; by individually piercing the veil (Parzival) of their illusions, we win something absolutely precious for all humanity.

A surefire way to allow Lucifer and Ahriman to wreak havoc is to mistake their identities, as has happened over and over in history. Most commonly, Lucifer is confused with God, and Ahriman with Lucifer. The names are legion by which Lucifer and Ahriman have been known, but once one has become acquainted with their misdeeds, it becomes possible to recognize the places and times of their influence. Let us begin close to home, in the year 1519, a century after the opening of the Piscean Cultural Age, the Age of the Consciousness Soul.

1. Gennadyi Bondarev, *The Crisis of Civilization: Anthroposophy at the Crossroads of the Occult-Political Movements of the Present Time*, (translated by Helga Schulte-Schröer, edited by Graham Rickett, from 1999 Lochmann-Verlag edition, p. 250

5: Who Could Shake the Foundation of Heaven?

Tenochtitlan
Proud of itself
Is the city of Mexico-Tenochtitlan.
Here no one fears to die in war.
This is our glory.
This is Your Command,
Oh Giver of life!
Have this in mind, oh princes,
Do not forget it.
Who could conquer Tenochtitlan?
Who could shake the foundation of heaven?
—Aztec poem

Growing up Mexica

Imagine for a moment that it is the spring equinox in the year 1467, and you have just been born into a Mexica (*may-shee-ka*) family living in the *capulli* (neighborhood) at the front of Chapultepec, the "grasshopper hill" along the western shore of Lake Texcoco. This is the place where your ancestors first settled after their arduous migration from the desert north. From the summit of Chapultepec, one can look east, following the causeway across the waters of Texcoco to the towering twin temple pyramids at the heart of Tenochtitlan (*tay-nosh-teet-lan*). On the face of the cliff—looking east toward the great city—are carved the countenances of the founders of the Aztec empire, Itzcoatl (*eetz-co-watl*), and his nephew Motecuhzoma Ilhuicamina (Montezuma I), the fifth Mexica emperor. Montezuma's image is still being sculpted by craftsmen; he has just ordered this as he is ill and fears he will die soon.

According to the *tonalpohualli*, the "count of days," you have been born on 12 Quiahuitl in the year 1 Acatl. The protector of the day is Quiahuitl (Rain), the provider of the *tonalli* (shadow soul) is Tonatiuh—the Sun God, symbol of the Fifth World, the present age. Quiahuitl is a day of relying on the unpredictable fortunes of fate; it is a good day for traveling and learning, a bad day for business and planning. The Mexica calendar is neither solar nor lunar, but instead is based on 20 cycles of 13 days, or *trecenas*. You have been born into the *trecena* known as *Tochtli* (Rabbit), which is the last *trecena* of the sacred year, signifying the end of one cycle and the beginning of a new one. This *trecena* is an auspicious time, when great Mexica unite in their goals, but it is also a dangerous time, requiring courage and diligence. For all Mexicans, it is the time when one's memory turns to the old god, the first god, who both divides and unites the worlds of dreaming and waking. Here between winter and spring, something wakes in the dreaming heart which endures across the cycles of Time. These are good days to focus on the needs of others, bad days to think only of oneself.

Before you were born, your mother would recite this prayer to herself: "Oh Lord, Creator, Master, Quetzalcoatl (*ket-zal-co-atl*), bring to me the precious necklace, the precious feather. Flake from yourself the precious necklace, place the precious necklace, here on my neck, upon my breast, in my hands." Now the midwife prays to Quilaztli, the goddess of childbirth, as she cuts the umbilical cord and places it in a special container for the burial ceremony. She wraps you in a cloth, and then the local *tonalpuhque* (priest) reads out your fortune, as determined by his reading of the *tonalamatl*, the book of horoscopes. The midwife then bathes you (unless it is a very inauspicious day, in which case a "second birth" is created by performing the ceremony on a more favorable day within the *trecena*) and places you in a cradle, giving you, if you are a boy, a small shield, bow, and arrows, and dresses you in a miniature loincloth and cape; if you are a girl, you are given a spinning whorl, skeins, a shuttle, and a reed basket, and dressed in a small skirt. Your father comes to give you a taste of *octli*, a ritual drink made from the fermented syrup of the maguey plant.

Within hours of your birth, your parents take you to the local temple, to dedicate you to either the *calmecac*—the religious school—or the *telpochcalli*—the secular "house of youths." If you are to enter the *calmecac*, a feast is given, during which the priest cuts you on the hip and chest—the scars intended to mark possession—and speeches are made that describe the special haircut that you will wear all your life. If you were destined for the *telpochcalli*, there was a different feast, where you were marked by having a hole made in your lip, for later placement of a lip plug. In both cases, the "Master of Youths" of the temple cradled you and sang songs to proclaim that your life was now dedicated to them, until you reached the age of marriage.

Every fourth year, during the month of *Izcalli*, the priests would hold a ritual to mark the transition out of infancy. The ceremony began at midnight, when the priest would pierce each child's ears, the first shedding of sacrificial blood. A cotton thread was placed in the wound, to keep it open for later placement of ornaments. Then the priest grabbed the child by the neck, symbolizing that he would grow tall. The ceremony culminated at dawn, when the children and their sponsors returned home to a day of feasting and drinking of *pulque*. There was much singing and dancing, with the adults taking care to instruct the children in the proper and exact words and steps.

At around age seven, children would be subjected to punishment for the first time, usually through the use of maguey spines to pierce the body. At age 12, differences in hairstyle for boys and girls first became apparent; up until this time, both wore their hair quite long. For the boys, this was incentive to achieve distinction as a warrior; once they had taken their first captive, the hair was shorn on one side. Only after the taking of the fourth captive was the remaining long tuft of hair cut off.

For boys, school began around age 15 or 16 (girls continued their education at home). At the *calmecac*, which was attached to a local temple, children learned the most elevated aspects of Nahuatl culture—history, painting, music, law, astrology, astronomy and the highly refined poetic language that was used exclusively by nobles and wise people. Some students also were trained in high quality craftsmanship—in lapidary arts, woodcarving, writing and painting, feather-working and precious-metal-working—and might eventually reach the status of *tolteca* (master craftsman). Students at the *telpochcalli*, on the other hand, received largely military training; drilling in martial arts and grueling periods of physical endurance prepared them for life as warriors. In both schools, instruction in singing and dancing prepared children for participation in the frequent and highly structured round of festivals of the Mexica religious calendar.

Boy or girl, noble or commoner, the most valuable lesson learned by Mexica youth was to always work hard and avoid laziness. The Mexica held that laziness led to ill behaviour—drunkenness, thievery, sexual promiscuity. These behaviors were severely punished by Mexica law, with children of nobles receiving the harshest sentences. Industry, duty, and productivity, however, led to a long, healthy, and prosperous life rewarded with status, responsibility and respect.

The Mexica Subtle Body

By the time that a young Mexica entered either the *calmecac* or the *telpochcalli*, he or she had an incredibly rich vocabulary for the human body. The Nahuatl language just before the arrival of the Spanish was simultaneously highly poetical in the sense of imaginative, but firmly grounded in empirical description. New words were always being formed, but very few came from outside sources. In Nahuatl, the most common name for the body was *tonacayo*, literally "the whole of our flesh." The same word was used for corn and other important fruits of the earth. In magical incantations, *chicomoztoc* was used to mean body, the word recalling the mythical place of origins of the Mexica in Aztlan, at the "place of the seven caves." Every Mexica was aware that the human body, like their ancestral homeland, had seven openings—two eye sockets; two nasal passages; the mouth; anus; and navel.

There is a surprising degree of convergence of the 16th century Nahuatl with modern English or Spanish in terms of the number of regions of the body for which there are separate words. The languages converge too in that the reproductive organs are particularly rich, full of spicy euphemism. Unsurprisingly, the male-dominated Mexica culture coined at least ten terms for the penis—from the straightforward *acayotl* ("the reed") to *cincul* ("the curved ear of corn"), *mitl* ("arrow"), *tepolli* ("the big ball"), *tototl* ("the bird"), *tlamazqui* ("the one who offers," i.e., the priest), and *xolo* ("manservant"). Occasionally Nahuatl words highlight the differences in body concepts from our own—there is no Nahuatl word for testicles, but there are half a dozen words for the kidneys which indicate that the Mexica held them to be sexual organs—"the gay ones," "the joyful ones," "the ticklish ones," "the voluptuous ones."

The sensual fidelity of the Nahuatl language can be heard in the words for the female breast (*chichihualli*), nipple (*chichihualyacatl*), and even the tip of the nipple (*chichihualcahuitzil*). The "*chichi*" is a beautiful onomatopoeic word that captures perfectly the sucking sound of the suckling infant.

The Spanish scholars who recorded the Nahuatl language after the conquest were keen to know how the Mexica conceived of that quasi-bodily entity that was such a mystery to the European mind—the soul (*anima* in Spanish). In 1555, Father Alonzo de Molina found that Mexica typically spoke of twelve different "animistic centers," but these really could be collapsed into three soul "entities"—the *tonalli*, the *yollia*, and the *ihiyotl*.

The *tonalli* is equivalent to the modern concept of the ego—the unique, personal self—but the Mexica word held in its three syllables wonderful worlds of cosmic correspondences. Literally, "what has been illuminated," *tonal* was associated with the primal Mexica myth of human origins, in which the gods gave independent existence to the human being by drilling fire into his chest. As the ego is the "Sun" aspect in much early modern art and literature from around the world, so it was in ancient Mexico. The verb *tona* ("to make warmth or sun") extended out metaphorically from solar heat to summer; day; day sign (*tonalli* also means the day sign when one is born); the destiny of a person according to his day of birth (thus *tonalamatl*, the book of horoscopes); the soul and/or spirit; even a term for personal property. Its linkage to the personal identity is seen in certain Mexica customs: its principal location believed to be in the head, it was dangerous to cut the hair from the back part because it might allow the *tonalli* to depart; stepping over a child's head was feared to harm his *tonalli*; twins and pregnant women suffer from a lack of *tonalli*.

The *yolia* was the term that the Spanish most readily identified with their word *anima*; indeed, *teanima* became an early Spahish loanword adopted into the Nahuatl language during the colonial era. The *yolia* was believed to be an animating force that survived after death. The related word, *yollotl*, meant both "heart" and "vitality," but even more directly, "movement," and thus is related to the *ollin* character, the day sign for motion, and essentially the Mexican equivalent of the swastika or yin-yang symbol. Sahagun said that the Mexicans believed that after death the *yolia* became a bird, and this belief may have helped Mexicans to adopt the Spanish iconography of winged angels and cherubs.

Yolia was most closely associated with the heart, and the Mexica believed that the heart received some divine force. Any brilliant individual was said to have a "divine heart" (*yoteutl*), while poor performers in art, divination, or other endeavors was *yolloquimilli*—a "heart wrapped in turkey feathers." As the heart principle, *yolia* was tied to the emotions. In modern esoteric parlance, the *yolia* is the "astral body."

The last of the three entities was the *ihiyotl*, which was identified with the liver, and implicated in the magical practice of the evil eye and the harmful emanations from the dead. The *ihiyotl* was known to be a source of energy which could be used for one own benefit or for others. A headache could be cured with the *ihiyotl* in the breath, or applying *ihiyotl* with the hand brought strength. But its promiscuous release, or its use with malicious intent, could cause catastrophic damage. Sorcerers breathed *ihiyotl* on their victims to bewitch or destroy them. Again, if we were to equate *ihiyotl* with a modern term from the vocabulary describing the human subtle body, it is the "etheric," known from Asia as *chi*, and in other places as *mana* (Polynesia), *orenda* (Iroquois), *manitou* (Algonquian).

All three animate entities—the "subtle bodies" that extended beyond the human physical body and connected it to the 13 heavens (and 9 hells)—were conceived as being constituents of the blood. In anatomical terms blood was *etzli*, but a more common way to refer to it was as *chalchihuatl*, "precious liquid." Tenochtitlan was a city soaked in human sacrificial blood at a time in history when most of the world's people had escaped the nightmare of bloodletting as a means of divine service. In the Mexica mind, a violent death allowed the gods to partake of the vital energy for which they were supposedly so greedy. Sacrificial blood was meant to revitalize the Sun, which, lacking nourishment, would languish to the point of failing to sustain the cosmic order. Rain, fertility, human health, military power—all were bought from the gods with the blood of sacrifice. The priests officiating at sacrifices anointed the lips of the stone idols with the blood of those killed in their rites, and they flung drops of blood to the four directions so that the gods of all four quarters would receive part of the feast. In this way the "precious liquid" invigorated all the lords of the universe.

Sacred Bloodletting

One of the earliest stories that Mexica children heard was how their people had first come to *Anahuac*—the "country of the waters," the Mexica name for their adopted homeland in the Valley of Mexico, and its imperial extensions. Centuries before, when they were merely the *chichimeca* (the *chichi* metaphorically describing their infantile state), a *tlamazqui* had had a prophetic vision of a new and glorious civilization that would arise in a marshy place marked by an eagle eating a snake while perched atop a cactus growing out of a rock. The eagle was the *nagual* (animal double) of the god *Huitzilopochtli* (*weet-zeel-o-poch-tli*), the "Hummingbird of the South."

Now imagine it is the year 1487, and you are twenty years old. You have performed well in recent conquests and have been initiated into the order of *ocelomeh* (the Jaguar Warriors). You have just returned from a battle with fresh captives for the ceremony that will dedicate the new temple to Huitzilopochtli, and as you watch from your place of honor at the base of the pyramid, a line of plebeian captives—their hands tied behind their backs, a leather choker around their throats—is coming through the Tenochtitlan gates. They are met by a band of priests who inspect them and waft incense about each one. Led to the bottom of the temple staircase, they are forced to do reverence before Huitzliopochtli's altar; they are marched to the palace to perform the same for Montezuma and his priest-advisor Tlacaellel (*tla-cal-yel*).

A line of captive nobles follows, and at Huitzilopochtli's temple they are made to place the richest gifts of treasure from their own lands. Kneeling before the altar, they pierce their tongues, legs, and ears with maguey spines, and then are compelled to make the ultimate gesture of surrender; they place their moistened finger in the dirt and then place it in their mouths. The highest of the lords has been coached by a priest, and makes his prayer: "I come to worship Huitzilopochtli, who gathers unto himself all nations; and now, as his creature, I come to serve him, bringing all my vassals and servants that they too may adore him and recognize him as their lord."

At daybreak the following morning, your captives are among the thousands who have been placed in a close single file line down the steps of the great pyramid (it is now over 100 feet tall, in five terraces), through the city out over the causeways, as far as the eye could see. At the ends of the lines there are pens full of thousands of captives, waiting for the line to begin moving. As you look out over the scene from the rooftop of the Jaguar Warrior compound, it appears to you that the lines of victims stretch to the very ends of the earth. Every road in Tenochtitlan was choked with traffic; today would see the greatest crowd ever gathered in the sacred city.

From your rooftop you can see the platform at the summit of the new pyramid, and the twin chapels to Huitzilopochtli and Tlaloc, their upper sections adorned with intricately carved aromatic wood. Four sacrificial slabs have been set up, one at the head of each staircase. Adorned in their finest royal cloaks, Tlacaellel and the three kings of the Triple Alliance— Tenochtitlan, Texcoco, and Tlacopan—approach Huitzilopochtli's altar, make prayers, and then take their places at the slabs. As the sun breaks over the horizon, the great snakeskin drums begin to throb, and almost synchronous with the beat of the drums, the slaughter begins. Each victim is seized by four priests, one on each limb, and then flopped across the sacrificial slab. A fifth priest slips a hook around the victim's neck, to choke off the sound of the screams, and then the officiant raises the great obsidian knife and lets it fall with the full force of his upper torso. The precisely-aimed stroke slices the chest in two, so that the priest can easily reach inside the pulsating pool of blood and tear out the still palpitating heart, to raise skyward in offering to Huitzilopochtli. The carcass was pushed off the slab and kicked over the top step, to tumble down to the base of the pyramid, where another group of priests waited to dismember the body.

The careful ceremonial protocol that marked the usual sacrificial occasions was impossible today—the scene at the temple was one of barely controlled mayhem. Over the course of the day, the red rivulets turned into rivers of fresh red blood running like lava over drying, darkening clots, which occasionally broke off and bobbed downstream. At the foot of the pyramid, where blood and bodies came to rest, the priests struggled to keep their footing as they butchered. Others bailed up blood in jars, then ran off with them to all of the temples in the city, to smear onto the faces of the idols there.

By afternoon, the stench of death hung over the central part of the city, and residents left to stay with friends and family in the outskirts. But the slaughter continued—for four days and nights—and even the guests of honor fled in panic from their flower-draped boxes in the central square. No ledger was kept of the killing spree, but some of the eyewitnesses told later Mexica chroniclers that 80,000 victims were sacrificed over the four days. Some accounts state that Tlacaellel and the most stalwart of his fellow priests continued the slaughter until month's end, butchering over 100,000 people to honor the Hummingbird.

The "Prince-of-the-House" and the Rise of Huitzilopochtli

> Huitzilopochtli,
> Only a subject,
> Only a mortal was.
> A magician,
> A terror,
> A stirrer of strife,
> A deceiver,
> A maker of war,
> An arranger of battles,
> A lord of battles;
> And of him it was said
> That he hurled
> His flaming serpent,
> His fire stick;
> Which means war,
> Blood and burning;
> And when his festival was celebrated,
> Captives were slain,
> Washed slaves were slain,
> The merchants washed them.
> And thus he was arrayed:
> With head-dress of green feathers,
> Holding his serpent torch,
> Girded with a belt,
> Bracelets upon his arms,
> Wearing turquoises,
> As a master of messengers.
> —*Hymn of Huitzilopochtli*

Chimalpahin, one of the most reliable Mexica historians, wrote:

There were many great kings who inspired fear far and wide, but the one who was the most courageous, the most illustrious in the state, was the great captain, the great warrior Tlacaellel. . . . It was he also who established the worship of the devil Huitzilopochtli, the god of the Mexicans. . . .

Before 1428, and the victory of Itzcoatl and Tlacaellel over Atzcapoltzalco, there had been no temples to Huitzilopochtli in Tenochtitlan or its environs. Tlacaellel—who was the nephew of Itzcoatl and half-brother of Montezuma I—had pronounced himself "Prince-of-the-House," and assumed command of the armies of the Triple Alliance. But more importantly, he created a new state ideology for the Mexica, with the following edict: "Huitzilopochtli is guiding the destiny of the Mexica. Anyone who opposes the Mexica opposes divine destiny."

All three states of the Triple Alliance had archives filled with codices, maps, and genealogical records that told a remarkably detailed history that extended back into the time of the *Tolteca*, the "master craftsmen" claimed by the Mexica as their ancestors. A widely held legend was that all of Anahuac's tribes had come to this continent under the guidance of a single omniscient deity, *Tloque Nahuaque*. Landing near what is today Tampico, they wandered the Gulf Coast north and south before heading inland. After long centuries had passed, their god took leave of them, making this farewell through the priests:

> Our Lord goeth bequeathing you this land; it is your merit, your lot. He goeth, he goeth back, but he will come, he will come to do his duty, he will come to acknowledge you. When the world is become oppressed, when it is the end of the world, at the time of its ending, he will come to bring it to an end. But [until then] you shall dwell here; you shall stand guard here. That which lieth here, that which spreadeth germinating, that which resteth in the earth, is your merit, your gift. He maketh it your birthright. For this you followed him here. . . .

After Tloque Nahuaque (also called *Ometeotl*; identical to the Maya *Hunab Ku*) had departed, the Tolteca, still living as a single tribe, moved north and settled in Teotihuacan, where they built the pyramid temples of the Sun and Moon, in a kind of foreshadowing of the principal temples at Tenochtitlan.

In the hands of Itzcoatl's royal historian, Cuauhcoatl, these myths were totally twisted to serve the purposes of the new rulers. An official state history was created and then widely disseminated; it replaced Tloque Nahuaque with Huitzilopochtli, saying that he ordered the Mexica to leave their land, and promised to make *them* princes and lords of all the rich lands of the other six tribes. The older histories were ordered destroyed by Tlacaellel, who declared: "It is not necessary for all the common people to know of the writings; government will be defamed, and this will only spread sorcery in the land, for it containeth many falsehoods." This became a key part of state policy; whenever a temple was destroyed—the ultimate symbol of conquest—its archives were put to the torch, so that the new history could begin unhampered by the old.

Perhaps the most important new myth was that of Huitzilopochtli's birth. From bits and pieces of ancient Toltec myths, Tlacaellel, Cuauhcoatl and the *Pipiltin* ("Sons of Lords," i.e., the aristocratic Mexica class) told this story: Coatlicue, the Earth Goddess, was one day sweeping the floor of her temple at Coatepec ("Snake Mountain") when a ball of feathers floated down from the sky and touched her upon the shoulder. With this, the child Huitzilopochtli quickened within her womb. When Coatlicue's daughter Coyolxauhqui heard of this shameful news, she incited her brothers, the Centzon Huitznahua (the Four Hundred Stars) to destroy Coatlicue, because her pregnancy brought disgrace on the family. While in the womb, Huitzilopochtli swore to defend his mother and at the moment of birth, he sprung forth in full battle armor and war paint. After defeating the Four Hundred Stars, Huitzilopochtli slew his sister and cast her down the Coatepec hill, where her body broke to pieces on striking the bottom.

Tlacaellel ordered the creation of a large round stone on whose face was sculpted the dismembered Coyolxauhqui. Placed at the bottom of the steps leading up the pyramid to Huitzilopochtli, sacrificial victims landed upon it after their hearts had been extracted. The priests of the cult of Huiltzilopochtli were presumed to reenact with every ritual murder, the heroic deed of the newly-born Sun God Huitzilopochtli. Tlacaellel had also founded the myth that Huitzilopchtli was "The One Who Makes the Day," inferring that Huitzilopchtli must daily be fed with human blood if the day would continue to be made by the sun's arcing path. With these two myths, Tlacaellel made human sacrifice the organizing principle of Mexica social, economic, and spiritual life.

In the new mythic universe of the imperial Mexica, Huitzilopchtli was always associated with Quetzalcoatl (*ketz-al-co-ahtl*), the Feathered Serpent, lawgiver, civilizer, creator of the calendar. In Tlacaellel's version of myth, demons tempted Quetzalcoatl constantly to commit murder and human sacrifice, but his love was too great for him to succumb. To atone for great sins, Quetzalcoatl threw himself on a funeral pyre, where his ashes rose to the heavens as a flock of birds carrying his heart to the star Venus. A mural in the palace at Teotihuacan shows his first entry into the world in the shape of a chrysalis, from which he struggles to emerge as a butterfly, the symbol of perfection. Quetzalcoatl's promise to return in a 1 Acatl year became the fateful catalyst for the Spanish conquest.

While Quetzalcoatl was clearly a god with a long history in Mesoamerica (in the Mayan culture, he is known as *Kukulkan*), Huitzilopochtli was very little known. In some older accounts that survived Tlaclaellel's *auto da fé*, the two gods are actually inverted in their characteristics—Quetzalcoatl is the bloodthirsty one, and Huitzilopochtli is a much milder, benevolent figure. But one of Tlacaellel's propaganda coups was that after his raising up of Huitzilopochtli to supreme divinity, the god was silenced. According to the empire's official history, Huitzilopochtli never speaks nor appears to anyone after the accession of Itzcoatl—and with him his trusted advisor Tlacaellel—to the throne. Under Montezuma I's rulership, there were enough skeptical voices to cause Tlacaellel to orchestrate a public relations stunt; they made a public claim that Huitzilopochtli's mother, Coatlicue, was still alive and residing in Aztlan. Tlacaellel organized an expedition to find her, and they met a sorcerer who conjured a demon who then carried the party to Aztlan via their subtle bodies. As the story went, somewhere beyond Tula they met Coatlicue, who haughtily demanded to know who sent them and why, and then gave them a new robe and sash for her son. The searchers carried these back with them and presented them to Montezuma, who promptly draped them over the statue of Huitzilopochtli in the main temple.

It was hardly a convincing demonstration; more convincing was the rein of terror that Tlacaellel instituted in tandem with the new stories. Immediately after issuing his second edict— that the Mexica's mission was to bring the worship of Huitzilopochtli to all peoples and nations, even if by force of arms —Tlacaellel sent emissaries to the lord of Xochimilcho to demand that he provide labor and materials for a new temple to be dedicated to Huitzilopochtli. When the lord refused, the Prince-of-the-House directed a swift attack; hundreds of captives were brought back for sacrifice to Huitzilopochtli. Other neighboring lords were similarly coerced, provoked, and then attacked. Soon there was a regular levy of sacrificial victims from all conquered territories.

Tlacaellel also coerced the *pochteca*—traveling merchants—into serving as his spies in the outlying territories, and then sent ambassadors to each region, demanding that they worship and provide sacrificial victims for Huitzilopochtli; recognize Mexica sovereignty; and pay tribute. If the ruling lords complied, Tlacaellel permitted them to continue worshipping their old deities along with Huitzilopochtli. When they refused, the Mexica legions swept upon them without mercy, confiscating property, enslaving or sacrificing a significant part of the population, and burning their temples. All statues and other representations of the local gods were collected and brought back to Tenochtitlan, where there was a special prison for rival deities.

In 1440, with Itzcoatl's death and the succession of Montezuma I, Tlacaellel again strengthened the stranglehold of the Huitzilopochtli cult. He assumed the title of *Ciuhuacoatl*—"Vice-Ruler," but literally "Snake Woman"—and had a duplicate throne placed for himself next to Montezuma's. He now was supreme oracle of the empire. The chronicles read: "Nothing was done in the realm without his orders, and thus he used the tiara and insignia of the king." One of Tlacaellel's first acts as *Ciuhuacoatl* was to create a new ceremony called *motlatocapaca*, literally "washing the feet in blood." Beginning with Montezuma, each time a new monarch was elected, he was expected to personally lead the army against some neighbor, in order to accumulate enough sacrificial victims for the public coronation ceremony. The king was then expected to begin the sacrificial slaughter with his own hands, and continue to tear out hearts until his feet were covered by the blood of Huitzilopochtli's victims.

Bit by bit, Tlacaellel insinuated Huitzilopochtli into nearly every ceremony in the elaborate Mexica sacred calendar, and so the demand for sacrificial victims quickly outpaced the supply. In addition, Tlacaellel argued that Huitzilopochtli demanded *fresh* victims, and the ever increasing distance to new imperial conquests made this difficult. His solution to this predicament was the *Xochiyaoyotl*, or "Flower Wars," which were prearranged military exercises that took place regularly, serving both to train young warriors and to provide captives for sacrifice. Tlacaellel told Montezuma:

> Our god will feed himself with them as though he were eating warm tortillas, soft and tasty, straight out of the oven. . . . And this war should be of such a nature that we do not endeavor to destroy the others totally. War must always continue, so that each time and whenever we wish and our god wishes to eat and feast, we may go there as one who goes to the market to buy something to eat . . . organized to obtain victims to offer our god Huitzilopochtli. . . .

The Attack on the Grail in Anahuac

Modern historians routinely make glib, dismissive statements about this episode of human depravity and carnage that should make us shudder and weep. For example, here is how one contemporary textbook concludes its review of these events:

Aztec sacrifice, once perceived as a ruthless practice committed by a 'tribe' seemingly obsessed with bloodshed, is now seen as no more or less brutal than what many imperial civilizations have done to 'bring home the war.' (*2008 World History Annual Editions*)

We cannot—we must not—shrink back from examining this holocaust any more than we could or should turn away from confronting the holocausts of the twentieth century, or our own time. From Maurice Collis's *Cortez & Montezuma*, you have heard the story of how the Mexican Empire collapsed under the weight of Montezuma's fatalistic dread of Quetzalcoatl's return. We can now appreciate the role of magic and myth in the Mexica's futile resistance to the Spanish. The magico-mythical Mexica "simply failed to arrive" in the face of the rational, perspectival consciousness of Cortes and the conquistadores.

In the images that were created by European artists of the god Huitzilopochtli, he is invariably portrayed with all the attributes of a demon—horns, cloven feet, bat wings, a devilish face staring out from his belly. At one level, it seems that we confront once again the same dilemma that faced Joan's judges—angel or demon, God or Satan? From our perspective a half millennium later, the Spanish appear as superstitious as the Mexica, wracked by fear of wholly imaginary entities. And yet we cannot ignore the stunning conclusion that the entire sacrificial system was dedicated to a single, bloodthirsty being. Would it not be helpful to know the true identity of that being the 15th and 16th century Mexica and their subject peoples called "Huitzilopochtli"?

The main reason that we cannot turn for the answer to the Mexica themselves is that, no matter how much they were still in a condition of consciousness that largely precluded rational, perspectival thought, *they were no longer clairvoyant for the spiritual world.* Apart from the newly created imperial myths of Huitzilopochtli and other gods, there was a vast reservoir of authentic myth and legend that, as in other places around the world, gave true imaginative pictures of past spiritual realities. But by 1428—note that the establishment of the Mexica empire occurs just twice seven years after the advent of the Consciousness Soul Era (1414)—the only individuals with clairvoyant communication with the spiritual world were the *tonalpuhque*, the priests. The original source of Tlacaellel's power was his claim to divine communication; one of the reasons that Tlacaellel could be so successful in substituting a false image of Huitzilopochtli is that only a handful of Mexica (principally the priests, who were initiated however by Tlacaellel, and thus under his sway) were able to communicate with the spiritual world, that is, the "third eye" was largely closed for the Mexica people, just as for the Europeans.

Something remains hidden from our view—like the stone idol of Huitzilopochtli that Montezuma ordered spirited away after the Night of Sorrows. In the years after the conquest, the Inquisitors uncovered many places where the old idols were still worshipped, and blood sacrifices still made. Often the secret altars were underground, in the caves that riddled the volcanic landscape of central Mexico. Bishop Zumarraga, charged with rooting out the persistent pagan heresies, often found that demon-worship was going on right in his own community, without his knowledge.

But there had always been dark magic hidden in plain sight, at the heart of the Huitzilopochtli cult. It is doubly masked from us, since both the Spanish at the time, and even more so we now, are uninitiated into the black arts. *The cult of Huitzilopochtli as practiced by the priests was a path of black magical initiation, centered on the act of ritual murder.* At first deep within the earth, in the lava tube caves, but after 1428, in the rooms of the temples, the priests were given detailed instruction in how to carry out black magical murder. They were instructed that in ripping out the still-beating heart of their victims, the priests would become filled with vast spiritual knowledge, stolen from out of the spiritual world. The bond forged between murderer and murdered was so powerful that the murderer, still alive back on earth, would be able to see and hear all the things that the murdered soul experienced in his journey through the upper worlds of the thirteen heavens. The initiates were also promised that by carrying out these murders, they could achieve a form of immortality. Tlacaellel, who lived to nearly one hundred, and whose vitality in old age was a constant source of amazement to others, demonstrates the vampiric quality of black magical initiation practices.

What was kept back from all but the most exalted members of the black magical order is that the spiritual effect of these murders was to drive the sacrificial victim's soul away from the Earth, with the intention never to return. These revolting mystery practices were thus ultimately aimed at creating an entire culture oriented toward fleeing the Earth. Under Tlacaellel's supervision, the Mexica were well on their way to founding such a culture, before the arrival of the Spanish put an end to the widespread practice of black magic.

Tlacaellel did not invent this system of black magic, but only stewarded the resurgence of an ancient practice. Fifteen hundred years before, in the caves below the ancient city of Teotihuacan, there had been a similar black magical mystery school, dedicated not to Huitzilopochtli, *but to Quetzalcoatl.* The being called "Quetzalcoatl" by both the ancient Toltec and the modern Mexica was and is identical with the being known in Abrahamic traditions (Christianity, Judaism, and Islam) as Lucifer. Even with all of the twisting that was done by Tlacaellel and the Huitzilopochtli cult, the fundamental iconography of Quetzalcoatl shows that he was perceived as a *serpent*, just as he was clairvoyantly perceived in the ancient Abrahamic traditions.

East and West, past and present, the gods go by many names, but we can best know their identity by the attributes that men give them. As the Dragon, Lucifer had brought knowledge to human beings of Asia. He was known there as *Tao*; in ancient Mexico, at the time of the Toltecs, he was *Taotl*. Looking back now upon Genghis Khan's mentor Kököchu's encounter with the god Tengri, one recognizes *Tao/Lucifer/Taotl*, who chose the boy Temujin to *drive human souls away from the Earth*. As another dragon-being—the "Plumed Serpent" Quetzalcoatl/Lucifer pursued this same goal on the North American continent, having won over the allegiance of Tolteca priests as the implementers of his diabolical scheme.

In earlier times, at Teotihuacan, the "birthplace of the gods," Quetzalcoatl had worked particularly through a skilled—the most skilled ever—black magician, whose powers had been won through a lifetime of committing ritual murder. In the very first decades of the first century AD, this magician had collected around him a devoted retinue of black magicians, all initiated through the same process of committing heart sacrifice on innocent victims. The Valley of Mexico, the heart of Mesoamerica, was at the turn of the first millennium AD becoming a Valley of Death, as it would become again fifteen centuries later.

Not all Toltecs accepted the Quetzalcoatl cult; opposed to it were individuals who were devoted to a being they knew as *Tezcatlipoca*. Once again, we must put aside the post-1428, Tlacaellel-created myths of the "Smoking Mirror," and seek the original myths. One of the most helpful indications is Tezcatlipoca's alternate name, *Yohualli Ehecatl*, usually translated as "Night Wind." One Nahuatl text describes Tezcatlipoca/Yohualli Ecatl as "*can iuhqujn ioalli, i ehecatl*," which translates as: "he was invisible, like the night and the wind." The related Nahuatl word *ceoalli* means "just like a shadow," and both point to his nature as an invisible, etheric being, who communicated with his initiates just as Quetzalcoatl did with his black magicians— through trained clairvoyance within the mystery practices.

At the center of the Tezcatlipoca mysteries was devotion not to heart sacrifice, but to *sacrifice of the heart*, that is, consecration of one's own inner self to the supreme god. Piety, chastity, purity of thought and deed—these were the core values of the Tezcatlipoca mysteries, which began to be adopted outside of the mystery centers, among portions of the Toltec people. While within the black magical schools novices gained power by inflicting pain and suffering, in Tezcatlipoca's school the novices adhered to the white magical principle that no power could be gained without the rigorous practice of selfless devotion. One could think of the Tezcatlipoca teachings as the "American Grail Mysteries," since the ideals and practices were so consistent with the Grail tradition that would develop in Europe in later centuries.

But, as would happen with the Mexica thanks to the devious workings of Tlacaellel, the Quetzalcoatl-inspired black magician gained the upper hand, and the pyramids of the Sun and Moon at Teotihuacan became drenched in sacrificial blood. One member of the Tezcatlipoca sect emerged to wage war on both the inner and outer planes against the Quetzalcoatl cult; *his name was Huiltzilopochtli*, the "Hummingbird of the South." Huitzilopochtli, though a human being and not a god, *was born of a virgin in the year 1 AD, the same year as the birth of the Quetzalcoatl cult black magician*. At the age of thirty, in 30 AD, the black magician and his followers had gained such a grip on Teotihuacan and its hinterland that the practice of heart sacrifice was spreading abroad under the Toltec imperial impulse. More importantly, the black magical practices were succeeding in driving souls away from the earth; with each ritual murder, the Quetzalcoatl priests gained more occult knowledge and succeeded in "detouring" the rightful path of human evolution in this part of the world.

For three years, Huitzilopochtli led a campaign against the Quetzalcoatl cult; the Tlacaellel-fabricated Mexica myth of Huitzilopochtli's birth preserves some memory of this in its tale of Huitzilopochtli's campaign against the Centzon Huitznahua—the Four Hundred Stars—who most likely represent the forces of the Quetzalcoatl cult. Then, in the year AD 33, Huitzilopochtli captured and crucified the black magician, and, by his own white magical means, placed a ban on the soul of this adversary of humanity, rendering both his knowledge and his activity powerless. Huitzilopochtli won back again for the earth all the souls who had been wrongfully compelled to follow Lucifer/Quetzalcoatl away to the region known in the mysteries as the "Eighth Sphere," an illicit incipient planet that could be thought of as equivalent to the "Death Star" of the *Star Wars* tale.

That this crucifixion by Huitzilopochtli of the black magician had occurred *in the year 33*—

the year of Christ's crucifixion at Golgotha—suggests that the activities of the spiritual being Quetzalcoatl and his human followers were intimately associated with the events that transpired half a world away, in Palestine, Jerusalem, and finally, at Golgotha, the Hill of Skulls where Jesus Christ was crucified. It was as if Christ's adversary, unable to vanquish the Grail in the Old World, laid plans to crush it in the New World. Christ's central mission was to bring into world history the higher Ego of humanity, and to offer with it a path of *inner sacrifice*, through the practice of Love. In the volcanic Valley of Mexico, the infernal powers bubbled up like magma to institute a culture based on a counter-image of Christ. This indeed is the hallmark of black magic, that always and everywhere it appears it is only merely the *ape of God*, since it possesses no truly creative powers of its own.

This aping—the mendacious inversion of the Good, the True, and the Beautiful—is written all over the deeds of the Mexica empire. Tlacaellel stole and twisted the story of Huitzilopochtli's virgin birth; stole and twisted the story of Huitzilopochtli's vanquishing of the 400 Stars; stole Tezcatlipoca's preaching of a culture of love, and assigned it to the adversary, Quetzalcoatl. Incredibly, outrageously, Tlacaellel completely reversed the qualities and deeds of the two gods and their earthly representatives—Quetzalcoatl and the powerful black magician; Tezcatlipoca and Huitzilopochtli. In the short space of a generation, aided by the coercive power of a cult of terror and backed by a militarist state, Tlacaellel turned white into black, black into white.

Here is the signature of *Druj*, the Lie, Ahriman. First through Tlacaellel and his murderous priesthood, and then with the aid of the *Pipiltin* aristocracy and the emperors, Ahriman was given every opportunity to suckle an entire civilization on lies. Reviewing last chapter's list of Ahriman's "attributes," we see Ahriman emerge from the figure the Mexica called "Huitzilopochtli." He certainly worked in the human will, both individually and collectively, in the fiendish, selfish manner of all empires. The rampant, murderous immorality of the Mexica priests and nobles was combined with a spectacular hypocrisy; the high ethical and moral standards that were supposedly held by the lords were instead routinely violated. Instead of justice, rote form and rigid law characterized Mexica rule. Though the Mexica placed great value in the acquisition of knowledge, it was only to the degree that the knowledge reified imperial aims and ambitions. The hand of the god the Mexica called "Huitzilopochtli" was in all these cultural patterns.

For all of their obsession with "honoring" spiritual beings, the Mexica were also prodigiously materialistic. When archaeologists began to excavate the lower levels of the ruins of the Huitzilopochtli temple in Mexico City, they found over 7000 separate offerings, most consisting of treasured, exotic objects from the farthest reaches of the empire. The priesthood was obsessed with honoring their dark god by way of the choicest material treasures. The sacrificial self-bloodletting of lords and peasants alike was another form of this acute materialism; *actual blood had to be shed*. Symbolic substitutes would not do.

In their attempt to shake the foundation of Heaven, Lucifer and Ahriman formed a cosmic "Double Alliance," a pincer-like action that for a few centuries, put the Grail in grave peril. The concerted, sustained attack by Lucifer and Ahriman over a millennium and a half suggests a sort of desperation on the part of these adversaries of the Grail, as if the sand in some cosmic hour-glass is running down to its final grains. This indeed is how Zarathustra's narration of the *Rig Veda* ends; he puts a time limit on Ahriman's activity, allowing him complete freedom to tempt and deceive human beings so that they will more fully develop their soul capacities, especially in the Age of the Consciousness Soul. Coming at almost the very beginning of that time period, the Mexica imperial onslaught was just a warning shot across the bow compared to what was yet to come.

Clothed with the Sun, the Moon Under Her Feet

Twelve years after Cortes arrived in Mexico, on December 9, 1531, the feast day of the Immaculate Conception of Mary, an Aztec widower named Cuauhtlatoatzin—called "Juan Diego" by the Franciscans who baptized him—was walking to church when he heard from the top of Tepeyac Hill an extraordinary chorus of songbirds, and someone calling his name in Nahuatl. Running up the hill, he saw coming out of the mists a beautiful woman, dressed like an Aztec princess. Calling him *Xocoyte*—"little son"—she asked him in his native language where he was going, and he answered by saying that he was on the way to celebrate the Virgin's feast day. The woman asked Juan Diego to tell the Bishop of Mexico, Juan de Zumarraga, that she wanted a *teocalli*—a sacred little house, to be built on the spot where she stood.

Juan Diego went to the bishop as instructed, but the Bishop, doubtful of the man's story, said that he needed some sign. Juan Diego returned to Tepeyac Hill and explained to the woman that the bishop did not believe him. After insisting he was not worthy and begging her to use another messenger, she instructed him to return to the Bishop, but still the skeptical Bishop demanded a sign. After she had promised one, he returned home to his uncle's house, and discovered him seriously ill. The next morning, concerned about his uncle's condition, he tried to skirt around Tepeyac hill, but again the woman stopped him, assuring him his uncle would not die. The woman, who referred to herself as *Coatlaxopeuh* (pronounced "Kwatlashupeh" the Nahuatl word means "She who crushes the serpent") asked Juan to climb the hill and gather flowers. Though it was December, when nothing would normally be in bloom, he found that the barren summit had been transformed into a garden, with roses from the region of Castile in Spain, the former home of Bishop Zumárraga. Coatlaxopeuh placed the roses carefully inside the folded tilma (cactus-fiber cloak) that Juan Diego wore and told him not to open it before anyone but the bishop. When Juan Diego unfolded his cloak before the Bishop, the roses cascaded out, revealing impressed upon the cloth an image of Coatlaxopeuh. The Bishop dropped to his knees before the image of the Virgin Mary.

Hearing "Coatlaxopeuh" as "Guadalupe," the Bishop recognized the image as *Nuestra Senora de Guadalupe*, a famous representation of the Virgin from his native region of Castile. The stars on her cloak, her dark face (the Guadalupe sculpture was one of Spain's Black Madonnas), the angel at her feet, her hands folded in prayer—all these features made the apparition meaningful to the Spanish. But when the story came back to Europe, *all* Europeans could recognize the symbolic language in the image. Her attire and hairstyle was familiarly that of a woman from the Holy Land. The nimbus around Her and crescent moon below was a reminder of *Revelations*

12:1: "the Woman clothed with the Sun, the Moon under her feet." The red, white, and blue feathers on the wings of the supporting angel symbolized loyalty, faith, and fidelity; his position beneath Guadalupe indicates that She is his Queen. Her blue mantle symbolized eternity and human immortality. The cingulum (sash) was worn by young unmarried virgins, a symbol of chastity. The whiteness of the ermine fur showed Her purity; the eight-pointed stars on her mantle represented baptism and regeneration. To any European of the sixteenth century, the stars also represented the heavens, and Guadalupe's role as Queen of the Heavens.

But more importantly, Coatlaxopeuh was immediately recognizable to the Aztec, who were even more adept than Europeans at reading the language of images. Standing in front of the sun, Coatlaxopeuh was therefore greater than the sun god Huitzilopochtli. Her skin was the color of a native Mexica; Her blue-green mantle was the color once reserved for the divine couple of Aztec myth—Ometecuhtli and Omecihuatl; the white fur at Her neck and sleeves and the gold border were marks of royalty for the Aztecs; the broach at Her throat bore the same black cross carried by Cortés and the Spanish Friars; the sash at Coatlaxopeuh's waist was worn by pregnant women in Aztec culture; the child She carried was clearly divine. Flowers represented for the Aztec the experience of the divine. The single four-petalled flower over her womb represented the *ollin*, the familiar Aztec glyph for the Fifth Age, i.e., the present era. The cross-shaped flowers on her garment were the *mamalhuaztli*, signifying new life.

Much has been made of the seemingly supernatural, or at least inexplicable, qualities of the tilma image—the method by which the image is imprinted into the fibers; the reflection of the Bishop's image in the eye of the Virgin; the survival of the image after an anarchist exploded a bomb next to it in 1921—but there are *natural* features that prove equally stunning. Depicted on the Virgin's cloak is an accurate star map for 10:30 AM local time on the day that the image appeared on Juan Diego's tilma. Spain was in 1531 still using the Julian calendar, so the winter solstice took place on Tuesday, December 12. The main constellations of the northern sky are laid out on the right of the mantle; on the left are shown the southern constellations that can be seen from Tepeyac Hill in winter at dawn. (In the Aztec style, East is at the top of the map)

The image is even dated according to Aztec practice—the three stars near the Virgin's foot represent the Aztec date of 13 Acatl, or 1531. Other groups of stars are placed not by their position in the sky, but to convey apocalyptic messages: the Corona Boreans (Boreal Crown) rests upon the Virgin's head; Virgo, the Virgin, is on her chest near her hands; Leo is on Her womb (she carries the Lion of Judah), with its main star Regulus, "the little king;" Gemini, the twins, are in the region of the knees; Orion, the Hunter, is over the angel.

Before the Spanish conquest, Tepeyac Hill was the site of a sacrificial pyramid dedicated to the Aztec lunar goddess Tonantzin, who was variously referred to as "Little Mother" (the patron of childbirth), "Goddess of Sustenance," and "Honored Grandmother." No doubt in some uncorrupted pre-Aztec form, Tonantzin had been a sustaining, nurturing, loving being, but in the hands of the post-Tlacaellel Aztec priests, she was a devouring, vengeful Spider goddess who ate her own children. Her fate was that of Huitzilopochtli and Tezcatlipoca, turned upside down by black magicians in service of the adversaries of the Sun Spirit.

Within weeks after she appeared to Juan Diego, Bishop Zamarraga ordered a shrine to be built where the Virgin had appeared. He entrusted the cloak with its miraculous image to Juan Diego, who moved into a small hermitage near the spot where the Virgin Mary had appeared, and he cared for the chapel and the first pilgrims who came to pray there, until his death in 1548. Even a decade before Juan Diego's death, only seven years after Coatlaxopeuh's appearance, 8 million Mexican natives were converted to the Catholic faith. Before the incident at Tepeyac Hill, the Franciscan and Dominican friars had been notoriously unsuccessful in their evangelization. Rebellions racked the countryside, and in the farther reaches of the old Aztec empire, heart sacrifice persisted.

Perhaps the original myth of a future return of a god to the Valley of Mexico had been true after all, but had centered on Huitzilopochtli, not Quetzalcoatl. As the New World emissary and ally of Christ—the Old World god—man who came to *end* human sacrifice—Huitzilopochtli's mission had been to institute a culture of *inner* sacrifice of one's heart to the Divine. Perhaps that myth, before Tlacaellel took hold of it and twisted it, *had* specified a return in a One Reed year. If so, "Cortez the Killer" (Neil Young's song title captures the widespread modern estimation of Cortes' legacy) truly did fulfill the prophecy, at least in part. The final fulfillment of the prophecy came only with Coatlaxopeuh's appearance at Tepeyac Hill, and the spreading of her mantle of stars over the Mexican people, finally free of the horror of the Flower Wars. The smell of brimstone and blood was finally lifted from their land.

6: The Disfigured Kingdom

IN THE NAHUATL LANGUAGE, the word for "human being" was *tlacatl*, but the literal meaning was "the diminished."[1] In this single word was preserved the sense that all Mexica shared, that the Golden Age of humanity lay in the *past*. While Cortes and his fellow Europeans were birthing the *future*, the Mexica—like many peoples all over the planet in the 16th century—were stuck in the labyrinth. In the Legend of the Five Suns, the only creation epic to have survived the destruction of the old manuscripts, the first human beings had been giants; with each successive epoch ("Suns") humanity had become reduced in stature. After the First Sun ended—the primal giant humans having been eaten by Jaguars—humanity was reborn in the Second Sun as monkeys, followed by a period as dogs. After a titanic flood in the Fourth Sun wiped out the Earth's people, Quetzalcoatl descended to the underworld to fetch the bones of the earlier generations, with which he repopulates the planet. In the Mayan *Popol Vuh*, a similar picture is given of human degeneration from a Golden Age; after he creates the world, Gucumatz declares: "Let their sight reach only to what is near; let them see only a little the face of the Earth!" With this declaration, Gucumatz casts a mist over the human beings' eyes, leaving them unable to see what the gods can see, and what the gods had formerly permitted man to see as well.

A whole complex of Nahuatl words expressed this sense of a Fall from a prior state of enlightenment. *Tlac* meant "half"; *tlaca* signified "reduced, depraved"; *tlacaellotl* was used to describe living things that had experienced a reduction in vigor or quality; *tlacaelleli* denoted someone deprived of his wealth, unfortunate, fallen into misery as a punishment for his harshness to the needy. The word is remarkably close to the name of the "Prince of the House," Tlacaellel. And yet, one more word from the *tlacatl* complex perhaps more accurately describes Tlacaellel; *tlacatecolotl* literally meant "man-owl," and was used for any malign supernatural being, particularly sorcerers.

That Europeans spoke of their own "enlightenment" shows that they did not share the pessimistic, backward-looking ideology of the Mexica. The future was theirs, and perhaps no development in the wake of the conquest symbolized this more than Cortes' decree ordering the immediate rebuilding of the center of Tenochtitlan. Upon the ruins of the Coatepantli—the snake-bedecked wall surrounding the ceremonial complex and royal palaces—he commanded that the victor's new ruling center should be built within 60 days. As the smell of death dissipated

---

1. Some Mexica used *Tlacatl* in the sense of the human being's essential qualities—peaceful, benign, friendly, compassionate, tender, merciful, modest, and generous. These were all the qualities celebrated within the *original* cult of Tezcatlipoca/Huitzilopochtli, and, since Guadalupe's appearance to Juan Diego, the possibility was offered for rededication to this lost essence of the human.

from the ruined city, the Cathedral Metropolitana rose into the sky directly across the square from the rubble of the Huitzilopochtli pyramid. The great stone serpents at the foot of the pyramid were buried as the cross was raised on the first steeple. While Tlacaellel's myth had Quetzalcoatl as the phoenix, it had been Huitzilopochtli all along who would experience resurrection. Perhaps the Mexica now understood why their Toltec ancestors had named him "Hummingbird," the tiny jewel that appeared to die and disappear each winter, to be gloriously resurrected in the spring.

Suffering the Tsars

At almost the same moment that the Spanish church was rising from the ashes of Tenochtitlan, Ivan the Terrible's Church of the Ascension was reaching skyward in Moscow. The eight onion domes, though calling to mind the Book of Revelation, were a departure from traditional Russian church architecture, in which a single, central cupola rose from a simple cube-shaped sanctuary. Before the Mongol invasions, the flat, often-featureless landscape of Russia was dotted with these single-domed churches, whose ground plan expressed a progressive, future-oriented sense of history that was absent in the Mexica pyramids. The four walls of the cube expressed the four members of the human being—physical body, etheric body, astral body, and ego—to which was added (via the cupola) a fifth element, the purely spiritual member that human beings would birth out of themselves in a future cultural epoch. Called "Philadelphia" in the Book of Revelations, this epoch was understood by Basil and other wonderworkers to be the *Russian* epoch, the period when the invisible City of Kitezh would once more become visible upon the Earth.

From a distance, these churches (many of which had survived the Mongol onslaught) give the impression of a pure, white salt crystal topped by an inverted cup or chalice. They bring to mind Christ's words: "You are the salt of the earth," (Matthew 5:13) and indeed, according to the Book of Revelation, it was in just this form of a cubic crystal of salt that the heavenly Jerusalem appeared to the clairvoyant vision of John on Patmos. As John's apocalyptic pictures were simultaneously revelations of the course of both individual spiritual transformation and the whole of human history, the cubic salt crystal was at once a symbol of individual and collective *resurrection*. In Russia, the festival of the Resurrection (Easter) had always been the principal Christian holiday, and even the most untutored peasant who passed through the church doors had an inner understanding of these great spiritual pictures made manifest in his local church.

In the same section (Chapter 21) of Revelations where John speaks of the salt-shaped heavenly Jerusalem, he describes it as having twelve gates, three facing each cardinal direction. In the old Russian churches, this was given architectural expression by means of vertical pilasters or columns that broke up the façade into three sections—the "gates"—which usually included a tall, narrow window. Round about these windows were sculpted fantastic, demonic animal and plant forms; it looked as if they were trying to gain entry into the church. Like the gargoyles of Gothic European churches, or the protective demon figures that adorn temples all over the world, the task of these sculptures was to draw down and enchant into stony immobility the evil forces that constantly attacked both the physical church and the future heavenly Jerusalem, through their attack on the Russian people.

The most common human figure sculpted on the outer wall of these churches was King David, sitting on a throne playing a psaltery (a stringed instrument similar to a lyre), surrounded by a host of fantastical animals and birds—all of which represented stages of inner development. Like the Greek Orpheus, David soothed with his music the surging passions and demonic entities that universally threatened to overwhelm the human being. This was exactly the image and ideal that was conspicuously absent in the Mexican mysteries, which were at the same time totally given over to these passions and demons.

The cupola of the Russian churches was usually covered with a thin layer of gold, and had the form of an upturned chalice. Eight narrow windows typically encircled the cupola, whose interior was ornamented with various designs, including the double helix enclosing images of saints, angels, and archangels. Entering the church, one was plunged into semi-darkness, while above, in the cupola, light poured in from outside. At certain times of day, it appeared that the light streamed *out* from the interior, a picture perhaps of the future condition of the transformed "salt of the earth," the human being as a radiant sun.

From the dark space far below, one looked up to see the paintings of the cupola bathed in streams of light. Like the great arches of the Gothic cathedral, the effect was to draw the soul upward, to come face to face with the Christ or the Holy Trinity, painted on the vault of the cupola. Sometimes Christ held in his hands a dove, surrounded by a halo of light, an image that would often come to life when, during a service, a bird might fly into the church, spiral up into the light in its search for an exit, and then disappear out one of the cupola windows. There was an old Russian custom of bringing doves into the Church to release during festival occasions; the special quality of devotion among the Russian people gave these experiences a heightened intensity. A "Grail mood" hovered around and within the Russian church, as surely as an "anti-Grail" mood surrounded the Mexica temples. This is something that we can of course still experience when we visit the great religious shrines of the world. The devotional aims and qualities of the celebrants create a distinct spiritual atmosphere that can either uplift or oppress, the moment one enters the church. In the great European cathedrals, the congregants often had an intellectual experience of their church. Under the dome of the simple Russian church, enormous heart forces within the people seemed to give them a direct, supersensible experience.

In Russia at the end of the 14th century, it became common to refer to a peasant by the word *krestyanin*, which was a slight modification of *khrestianin*, a Christian. This linguistic migration was founded upon the recognition that a Christian was someone directly connected with the earth. Whether directed downward toward the Earth, or upward to the spiraling dove, the Russian people had a unique capacity for empathy. As Christians, this empathy was transformed into compassion. Remember St. Basil, going about Moscow with his beggar's bowl, honored at the end of his life by the Tsar himself? This reverence for the beggar was not unusual in Russia, where all suffering, all injustice, was seen as noble, since these brought one closer to the experience of Jesus Christ. In practicing mercy to the least of their brethren, the Russian extended mercy unto Christ.

A study of Christianity's establishment across the vast plains of Russia suggests that while in other places around the globe the strenuous efforts of missionaries and monks were necessary to promote adoption of the new faith, in Russia there was an immediate and widespread affinity for the ritual forms brought in the late Middle Ages from Byzantium. That affinity was rooted not in the profundity of the liturgy, but its sheer *beauty*. All ritual activity—particularly when it is beautiful—has a strong effect on the etheric body of the participants, and the artistic forms of Byzantine Christianity wove themselves harmoniously into the etheric bodies of the Russian people. The effect of this was to strengthen the Russian's capacity for *patience*. This capacity also colored their relationship to suffering; *all* suffering—even when it was undeserved—was worthy of respect, reflecting as it did Christ's earthly suffering. There is something deeply true about the Russian's name for themselves—*Slavs*.

That slavery had begun in the 13th century, and lasted into the 15th century, under the Mongols. Early twentieth century writer Hendrik van Loon describes the Mongol "yoke" in this harsh but basically accurate caricature: "It turned the Slavic peasants into miserable slaves. No Russian could hope to survive unless he was willing to creep before a dirty little Mongolian who sat in a tent somewhere in the heart of the steppes of southern Russian and spat at him. It deprived the mass of the people of all feeling of honour and independence. It made hunger and misery and maltreatment and personal abuse the normal state of human existence. Until at last the average Russian, were he peasant or nobleman, went about his business like a neglected dog who has been beaten so often that his spirit has been broken and he dare not wag his tail without permission." Though the outer yoke of Mongol rule was eventually broken, it left a legacy of "inner Mongolism," a spiritual heritage of the acceptance of a centralized state. The first to manifest this inner Mongolism were the Muscovite princes, who successively turned their backs on the models of pious Christian princes celebrated by the *bylini*. The meeting of the rulers' "inner Mongolism" with the "Grail mood" of the *krestyanin* would prove disastrous for centuries.

In the late 15th century, even as Russia was finally liberated from the Mongol yoke, Ivan III (1440–1505) substituted a new form of tyranny, extending by violence Moscow's reign. Ivan gave himself the title *tsar* (from the Roman *Caesar*), and loved to proclaim that "Above Russia stands Moscow; above Moscow the Kremlin; and above the Kremlin stands God!" His cruelty paled in comparison to his grandson's, "Ivan the Terrible" (1530–1584). Ivan played childhood games humiliating other children and killing animals; at thirteen, he ordered a young Prince torn apart by hunting dogs while he watched. At sixteen he proclaimed himself Tsar, declaring Moscow the "third Rome" and himself God's representative on Earth. After a series of military victories that extended the Slavic territory of Russia, Ivan attempted to eradicate the entire Muscovite aristocracy; to assist this destruction, in 1565 he established the *oprichnina*, theoretically a personal royal bodyguard, but in practice a totalitarian terrorist organization.

In 1570, just a dozen years after he laid Basil to rest in the graveyard of the Church of the Intercession of the Virgin, Ivan launched an attack on Russia's most progressive city, Novgorod, where, despite the heavy tax burden imposed by Moscow, the people had created Russia's only real "European" city. The expedition had sacked each town and village along its way, and arriving in Novgorod, murdered 80% of the population—over 60,000 people. The chronicles record that the corpses dammed up the River Volkov, flooding the destroyed city.

Ivan professed that his principal motive for carrying out this destruction was that he was fulfiller of a higher will. "God's will is that man acts well and suffers. If you are righteous and good, why do you not want to suffer sorrow through me, your recalcitrant ruler, and so receive the crown of life [i.e., martyrdom]?" Here was another cruel inversion of the Grail ideal of sacrifice. Ivan's declaration was also a clear echo of Genghis Khan's claim that he was doing the bidding of the god Tengri. Even as Lucifer had been defeated in the New World, in the Old World he was working his old black magic through the tsars.

The response of the Russian folk to this Luciferic force of evil was to simply flee. By the end of the 1570s, the country around Moscow was deserted. While it is tempting to see this lack of resistance merely in van Loon's terms, a more accurate reading would be to understand this withdrawal as an inner as well as an outer one; despite their deep love for their native soil, the *krestyanin*'s sacrificial remove allowed them to remain true to the Grail mood in their soul.

Upon Ivan's death in 1584, he was succeeded as tsar by his second son Fyodor, but Fyodor's weakness allowed his brother-in-law Boris Godunov to rule from behind the scenes, until he became tsar at Fyodor's death in 1598. Although Godunov was from an old Mongol family, he embodied not the traditional feeling-bound ways of the Sentient Soul, but the advent in Russia of the Intellectual Soul—capacities that had long development of European nation states. While Godunov's predecessors had ruled ruthlessly and often arbitrarily out of their inflated passions, Godunov carried out his political agenda wholly within the calculus of modern statecraft. He waged the first campaign to transform the Russian state into a European power. Totally lacking in any education himself, and unable to read or write, yet Godunov attempted to establish in Moscow the first Russian university; he founded open-admission schools; he provided stipends for the sons of aristocratic families to study science in Germany and France. His own son Fyodor, heir to the throne, he brought up a European; Godunov even tried to secure John Dee— Queen Elizabeth's magician and alchemist as well as mathematician—as his son's tutor.

Though a "new" sort of Russian ruler in aspects of his cultural affinities, Godunov was like the previous tsars still modeling his idea of the Russian state after the Roman Empire. Furthermore, he followed his predecessor tsars (and Roman caesars) in his treachery against political rivals; in 1591, Godunov ordered the assassination of the 8½-year-old Tsarevitch (heir to throne) Dmitri, Ivan the Terrible's son, who was the only obstacle to Godunov's gaining the crown. Among the Russian folk, Godunov was widely recognized as having murdered the young heir, and when, after he was made tsar, crop failures led to famine and plague in the countryside, and refugees overran the cities, people blamed Godunov for bringing these disasters upon them as retribution from God for the killing of Dmitri.

This "Time of Troubles"—the interregnum between Fyodor's death in 1598 and the establishment of the Romanov dynasty in 1613—can be understood as an expression of the spiritual battle that was being waged for the soul of Russia. Destined to become in the *next* zodiacal period (Aquarius, AD 3574-5734) the place where the Consciousness Soul would find its highest development, Russia had many centuries in which to make the transition from the condition of the Sentient Soul to that of the Intellectual Soul. The new impulses in human consciousness always appear in particular places and among particular peoples, and experience long preparation. That the Intellectual Soul had first developed in Greece and Rome thousands of years before AD 1414—i.e., the advent of the Consciousness Soul—meant that southern Europe could adequately steward the radical cultural changes that the new consciousness would bring. In Russia, where most of the people were still within the condition of the Sentient Soul, forces were acting to try to bring in social, economic, and political innovations consistent with the Intellectual Soul, but in a premature, precipitous fashion. In the Spanish conquest of the Mexica, and all around the globe where European colonizers met native peoples, there was a dramatic clash of the Sentient Soul (the magico-mythical worldview) with the Intellectual Soul and young Consciousness Soul forces (in the form of rationalism, mercantilism, and other modern worldviews). A "Time of Troubles" was always the result. In Russia at the end of the 16th century, the clash of consciousness took place without a process of external colonization by a European power, but the conflicts all stemmed from European-style thoughts and deeds finding inroads before their proper time.

No episode dramatized this more clearly than the affair of the "false Dmitri." In 1603 a young man calling himself "Dmitri" appeared in the Polish-Russian Commonwealth, claiming to be the heir to the Russian throne. There was such widespread discontent with Godunov that a large number of Russians accepted the impostor's claim; indeed, there had always been rumors of Dmitri's survival, born out of the naïve hope that a rightful heir would put an end to Godunov's disastrous rule.

The false Dmitri had been educated at first by Russian boyars (the highest rank of Russian nobles) opposed to Godunov, and then came under the tutelage of Polish Jesuits, who convinced him that he was the true heir to the Russian throne. He firmly believed that he had escaped the attempted murder at Godunov's hands, and was destined to regain the throne. In June 1605, shortly after Godunov's death, the false Dmitri entered Moscow with 2,000 Polish troops. He was accompanied by his tutor-advisor Andrzej Lawicki. The Jesuits' aim was to replace Russia's Orthodox faith with Roman Catholicism, and obedience to Rome. This would have—just as had the Mongol invasions—stymied the rightful growth of the Russian people toward the future development of the Consciousness Soul.

The false Dmitri's disdain for Russian customs, and the Polish army's pillaging and desecration of Orthodox churches led the Russian people to quickly turn against the new ruler. A group of boyar conspirators killed the pretender, and eventually drove Polish troops from Moscow. But a third threat against the rightful development of the Intellectual Soul then appeared with the accession of the Romanov dynasty in 1613. While the first two Romanov tsars –Michael and Alexei Mikhailovich—established a footing for a gradual adoption of some European ways, Alexei's successor, his son Peter I, sought to destroy Russia's connection to her historical and spiritual past in his obsessive pursuit of Westernization. Tsar Alexei earned the nickname "the gentle" because of his gradual introduction of European customs. An important avenue of European influence was the arrival of foreigners; among Moscow's population of 200,000, 28,000 were foreigners (mostly German). The tsar employed Dutch painters; an English engineer was building the great tower of the Kremlin; a German pastor founded Russia's first theater company. Boyars cut off their beards and took up smoking, snuff, and Western dress. European tools and techniques made inroads in factories and mills. Moscow opened the first medical school in 1652. Literature, art, music, and architecture all began to show signs of European influence.

The True Dmitri?

All of these developments, however, were confined to the aristocratic class, and never took hold among the Russian folk. The most precious gift of modern Europe—the ending of medieval serfdom—never accompanied these superficial, largely aesthetic waves of acculturation. Indeed, with the *Ulozhenie* of 1649—a legal code enacted under tsar Alexei—Russian peasants were stripped of their one freedom—the right to change landlords once a year, on St. George's feast day, the 26th of November. The new code gave legal justification to serfdom, preparing the way for further exploitation by landlords.

To speak of "rightful destiny" of a people, or to suggest that anyone could know with certainty even the general outlines of a particular culture or nation one or two millennia in the future seems preposterous to us, and yet this Book of Wonders keeps bringing before your consideration instances of "seeing the future." The Grail legend as narrated by Wolfram von Eschenbach's *Parzival* tells of the progression of humanity through the stages of the Sentient, Intellectual, and Consciousness Soul, and thus contains a prophetic vision of Russia's path of destiny. At the beginning of *Parzival*, the story is told of the founding of the Grail stream by Titurel; he is succeeded as Grail King by Amfortas, and then Parzival. In these three figures we find the three stages of human consciousness evolution—Sentient, Intellectual, and Consciousness Soul. The drama of their succession as told in Wolfram's 13th century tale is a clairvoyant picture of what would come to pass on the plane of history, in Europe and Russia, over the course of the epoch of the Consciousness Soul, i.e., from AD 1414 to 3574. At the same time that Titurel, Amfortas, and Parzival are characters in a legend, *they also were actual historical characters*. Titurel lived in the 8th century, and initiated at that time a circle of twelve advanced pupils of the mystery school he had founded. Titurel named Amfortas—again, a real person—as his successor and thus "Guardian of the Grail." During the period of Amfortas' leadership of the Grail school, "Parzival" was the term used for a certain stage of initiation. Amfortas had himself been through that stage, and thus had at one time been a "Parzival."

Mystery schools are essentially a program for the accelerated evolution of consciousness; with the assistance of initiates, individuals who undergo proper training are brought stepwise into *future conditions of human consciousness*. In the Grail Mysteries of the 9th and 10th centuries, 500 years before the Consciousness Soul would "appear" on Earth in the person of individualities like Leonardo da Vinci, initiates could experience in advance some of the insights, ideas, and perceptions that would come to form the cognitive matrix for all human beings at a future stage of their development. At the Parzival stage of initiation, one received the secrets of the Intellectual Soul, *from one's teacher*. Wolfram's Parzival—the son of Herzeloyde—becomes the first to reach the stage of the Intellectual Soul *by his own powers*, thereby "piercing the veil" and winning *for himself* the name. Parzival's emergence from the Soltane Woods and his adventures as an errant knight are an imaginative picture of his achievement of the stage of the Consciousness Soul; he rightly replaces Amfortas as Grail King, and assumes the role of preparing a new circle of the twelve for even higher stages of initiation, and thus consciousness.

If Boris Godunov, the false Dmitri, and the Romanovs were the "unlawful" Amfortas—in the sense of improper leaders of Russia into the experience of the Intellectual Soul—one might ask the question: was the true Dmitri the true "Amfortas"? Would he have shepherded into Russian life the proper path out of the Sentient Soul, through the Intellectual Soul? Would his reign have avoided the crises of the 17th century—the schism in the Russian church into Old Believers and the Orthodox Church; the crushing "reforms" of Peter; and the introduction of legal serfdom, with the *Ulozhenie* of 1649? If the true Dmitri had been true to the "Grail mood" of the Russian people, and, as a Grail initiate, had possessed vital knowledge of the true destiny of Russia, would Russia have taken a different path in the 20th century?

Peter the Great, "Father of the Fatherland"

With Peter I, Russia's long struggle to birth the Intellectual Soul in a healthy way undergoes a challenging intensification. For "It Matters" historians, Peter I—who christened himself "Peter the Great" after a military victory in 1721—is a compelling figure for both his rapid introduction of Western ways into Russian culture, and for his leadership of Russia's imperial expansion. These historians have long debated whether Peter was Russia's great benefactor (for his imperial triumphs and his establishing a European culture in Russia) or nemesis, given that he forced the country away from its indigenous self, onto paths alien to its nature. Orthodox historians tell of Peter's subjection of the church to the power of the state; his building of a great naval fleet, reorganization of the army, and buildup of an indigenous armaments industry; his creation of the *Duma* and the secret police; his founding of schools, military and naval academies, and scientific institutions; his repressive system of taxation to finance all this, not to mention his tyrannical rush to build the new capital, St. Petersburg. They can agree that Peter's ultimate objective was to create an all-powerful state, to which every aspect of human life was subject.

Peter's relentless program of "reform"—the radical subjection of all domains of Russian life to the state—produced a host of new burdens on the already suffering Russian people. A lifelong recruiting system was instituted for military service; training was so harsh and provisions so poor that soldiers were put in irons to prevent their fleeing, and every recruit had a cross burnt into his left hand. A massive network of secret police was created—while other tsars had similar organizations, Peter's bureaucratic instincts put them on a footing so that they persisted until the 20th century.

"It Matters" history also is able to discern the streak of sadism in Peter's biography. As a child Peter's restlessness led him to endlessly seek diversion, particularly at the expense of others. During *sviatki*, the period of carnival between Christmas and Epiphany, Peter would delight in seeing fat men falling through chairs, and peoples' clothes torn off. Peasants were made to sit on blocks of ice, and then to suffer having candles shoved up their backsides and blown with bellows. At least one person is said to have died from this. He organized mock battles between groups of children provided to indulge his caprices. In winter, he would have holes cut in the pond ice, and then compel overweight lords to drive their sleds over them to watch them fall in. He was obsessed with fireworks, and felt no remorse at all when an explosion injured or maimed an innocent bystander. All his adult life, Peter continued to enjoy inflicting physical violence on friends as a joke.

Though his entire reign is characterized by episodes of brutal violence, two incidents stand out as characteristic. They are "bookends" to an important period in Peter's life—the "Grand Embassy" of 1697-8, when he traveled in Europe, ostensibly for diplomatic purposes. Just before leaving for the Netherlands, Peter learned of a supposed plot against his life by an officer of the *strel'tsy* (the Russian guard, created by Ivan the Terrible) in league with two boyars. In reality, the officer had merely complained about being posted far from Moscow, and the boyars criticized Peter's fondness for foreigners, and other behavior unseemly for a Russian royal. The Tsar had ordered all three beheaded in Red Square; he had the remains of a long-deceased rival disinterred and set up next to the execution platform. The coffin—which, as an added touch, had been hauled there by a team of pigs—was drawn up before the chopping block, and its lid was laid open so that the blood from the executed men would spatter the dead rival's corpse.

While visiting Vienna a year later, Peter got word that four *strel'tsy* regiments along the Polish frontier had risen in revolt due to the intolerable living and working conditions. Headed to Moscow to join their families, they had threatened to kill anyone who opposed them, but they were overcome by force of cannon and imprisoned, after the execution of 130 on the spot. Peter arrived to find 1700 *strel'tsy* in prison; he put them to torture—on the rack, with flogging, and by fire—over the next six weeks. When one man (falsely) accused Peter's half-sister Sophia of having hatched the insurrection, Peter had her shorn and confined to a convent. He they turned to executing the rebels who had survived the torture chamber. Peter goaded members of his *kompaniia* into serving as executioners, and it was rumored that he wielded the ax himself. Nearly 200 were hung right outside the convent walls, and the three accused of conspiring with Sophia were left dangling outside her convent tower window for five months.

"It Matters" history also usually takes into account Peter's "irreligion." While as tsar Peter often used the church to accomplish his aims, he was constantly abusing the church. He put impossible restrictions on the taking of religious vows; he called the monks—who under his rule were subject to persecution and high taxes (and even military service!)—"gangrene"; he declared that he saw no difference between Protestantism and Orthodoxy; confession was abolished by Peter's decree, and all priests were made to report to secular authorities. He disdained prayer: "They are all praying. What is the good of that to society?" The "Holy Synod" he established to rule over all ecclesiastical affairs turned church dignitaries into civil servants; all members were required to swear an oath of fidelity to the tsar as "the highest judge of this spiritual college." The Old Believers declared Peter the "forerunner of Antichrist," and there was a widespread belief among the folk that the tsar was possessed by a demon.

The Unholy Council

Indeed, despite all of Peter's divine titles—"Most Merciful," "Great Sovereign," "Father of the Fatherland"—his actions were indeed more demonic than divine. This was all the more pronounced because he routinely inverted the sacred symbols and actions and stories of Christianity. "It Matters" history sees Peter the Great as a rabid secularizer; he was, but while carrying out that frenzy of secularization of a country still largely dwelling in the pious comfort of the Sentient Soul, the "Father of the Fatherland" held a completely religious view of his personal political mission. Only through his calculatedly antinomian, anti-Christian gestures can Peter the Great be understood.

Both during his own lifetime and now, Peter's most notorious mockery of the Church was his creation of the *vseshuteishii i vsep'ianeeishii sobor* (C'mon, try saying *that*!)—translated variously as the "All-Drunken Council," the "All-Drunken, All-Jesting Assembly," or "The Most Comical, All-Drunken Council"—which adapted the indecent language, dress and games of the traditional *sviatki*. Mocking the symbols and sacraments of both the institutional church and the sacred tradition upon which it stood, the "Council" would ordain a pretend patriarch (the title for the leader of the Orthodox Church in Russia), dressing him in counterfeit hierarchical vestments, closely tailoring the blasphemous ceremony to the instructions given by the Orthodox service book. The congregants would then profess their devotion to *nekoego Baga*—i.e., Bacchus, the God of Wine & Intoxication. In Russian, God is *Bog*, while Bacchus is *Bag*; this sort of wordplay was common in Peter's burlesques. Each participant had a mock office and title and associated costume and duties, usually modeled after a particular member of the church hierarchy.

For two to three weeks after Christmas, the Tsar and his entourage would ride, in costume and always inebriated, to the houses of the leading members of the actual church members, singing Christmas carols and demanding payment from their hosts. This was very close in spirit to the tradition of carnival, except that the true *sviatki* was a ritual performed by the folk, who were permitted to engage in this reversal of authority but once a year, as a way of ritually escaping the fetters of social class that bound them the rest of the year. When the Tsar and his retinue engaged in this ritual, it was not carnival but its true *antithesis*; everyone but Peter was *compelled* into the charade, or lose the favor of the capricious and cruel sovereign. The Tsar's authority was celebrated as sacred, even as he always took the role of some lesser member—"Humble Deacon Peter," Proto-Deacon Pitirim," and the obscene "Crams-with-His-Prick Mikhailov, servant of the Arch-Prince-Pope"—of the Unholy Council.

At first, the Unholy Council would convene at the royal estate of Novo-Preobrazhenskoe (literally, the "New Transfiguration") but Peter found other theatrical stages on which he could simultaneously inhabit and ridicule the central rites and symbols of Christianity. There was a long tradition of the Russian tsars publicly demonstrating their respect for the wonder-working saints of the Orthodox Church by making pilgrimages to sacred shrines. These visits had the political benefit of reminding the public of the tsar's role as mediator between Heaven and Earth. For Peter, such pilgrimages became a way to get around restrictions on his activities; when he wished to go visit dockyards and wharves to indulge his fascination for naval technology, he offered to make a pilgrimage to a nearby monastery. In 1694, on such a "pilgrimage" to the Transfiguration Church at the Pertominsk Monastery, the boat carrying the tsar and his entourage nearly capsized in the Arctic waters directly in front of the church. Though his real reason for visiting the region was to make contact with foreign experts, test the latest technology, and get some nautical experience, his stated purpose was to pay homage to two famous saints whose relics were housed at the church. In monastic and local tradition, Vassian and Iona had drowned in a storm in 1561; the church dedicated to the Transfiguration of the Savior was built to house their relics, and the local people credited a number of miracles to the two saints.

After the royal yacht (the *St. Peter*, of course!) was brought in safely, the Tsar declared that their lives had been saved by the miraculous intercession of the saints. Peter ordered their relics exhumed, had a local archbishop officially recognize them as sanctified, and then held a service of thanksgiving at which the Tsar read from the "Book of the Apostles." He then made a gift of money, supplies, land, and fishing rights to the monastery.

All of this is easily seen as posturing meant to affirm and augment Peter's own personal charisma, but Peter went on to a final performance that at first defies explanation. Calling himself the *bol'shoi ship'ger*, "The Great Skipper," Peter decided to commemorate his rescue by personally carving a 10 _-foot tall pine cross, upon which he inscribed: "This cross was made by Captain Peter in the year of our Lord 1694." Just before the yacht set sail, the Tsar carried the cross down to the shore on his back, and erected it. Peter had always loved to play the role of the humble carpenter, and he delighted in substituting himself for Christ; in this charade, he got to reenact Jesus' procession to Golgotha, not as humble servant of the Lord, but *as the Lord*, whose disciples (his courtiers) all were gathered as witnesses.

Peter could easily carry a ten-foot-tall cross, as he was himself over 6 _-feet tall, and had powerful arms and legs; he literally towered over every subject in his empire. But he had a disproportionately small, perfectly spherical head, at the end of a thin, unusually long neck. It was as if in Peter's disfigured physique Lucifer—the torturer/executioner's strong arms—and Ahriman—the point-like head of the cold intellect—had left their signatures, as surely as they left them in the culture-crushing combination of Luciferic cruelty against the Russian people and the Ahrimanic abstract, legalistic state apparatus fashioned by Peter's "reforms." In Peter's crucifix-carrying charade, and a host of other improvised mockeries of the Christ, Peter enacted not a New Transfiguration, but a new *disfiguration*. His perverse talents were perfectly suited to destroying the tender shoots of the Intellectual Soul, just then breaking through Russia's soul/soil. He was also totally indifferent to the incipient developments of the Consciousness Soul; in 1698, during his stay in England, Peter was taken to Parliament and allowed to observe the debates through a peephole. His hosts explained the workings of the parliamentary body, but he showed not the least understanding nor interest.

Another small but significant gesture suggests that Peter's body and soul was not wholly his own; he suffered from a severe facial tick, and mild seizures in which his eyes would roll back, leaving only the whites showing. Demons had made their home in his gigantic body and shrunken head, and in these convulsive episodes, they showed themselves as surely as in Peter's seizure of the title "God & Christ," while hell-bent on acting against both.

* * *

In October 1812, nearly a century after his death, a document that became known as "The Testament of Peter the Great" appeared in Paris—first in a book by a French historian, then on circulars posted on public buildings, both in Paris and throughout France:

1. The Russian nation must be constantly on a war footing to keep the soldiers warlike and in good condition. No rest must be allowed, except for the purpose of relieving the state finances, recruiting the Army, or biding the Favourable moment for attack. By this means peace is made subservient to war, and war to peace, in the interest of aggrandizement and increasing prosperity of Russia.

2. Every possible means must be used to invite from the most cultivated European states commanders in war and philosophers in peace; to enable the Russian nation to participate in the advantages of the other nations without losing any of its own.

3. No opportunity must be lost in taking part in the affairs of Europe, especially in those of Germany, which from its vicinity, is of the most direct interest to us.

4. Poland must be divided, by keeping up constant jealousies and confusions there. The authorities there must be gained over with money and the assemblies corrupted so as to influence the elections of the kings. We must get up a party there of our own, send Russian troops into that country and let them sojourn there so long that they may ultimately find some pretext for remaining there forever. Should the neighboring states make difficulties, we must appease them for the moment, by allowing them a share of the territory, until we can safely resume what we have thus given away.

The Testament's great interest in the affairs of Europe and its appetite for expansion sounded like Peter, but the document was clearly a forgery. Its real author was General Michel Sokolnicki, who had spent two years in a St. Petersburg prison along with other Polish patriots, including Thaddeus Kosciusko. That such a manifesto would appear in France during its Napoleonic war with Russia is not surprising; it would continuously appear for over a century, whenever Russia's expansionist aims were on the ascendant. During World War II, it turned up at business luncheons in New York City and among the refugee camps of central Europe. Each time it was printed, it was accompanied by a commentary that drew attention to how closely the policies of the Russian Empire after Peter's reign had followed the "Testament's" propositions. There was also typically mention of "secret archives" in Moscow, where this plan was rumored to be preserved.

Point # 7 of the Testament begins: "We must be careful to keep up our commercial alliances with England. . . ." These words held the key to the real secret behind the Testament, and to the policies of the actual Peter the Great. Objective historians as well as Russia's enemies have detected a common authorship in Peter's policies and the devious statecraft recommended by the Testament, whose ultimate aim was the destruction of central Europe. The desire for this destruction was not centered in Moscow, *but in England, where it was the central doctrine of the Freemasonic lodges.*

This doctrine, founded by King James I, had at its foundation the belief that, just as Rome had "nursed" western and central Europe in their infancy, the Anglo-Saxon would be the guardians and guides of eastern Europe, which James and other English occultists knew was the seedbed of the next stage in human consciousness evolution. It also sought to derail the proper development of the Consciousness Soul, which needed the fertility of mainland Europe's diverse cultures, folkways, languages, and politics to grow and thrive. For all of its strengths, Great Britain's island isolation, northern clime, and Saxon heritage was far too parochial—and materialistic—to shape such a precious heritage alone.

But this is just what King James's wedding of occultism to politics aimed to achieve—to dominate the Slavic soul, and by so doing not only influence future consciousness evolution (in the Sixth "Slavic" Cultural Age of Aquarius), but also to squeeze out the proper guardian of that Slavic epoch—Germany, which was the rightful guardian of the Grail of human consciousness in the Piscean Epoch. As a high-ranking Freemason, and perhaps the most studied occultist of his age (his *Daemonologie* (1597) set the standard for the era's witch hunters), James was well-aware of the ancient mystery traditions' teachings of the rightful course of human consciousness evolution. At almost the same moment that the false Dmitri, backed by the Polish army and the Roman Catholic hierarchy, invaded Moscow, the newly crowned King James sent his agent Sir Thomas Smith to Boris Godunov to propose an economic and political alliance with England.

There is such a tangled thicket of events here! One of these events is the Gunpowder Plot of November 1605, when a group of Catholic conspirators tried to blow up King James and the entire English parliament. The film *V for Vendetta* has brought this extraordinary event before the public eye once again, and yet only to further obscure the real forces and objectives behind the plot. In April 1605, as Sir Thomas Smith was returning with gifts and promises from Boris Godunov, the tsar died. Two months later the false Dmitri entered Moscow and immediately dispatched his own courier to Smith, demanding Godunov's letter to James.

What is this tug of war all about? While James and a small elite of his Masonic brethren played Russia from the "right," hoping to bind its destiny to England, the false Dmitri's Jesuit backers made an equal bid from the "left." In either case, Russia's true destiny was consequently neglected, abandoned, obliterated. This battle between right and left continued right up to the reign of Peter the Great, who, in a very short time, gave the English puppet masters—the Freemasonic brotherhoods—everything they desired, in his attempt to remake Russia in England's image. Peter began that effort to transfigure his kingdom only after his 1697-8 journey to England, where he made contact with Freemasons. A number of legends exist about these contacts, including some that insist Peter was the first Russian Mason, initiated by the Grand Master of the London Lodge.

When Peter was in England, he played at another masquerade. Dressing himself as a junior naval officer, the Tsar presented himself as "Peter Mikhailov," and managed to attend incognito many diplomatic sessions and official receptions, while his chargé d'affaires François Lefort conducted the necessary business. But within the walls of the Freemasonic lodges, Peter was himself, and the Lodge members performed the masquerade, for as they pretended to impart both fraternal fellowship and secret wisdom to the Tsar, the Masonic elite were actually using occult means to take hold of Peter's soul and spirit. By means of ceremonial magic—which Peter, with his penchant for ritual and pretense, adored—the London Lodge members were able to take hypnotic control of the Tsar, and plant a series of simple but powerful suggestions into his consciousness. The explosion of Westernizing reforms that Peter undertook upon his return to Russia can be traced to this source.

The Tsar's return to Moscow from England was marked by the bloody reprisals against the *strel'tsi*, followed by his first set of commands aimed at aping the West; under threat of severe punishment, Peter made compulsory the wearing of Western-style clothing and the prohibition of beards. He even substituted the Western calendar for the Orthodox one. His bizarre behavior led to a rumor among the Russian folk that he was an impostor, substituted by foreigners who had imprisoned or killed the true tsar.

This perception of some fundamental change in Peter's character was accurate, for the English lodge masters, in their magical manipulations of Peter's consciousness, had allowed demonic beings which already haunted him, to gain a firmer grasp upon his soul. Through Peter's violent, elemental fury, Lucifer attacked the entire Russian people; Ahriman's attack came in the calculated creation of an iron-fisted state apparatus. To collect the massive taxes to build the new state, Peter divided the country into eight administrative regions, further subdivided into 47 "provinces," each of which was ruled by a "governor" bound to Peter's will. The push to create a fourth Rome was seen most spectacularly in Peter's founding of the new imperial capital, St. Petersburg. Hundreds of thousands of peasants, soldiers, and craftsmen were conscripted to a marshy, uninhabited region and made to build the drainage canals, roads, forts, and palace of the new city, whose geometrical plan and classical architectural style made it more like Paris or Rome than a Russian city.

These domestic disfigurations of Russian destiny were accompanied by an even more important fulfillment of the English lodge masters' aims, and in the name of "Pan-Slavism"—the movement for the unity of all Slavic peoples—Peter waged war upon central Europe, from Sweden to France and eastward to Turkey. Undertaking a second European journey in 1716–17, Peter extended Russian influence in France and Russia via a peace treaty following the Northern War. While in Amsterdam to negotiate the treaty, Peter came once again under the hypnotic influence of Freemasonry, this time through the Scottish followers of the House of Stuarts. Point by point, the Testament of Peter the Great—in actuality the doctrine of the occult brotherhoods of the West—were gradually achieved under Peter's and his successors' disfigured kingdom.

The demonic polarity—between Lucifer and Ahriman—that gripped Peter also gripped Russia itself, which was subject to Jesuit as well as Freemasonic machinations. After the failed attempt to install the false Dmitri, the Jesuits continued their attempt to substitute Rome's authority for the indigenous Orthodox patriarchy. This can be seen most clearly through their attack on the only manifestation of the true Grail impulse in Russia—the Rosicrucians. Russian Rosicrucians worked tirelessly in the late 18th century to improve the spiritual and moral life of the serfs, through the establishment of schools, distribution of textbooks, founding of bookshops and libraries, and encouragement of resistance to the corruption of civil servants, the tyranny of landlords, and the debauched conduct of the imperial court. Through lodges established in many Russian towns, Rosicrucian leaders encouraged inner development as well as spreading knowledge among the folk. They published Russian language editions of Europe's great mystics, and worked to elevate the stature and conduct of the Orthodox Church.

The imperial leadership, who remained under the sway of the Jesuits, fought all of this Grail activity by the Rosicrucians. Catherine II ordered the arrest of prominent Rosicrucians and the banning altogether of Rosicrucian lodges. Catherine's successor, Paul I—who, at the very same time that European nations had prohibited the Jesuits, gave them official sanction in Russia—allowed the Jesuits to establish schools in Moscow and St. Petersburg. He even considered turning over the entire educational system to them.

The Time is at Hand!

Of the many secret historical streams that we have touched on so far, none is more important for an understanding of Western spirituality, science, and culture—and also for the future of the whole earth—than Rosicrucianism. Though born in the 15th century in central Europe, its presence in 18th century Russia suggests that future role. The German poet, playwright, and natural scientist Johann Wolfgang von Goethe first formulated the central question of Rosicrucianism in his poem, "The Mysteries": "Who added the wreath of Roses to the Cross?" In other words, "Who added love to knowledge?" The Rosicrucian task was to unite the inner mystical path with an outer, alchemical path of knowledge about the world. The West has excelled in cultivating purely rational sciences—like chemistry. Rosicrucianism has cultivated the science of alchemy—the science of the transmutation of substances—as one of the alternatives. Alchemy aims at the "resurrection" of matter. If the task of humanity is to transform wisdom into love—remember Trithemius' formula—then the substance of the earth *must actually become love*. The Rosicrucians practiced a kind of full-time sacramentalism, that is, believing that God can work only through anything and everything as channels of divine love, they transformed themselves into crucibles of just such transformation.

The "founding document" of Rosicrucianism was German theologian Johann Valentin Andrae's *The Chymical Wedding of Christian Rosenkreutz in 1459*, published in 1616. In 1786, more than a decade after he had experienced his own personal initiation into the Rosicrucian mysteries, Goethe read the work and wrote to a friend that he would one day like to turn it into a fairy tale.

When was the last time that you read a fairy tale? So many times in life, we find that something deeply pleasing, something that has contributed a great deal to our development, has completely passed out of our life. It is as if we had forgotten an old, dear friend. It is never too late to get in touch with an old friend, and it is never too late to reconnect with past pleasures.

As an adult, you will someday be shocked when you suddenly remember it has been 5 years since you picked up your guitar; 10 years since you rode your old bike; 15 years since you went back-packing; 20 years since you went skinny-dipping…

When you have children, you get the chance to revisit the pleasures of childhood, including the reading of fairy tales. But in asking you to read Goethe's *Fairy Tale of the Green Snake and the Beautiful Lily*, my purpose is not to have you revisit childhood, nor even to encounter a 'primary source' from the late 18th century. I introduce you to this tale because it is truly a secret revelation, a small Apocalypse, in that it gives a picture of the future condition of humanity, and illustrates in beautiful pictures a path to attain that condition. We have in our course continually encountered "pictures of the future." Do you wonder what pictures of the future—what true fairy tales—are being told or written today?

Like all great stories, Goethe's fairy tale—which opens with the image of a river separating two lands of great contrast, the land of the senses and the land of the spirit—can be read on many different levels. You will likely read the "Youth" as an individual boy on a journey, and this is certainly true, for one level of the tale describes an individual path of initiation. Having just considered the path of Russia over the course of the 14th through the 18th centuries, we can now think of the Youth as particularly the Russian people. Indeed, most of this chapter's consideration has been of how modern Russian history is a story of struggling toward the stage of the Intellectual Soul, within a period where Europe is at the next stage—the Consciousness Soul. The Russian people are "youthful" in this sense of remaining "behind" in the evolution of consciousness. But this is so that they will come into the 6th Epoch with a "Grail mood" that is not possible in central Europe, the Americas, or anywhere else on the planet.

The future that Goethe's fairy tale presents is the 6th Post-Atlantean Epoch, the "Russian Cultural Epoch," which will last from AD 2375 to AD 4535. The wonderful thing about looking off into the future through stories is that these stories can tell us what we should be doing *now*. Unfortunately, the modern world was built to distract you from your life's purpose—another temporary triumph of Ahriman—but there is nothing like a fairy tale or legend to get us back on track. For the Slavic peoples, the legend of the Invisible City of Kitezh gave an image of *losing* the Grail kingdom; the *Fairy Tale of the Green Snake and the Beautiful Lily* gives an image of how to regain it. One of the most important aspects of the tale is that it promises that when the 6th Epoch comes, *everyone*—not just initiates—will be able to cross over the river and reach the risen temple on the other side. The last words of the tale are: "and to the present hour the Bridge is swarming with travelers, and the Temple is the most frequented on the whole Earth."

That Bridge is built the first and second times by the body of the Green Snake, who moves east, then west, and finally east again. When she first appears, the Snake is gobbling up pieces of gold shaken off the bodies of the Will o' the Wisps—elemental beings of Nature. This gold causes her whole body to become radiant, and she is then able to see her way in the underground temple. The Snake is central Europe in the Age of the Consciousness Soul, whose abstract knowledge of Nature must be taken in and digested in order to spiritualize it. Goethe himself was one of the first to do this, as shown by his contributions to science—his discovery of the intermaxillary bone; his supersensible perception of the archetypal plant; his color theory.

The light that shines out of the snake allows her to see—i.e., understand—all that is around her. This is a great promise for a spiritualized natural science, that it can bring understanding of even the darkest mysteries of Nature.

That the Snake sacrifices herself for the sake of the Youth suggests that the higher knowledge she acquires cannot be gained out of selfishness. The knowledge must be placed in the service of mankind. From materialist astronomy to neo-Darwinian theory to "It Matters" history, all of the gains made by European science must be sacrificed, and transformed through spiritual awareness. The Snake's sacrifice brings the sleeping Youth back to consciousness; this is the 5th Cultural Age's gift of the foundation of a new culture to the 6th Age—the Russian Cultural Epoch. At her sacrifice the Snake becomes "thousands and thousands of shining jewels" which form the bridge to the future.

Like the Youth, the Russian people have a penchant for higher worlds, to such an extent that the immediate physical environment is often neglected. At first, the Youth experiences paralyzing illness. The situation is so desperate that the Snake fears that at "every moment the Sun would set." Russia's four-century struggle to overcome both "inner Mongolism" and the tyranny of Westernization is that paralysis. But the Youth gains the Lily, i.e., Russia in the 6th Epoch *shall* achieve clairvoyant consciousness. The Lily is the true Sophia, the Eternal Feminine to whom Russia has so long remained faithful, and with whom a full reunion is an image of the transformed Consciousness Soul.

The fairy tale even looks out another 2000 years beyond the end of the Russian Epoch in AD 4535, to the 7th Cultural Epoch. The Giant and his shadow are images of the West, particularly America, whose materialistic intellect even now seeks to envelop the entire earth in its shadow. America projects its military and economic might around the globe. The shadow in the future will be more challenging, when the dark web of electromagnetic radiation that America has spun over the Earth becomes an apocalyptic reality. The Snake could be speaking of Ahriman as well as America when she tells the Will o' the Wisps: "with his body he has no power; his hands cannot lift a straw, his shoulders could not bear a faggot of twigs; but with his shadow he has power over much, nay all."

Redemption is again promised though! The Giant's shadow is transformed into a majestic sundial that stands outside the Temple. Goethe gives us this image: "[The Giant] stood there like a strong colossal statue, of reddish glittering stone, and his shadow pointed out the hours, which were marked in a circle on the floor around him, not in numbers, but in noble and expressive emblems." What an extraordinary image to contemplate, as America at this moment, in 2009, is engaged in renewing the Cold War against Russia. Though it may take thousands of years, one day America will be in service to Russia, and Russia in service to America. Just as the Snake—Central Europe in the 5th Cultural Epoch—birthed the Youth—Russia in the 6th Epoch—in his leadership of the Sun Temple births the 7th Epoch—the spiritually transformed West, especially America. At the end of the tale, a grand procession crosses the river to the Temple, which we may now recognize as identical with the risen City of Kitezh. "...and to the present hour the Bridge is swarming with travelers, and the Temple is the most frequented on the whole Earth." How much more satisfying a conclusion than "And they lived happily ever after"!!!

Three times over the course of the fairy tale, the words *"The time is at hand!"* ring out, echoing *Revelations* apocalyptic pronouncement: "the time has come." For all of its attention upon the far future, *The Fairy Tale of the Green Snake and the Beautiful Lily* is eternally directed at the present. It was in 1796, when Goethe wrote the story; it is now, and shall be in centuries and millennia to come.

7: Manifest Destinies

Pakwanonzian! You, dear reader, still do "look brand new to me," that is, we still are only partially acquainted with one another, and so in each exchange, with each gesture, we are still discovering each other, explaining ourselves to each other. This chapter needs a word of explanation: it steps outside the narrative arc that I've been following so far—of the Grail and "anti-Grail" struggle in Asia, Europe, Mexico, and Russia—to return "home" to America. I focus in this chapter on a very small but extraordinary corner of that new nation (the United States was only 41 years old when Henry Thoreau was born, and he grew up among many neighbors who had lived through the events of the American Revolution)—Concord, Massachusetts, and principally upon one young man, Henry David Thoreau. Thoreau draws my—and, I hope, your—attention because he is a unique national treasure, a "creature of a different destiny" whose life is full of heroism, mystery, and magic.

Thoreau's life is a stunning witness to the truth that the Grail path is open to all, at any time in history. His words and deeds are rare gifts to America and the world, full of the promise of independence that America was founded upon, and that continues to unfold for both good and ill. Thoreau used to often write in his journal, "How long?"—a question prompted by Thoreau's perennial desire to live deeply into the unfolding biological activity about him. How long since a plant he encountered had flowered, fruited, or leafed out? He wished to be a silent witness at the birth of every natural phenomenon in the local landscape, and in his brief life, he went a long way to meeting such a desire. But his question carries an existential ache as well, a prophetic plea that rings far beyond Concord. How long before America becomes naturalized, becomes, like the plants and animals whose life histories he tracked, symbiotically imbedded within its physical surround? How long before America discovers its true destiny?

At the very historical moment when America seemed to be gaining its full independence from Europe, to realize what many felt to be its "Manifest Destiny," Thoreau's cranky voice kept insisting that America had an altogether different destiny. Seeing his country's task as one of redeeming its dark colonial past by forging a new relationship with Nature and History, he called attention to this task by way of his own personal lifelong pilgrimage. His daily meanderings within a tightly circumscribed corner of a rapidly expanding nation made him as acute an observer of civil society as he was of the local society of pickerel, turtles, and field mice. Thoreau's entire biography can be conceived of as an exquisite attempt to "go native," to meet the "expectations of the land," both as to how Americans will live in relationship to the land, and to each other. His life and words have become a measure against which America rests uncomfortably.

Another reason that I choose to stop and linger with you by the shores of Walden Pond is that a few years ago, I did literally linger at Walden Pond, and visited the replica of Thoreau's cabin there. Inside there is a guestbook in which thousands of people have written. I was so sad to read a number of remarks from guests who accused Thoreau of faking a wilderness experience when he went out to Walden to live for two years. "Henry went home on Sundays for turkey supper," or "His friends used to bring him a pie" and other cynical comments punctuated the guestbook. Such remarks completely mistake Thoreau's experiment in living! He went to the outskirts of his settled village to cultivate his spirit at a time when materialism was making it very easy for a young, talented, intelligent, curious, and uniquely destined person to lose his way, to neglect his calling, and also neglect the spiritual beings which have and shall always shepherd each and every one of us. Each of you are young, talented, intelligent, curious, and *uniquely destined*, and I stop with you to get to know Henry Thoreau in hopes that his life can be an inspiration to you to follow in your own way his philosophy of life. "Do what you love. Know your own bone; gnaw at it, bury it, unearth it, and gnaw it still. Do not be too moral. You may cheat yourself out of much life so. Aim above morality. Be not *simply* good—be good for something."

I have set Thoreau's life among some pretty odd subjects here, in order to both dramatize the uniqueness of his spiritual path when compared to his contemporaries, but also to show that most of the history we are taught is very narrowly circumscribed (I love that word, as did Thoreau, a surveyor who knew all about drawing and walking circular lines around things). It tells us that the world—especially America in the nineteenth century—is an altogether rational place, full of the deeds and thoughts of rational people who do not travel back and forth in time, see fairies, communicate with the dead, or make material objects appear and disappear. That may have been true of the Mongols in the 13th century, we think, but certainly it was not true of educated Yankees in Massachusetts in 1845! The railroad line already passed right along the shore of Walden Pond in 1845, and while Thoreau was living there, a telegraph line was erected. Trains and telegraphs do not encourage the exploration of the spiritual world… or do they?

Secrets

On July 4, 1837 Ralph Waldo Emerson was the obvious speaker of choice for the Concord, Massachusetts Independence Day ceremonies, which were especially auspicious as they were the occasion for the unveiling of the North Bridge Battle Monument. Emerson could not attend, but the audience—which included his young friend Henry David Thoreau, who sang in the choir—heard Emerson's commemorative verse "Concord Hymn" read in absentia. "By the rude bridge that arched the flood,/Their flag to April's breeze unfurled,/Here once the embattled farmers stood/And fired the shot heard round the world."

Emerson had been a member of the committee that crafted the inscription borne on the twenty-foot-tall granite obelisk: "The first forcible resistance to British aggression." Locally, the opening battle of the American Revolution was known as "Concord Fight"; but there was a second Concord Fight raging, which was, by the dedication of the monument, seemingly being brought to a truce. The fight was over where the commemorative monument would be located; one faction wanted it in the center of Concord Village, the other, led by Dr. Ezra Ripley—the "Pope of Concord," Congregationalist minister, leader of the local aristocracy, and founding member in 1798 and Grand Chaplain of Concord's Corinthian Lodge of Ancient and Accepted Masons—wanted the historic marker out at the North Bridge, believing that a patriotic pilgrimage needed to transport the pilgrim from the profane bustle of everyday life to a sacred space, and that the North Bridge site was the proper setting for such sacred communion. The fact that Ripley owned the land on either side of the Concord River there was—despite his 'generous' offer to donate the land for the monument—just salt in the wound of Concord's more humble citizens, who still bore a great deal of suspicion toward aristocracy, particularly Freemasons.

In 1826, the kidnapping and murder of New York Freemason William Morgan had shattered American Freemasonry and led to the rise of the Anti-Masonic party. The populist fear of Freemasonry as a conspiratorial alliance of aristocrats led to the demise of hundreds of lodges throughout America, but the Corinthian Lodge, though it ceased regular meetings in 1831 and enrolled only three new members between 1832 and 1844, never surrendered its charter. Indeed, in the year following the Morgan affair, ten new members were initiated, including Concord publisher and editor Herman Atwell. But by 1833, even the Boston region, heart of Revolutionary-era Freemasonry, was wracked by Anti-Masonic fervor, thanks largely to the revelations of Atwell, who published a series of editorials attacking Freemasonry. In March 1834, Atwell appeared before an investigative committee of the Massachusetts legislature to give testimony about the nature of his initiation into the first three Freemasonic degrees. He described being stripped naked, 'hoodwinked'—a black hood placed over the eyes—and a noose placed around his neck before he was led to the altar to take a series of oaths. The secret initiatory practices of Freemasonic lodges were widely known after the publication of Morgan's expose; what set Atwell's revelations apart was his insight into the rationale behind the initiation rituals. He understood that the ceremonies were designed to confuse and terrify the candidate in order to put him completely in the power of those doing the initiation. Most damning was Atwell's testimony that during the summer of 1833 he had heard a prominent citizen of Concord who was a Royal Arch Mason state "in a calm, dispassionate manner" that he approved of the murder of William Morgan as just punishment for his having violated his pledge of secrecy.

Early nineteenth century America had a passion for secrets, for their crafting, exposure, celebration, and damnation. The suspicions and scrutiny leveled at Freemasons, Catholics, and Mormons were also democratically directed toward peddlers, stage entertainers, and politicians, all of whom were seen as potentially criminal keepers of secrets. In 1834, in Charlestown, outside of Boston, a mob stormed and ransacked a Catholic convent, driven to this violence by their uncontrollable curiosity about the mysterious rites they imagined performed within. This tragic attack on cloistered, powerless religious women highlights the limits on America's distrust of secrecy; no similar mobs tore up the Masonic altars where influential men gathered to exchange secret oaths. But the rhetorical attacks upon Freemasonry show just how virulent a poison Masonic secrecy was seen to be.

The secret that drew in many hopeful candidates was the same Promethean power forever sought by humanity—the knowledge of nature. In the Second Degree ceremony the Masonic candidate was asked: "What are the peculiar objects of research in this degree?", to which he was required to answer: "The hidden mysteries of nature and science." On completion of the ritual he was told: "You are now expected to make the liberal arts and sciences your future study." Few Freemasons actually gained the knowledge promised of nature's arcana, and the ones that did came by that knowledge not from fellow Freemasons but from their own study. While most Masons were content to gain the expected business or social advantages conferred upon the elect, others—like Herman Atwell—were disappointed to learn that the Lodge was built not upon Solomon's wisdom but on ersatz mysteries designed principally to bind the initiated to ignorance.

In the ancient mysteries, the picture language and ritual procedures— particularly the mock "death" experience—were designed to open the candidate's spiritual sight. For the modern consciousness, the secret handshakes and arcane symbols on the letterboards and aprons that once held the key to a language of correspondences were mere atavistic obfuscations. As had happened in European Freemasonry, the rituals had been co-opted by a small, secret politically-motivated elite who employed the dramaturgical rites and binding oaths to gain magical control of the unsuspecting members.

"Sacred" and "secret" shared the same linguistic root, but they now needed to branch apart, as the new natural sciences were daily demonstrating. Ralph Waldo Emerson's book *Nature* invited the open-air exoteric exploration of Nature's correspondences at the very moment when the esoteric path was exhausting itself in the decadence of Freemasonry. In his emphasis upon the individual spirit as the crucible for knowing nature—"a dream may let us deeper into the secret of nature than a hundred experiments," Emerson declared in the concluding section of *Nature*—Emerson allied himself with the ancients, but he was preparing a wholly democratic, demonstrative, declarative –and yet still sacred—science. Its emblems and symbols could not be pyramids and trowels and compass and square, nor its oaths bound with secret handshakes. Little did Emerson know that the new spiritual science's first emblems would be drawn from his own woodlot at Walden Pond on the outskirts of Concord.

"The creature of a different destiny"

The morning after Independence Day in 1845, Henry David Thoreau wrote in his journal: "Yesterday I came here to live." Though in later years when he lectured or wrote about his "experiment" at Walden, he would say that it was an "accident" that it began on the Fourth of July, he knew full well that he was enacting a myth, and that mythic acts demand mythic timing. On his fourth day at Walden, sitting on the stoop of his cabin, contemplating the pitch pine sentinel that had not succumbed to his axe, Thoreau fancied himself a "fellow-wanderer and survivor of Ulysses." A week later, on his twenty-eighth birthday, he made no entry at all, perhaps because he was so keenly occupied with the vocation of living. But on the 14th of July, he gave voice to the conviction that stands behind the triumphs of all heroes: "Sometimes, when I compare myself with other men, methinks I am favored by the Gods. They seem to whisper joy to me beyond my deserts, and that I do have a solid warrant and surety at their hands, which my fellows do not. I do not flatter myself, but if it were possible *they* flatter me. I am especially guided and guarded."

Thoreau's sense of good fortune came from a series of curious incidents where, as if by magic, his thoughts or words *manifested actual objects*. Once, out searching for Indian relics with his brother John, their "heads full of the past and its remains," they had stopped at the brow of a little hill near the mouth of Swamp Bridge Brook. Thoreau, gesturing dramatically toward a nearby hill, broke into an inspired speech about the local Indians and their chief Tahatawan: "How often they have stood on this very spot, at this very hour . . . and communed with the spirits of their fathers gone before them, to the land of the shades!" "Here," he continued, "stood Tahatawan; and there is Tahatawan's arrowhead." Reaching for an ordinary stone and picking it up, it "proved a most perfect arrowhead, as sharp as if just from the hands of the Indian fabricator." Similar incidents happened to Thoreau when he was botanizing; he would desire to see a certain plant, and soon it would present itself to him.

Thoreau shared his sense of being divinely favored with all America, whose destiny was manifesting apace. On March 1, just weeks before Thoreau had begun clearing the lot for his cabin, President John Tyler had signed a bill annexing northernmost Mexico to the United States. If there were Americans who were discomfited by their nation's aggressive acquisitiveness, they were far outnumbered by those who believed that God's especial providence for the United States equated to territorial expansion. The same week that Thoreau moved into his cabin, influential editor and Democratic leader John L. O'Sullivan published an editorial championing America's right to encompass the entire continent, calling it "our manifest destiny." O'Sullivan looked to nature as the model for America's prodigious physiology: "It is right such as that of the tree to the space of air and the earth suitable for the full expansion of its principle and destiny of growth."

Thoreau already was coming to understand that the growth of trees was a rhythmic, almost musical process, and although he could confide to his journal that "Next to us the grandest laws are being enacted and administered," he could not fully see how his own biography exemplified grand laws of cosmic rhythm. Thoreau's life demonstrated Martin Luther's aphorism that "The seventh year always transforms man. It brings about a new life, a new character, and a different state." In his twenty-first year, Thoreau had met his destiny in a sort of stepwise fashion, encountering in the spring of 1837 first the transformative essay *Nature* and then its author, who in turn, just three months into his twenty-first year, had set Thoreau upon a task that was to become his greatest life's work—the keeping of a journal.

At Walden, Thoreau would fully live the truth he had uttered years before: "Surely joy is the condition of life." During Thoreau's life, that perennial condition always intensified at rhythmic seven-year intervals. His ecstasies grew stronger, his sense of his own heroic destiny more intense on or around the day of the septennial anniversary of his birth. The feeling of being specially "guided and guarded" was conveyed to him by the elemental world, the fairies who were just now fading from his view. Of all human emotions, joy passed most fully and fruitfully across the membrane separating the visible and invisible worlds, and Thoreau and his sister sylphs and undines experienced at seven-year intervals a particularly intense celebration of life's majesty. Born in the seventh month of the year, the rhythm of the seven was seemingly inscribed into Thoreau's most significant experiences and tasks: it took seven years for him to complete *A Week on the Concord and Merrimack Rivers*, his first book, and one whose seven chapters echoed the archetypal rhythm of the seven days of the week; his masterwork *Walden* would in seven years undergo seven revisions before publication. Other critical moments in Thoreau's life – such as the tragedy of his brother John's death and also the first articulation of the desire to live at Walden—occurred at the exact midpoint of the seven-year periods. Thoreau's move to Walden Pond on the eve of his twenty-eighth birthday would be a destiny event that rippled through the rest of his life; it would also ripple down through Time into the hearts of Americans and people from all over the planet.

Sevens played throughout the lives of the era's chapbook heroes and fairy tale characters, most famously Thomas the Rhymer, whose seven-year bondage by the Faerie Queen ended simultaneously with his being given the gift of prophecy. Though clairvoyance for the fairy world had mostly vanished among the modern peoples of the nineteenth century, even in England, western Europe, and North America, this and other atavistic forms of consciousness survived in children, but tended to end in or around the seventh year, at about the time of the eruption of the permanent teeth. Thoreau clearly kept an episodic clairvoyance for the faerie world into his adult years, but his last recording of a faerie encounter came at almost precisely age twenty-eight. In late July, he wrote this poem in his journal:

> Tell me ye wise ones if ye can
> Whither and whence the race of man
> For I have seen his slender clan
> Clinging to hoar hills with their feet
> Threading the forest for their meat
> Moss and lichens and bark & grain
> They racke together with might & main
> And they digest them with anxiety & pain…
>> They are the Titmans of their race
>> And hug the vales with mincing pace
>> Like Troglodites, and fight with cranes
>> We walk 'mid great relations feet
>> What they let fall alone we eat…
>>> A finer race and finer fed
>>> Feast and revel above our head.
>>> The tints and fragrance of the flowers & fruits
>>> Are but the crumbs from off their table
>>> While we consume the pulp and roots
>>> Some times we do assert our kin
>>> And stand a moment where once they have been
>>> We hear their sounds and see their sights
>>> And we experience their delights—
>>> But for the moment that we stand
>>> Astonished on the Olympian land…

This slender, unseen (except by Thoreau and others who were clairvoyant for the fairy world) forest-dwelling "race of man" is brave, immortal ("elder brothers" walking "with larger pace"), and in some sort of economic relationship with human beings. Directly following the poem, Thoreau wrote: "In my father's house are many mansions. Who ever explored the mansions of the air—who knows who his neighbors are. We seem to lead our human lives amid a concentric systems of worlds of realm upon realm, close bordering on each other—where dwell the unknown and the imagined races—as various in degrees as our own thoughts are. A system of invisible partitions more infinite in number and more inconceivable in intricacy than the starry one which Science has penetrated." In another poem telling of his having met fairies, Thoreau declared that they were "creatures of a different destiny." So was he. For some reason, he had been afforded a glimpse of the Otherworld into full adulthood. He was hardly alone in this, but in the early nineteenth century, adult ability to perceive the fairy world was typically restricted to uneducated rural folk. Among Thoreau's scientifically sophisticated peers, it was safe to show an interest in the "second sight" of New England cunning men and women, or of simple Irish peasants, but to claim such clairvoyance for oneself was surely beyond the pale. Thoreau's curiosity and honesty demanded that he report his encounters with these ethereal beings, but his inner compass guided him to an understated, cryptic form of reporting.

If Thomas the Rhymer's Otherworld "bondage" was an image of the capacity to perceive faerie beings, his release and accompanying prophetic gift was an image of a universal human process—the maturation into a new form of clairvoyance. In perfect rhythmic fashion, with his move to Walden Pond, Thoreau was living out that mythic tale of humanity's dance between the greater Gods above and the lesser gods below. Age twenty-eight had for centuries in Western legend and folklore been thought of as the "noon" period of life, when the individual had to learn to heed his own inner voice, having in the previous seven years since age twenty-one gone forth into the world to acquire outer experience that might be turned into inner knowledge. Like Parsifal at the Grail Castle, Thoreau at age twenty-eight was faced with the challenge of asking the right question, of realizing what his mission on Earth was to be, and then of dedicating himself to the task of authoring his own destiny.

Building Temples

It was fitting that a man whose days were so marked by rhythm should be graced with the rhythmic visitation of gods of all stature. At Walden, even more than he had up to this point in life, Thoreau lived in to the rhythms of both the natural world and the spiritual world, feeling their pulse. His daily "routine" in his new home was rhythmic: "After hoeing, or perhaps reading and writing, in the forenoon, I usually bathed again in the pond, swimming across one of its coves for a stint, and washed the dust of labor from my person, or smoothed out the last wrinkle which study had made, and for the afternoon was absolutely free." Far inland from the regular rhythms of the sea, Thoreau in his leisurely life at Walden of walking, swimming, paddling, thinking and praying became a being of rhythm. He spoke rhythmically to the gods in a series of poems composed this summer.

I make ye an offer,
   Ye gods, hear the scoffer,
   The scheme will not hurt you,
   If ye will find goodness, I will find virtue. . . .
   If ye will deal plainly,
   I will strive mainly,
   If ye will discover,
   Great plans to your lover,
   And give him a sphere
   Somewhat larger than here.

In another poem he describes the "great friend" whose "native shore is dim," and in "The Hero," makes a prayer that he be given by this unnamed friend "some worthy task." The task he outlines–essentially to live authentically into the soil below him, and "forever to love and to love and to love"—is the very one that he took up with the move to Walden.

A more mundane task Thoreau took up was the accounting of his experimental economy at the pond. In late fall he worked on what would become the first section of *Walden*, a wry critique of his fellows' failure to live lives of higher purpose, followed by a ledger of his cabin's construction. Thoreau was a man who loved to count and measure, and although he says that he gives the details to highlight how removed most people are from the making of their own homes, it is clear that he loves listing that the boards cost him $8.03½; the laths $1.25; second-hand windows $2.43; a thousand old brick $4.00; hair and lime for plaster $2.71; nails $3.90; hinges, screws and latch 24 cents; chalk a penny. The whole edifice cost $28.12½, comparing quite favorably with the $30 per year rent Harvard College collected from its students for a room of similar size.

Visitors to Thoreau's cabin saw a rude, if clean and tidy, spare structure with the barest of furnishings, but almost all failed to see the magnificent temple he had built in the invisible world hovering about the pond. He and other lovers of the pond's beauty and tranquility— Ralph Waldo Emerson and his family, and a host of other Concord residents– had over the years constructed out of their devotion a cathedral housing a host of benevolent entities. Traditional tales of the Faerie world always pictured them as dancing or singing, two of Thoreau's other favorite activities. The music of the spheres that he so frequently heard at Walden was the echo of the movement in rhythm of the invisible beings attracted to the airy mansion of the pond's environs by the beatific thoughts and emotions felt there.

Unadorned by a single graven image, cluttered with no relics or statuary, fronted by no massive portal and bearing no towering steeple or spire, Thoreau's Walden temple yet presented more beauty than the eye might imagine, and had a thousand entrances of the most splendid form. Divinity leapt from every niche and transept of the Walden woods while a cathedral choir was ever singing ethereal hymns. Working on the manuscript of *A Week*, Thoreau was composing holy scriptures for his time, not sermons but myths and fables, letting the myths and fables of past times buoy him. Recognizing the ancient myths as "hints for a history of the rise and progress of the race," Thoreau expected no less of his own day, when "other divine agents and godlike men will assist to elevate the race as much above its present condition."

While Concord Transcendentalists saw unadorned Nature as a temple that might elevate the human being, other Americans built more traditional temples. In November 1845, as Thoreau was getting ready for winter by building with secondhand bricks a chimney for his cabin, followers of the Mormon Prophet Joseph Smith were finishing construction of the main section of the Temple at Nauvoo, Illinois. Devoted Mormon saints had tithed their labor to quarry, haul and lay up the massive limestone blocks quarried from a site on the Mississippi, while Mormon women donated precious heirlooms to raise funds and prepared food for the laborers. The frontier town of Nauvoo was essentially founded to carry out construction of the temple, which was to be one hundred twenty eight feet long, eighty-eight feet wide, one hundred sixty five feet high to the top of the spire. Having begun just a few months after Joseph Smith in January of 1841 received the revelation to build the temple, the Nauvoo Mormons had been guided throughout the construction by Smith's continuing divine revelations, both as to temple architecture and to the rituals and rites that would be carried out among the elect once the temple was finished. Ever since receiving the Book of Mormon on a set of buried gold plates from the angel Moroni at the Hill Cumorah in Palmyra, New York in 1828, Joseph Smith had been a fount of odd apocalyptic revelation, but while other American prophets such as William Miller (who predicted the Second Coming in 1844) saw their flocks disperse as their revelations flopped, Smith's following grew steadily throughout the 1830s and 1840s.

Smith promulgated the Book of Mormon as a sacred canonical text, a new dispensation of truth that God delivered to humankind through the angel Moroni to himself, the Prophet. Smith's followers saw the Book of Mormon as God's third and final dispensation, signaling the fulfillment of John's Book of Revelation. The Book of Mormon identified Joseph Smith as the one who—aided by revelations from God—would prepare the way for Christ's Second Coming. After armed conflict in 1839 with neighbors in Missouri, Smith and nearly 15,000 followers fled to Commerce, Illinois, which they purchased and renamed Nauvoo. By 1844 Nauvoo had become the largest city in Illinois, an independent municipality with its own court system and militia. Smith's church was an elaborate hierarchy supposedly modeled on the ancient Hebraic church, with Smith the sole authority for receiving direction from God. In 1844, after revealing God's plan for organizing the Kingdom of Heaven on earth with himself as King, Smith declared his candidacy for President of the United States. This was only the latest of Smith's outrageous "revelations" guaranteed to anger "Gentiles"—both Christians and nonbelievers. In 1838 he revealed that Adam had lived in the area that became western Missouri; in August 1839 he declared that angels have flesh and bones; in April 1840 he preached that God was once a man; in 1841 he said that God also was made of flesh and bone, and that the earth had been formed out of other planets that had broken apart; in 1842 Smith's newspaper, *Times & Seasons,* printed a translation from the Book of Abraham that said the Elohim lived near the star Kolob and Smith also introduced the doctrine of plural gods; in 1843, Smith, who had 33 wives at the time, announced a divine revelation in favor of plural marriage. A few months later he advocated decapitation or throat-cutting for certain crimes and sins. By 1844, church population was over

25,000, and the Mormon Legion, Smith's private army, had over 3000 men. The United States Army had but 8000 troops. If not elected, many feared that Smith would seize the presidency by force.

Smith—who had been arrested nearly as many times as he had wives, for crimes including murder, high treason, burglary, arson, and larceny—was jailed with his brother Hyrum and two other Mormon leaders in Carthage, Illinois, for having ordered the destruction of the printing press, offices, and records of a Nauvoo newspaper critical of Smith's teaching polygamy and polytheism. On June 27, 1844, a mob of over two hundred fifty black-faced militiamen stormed the jail and killed Smith and his brother. Firing a gun smuggled to him by a confederate, Smith managed to kill two and wound another of his assailants. To his last breath, the Prophet acted as he had throughout life—violently, and with the aid of magic. Just before his death, Smith made the Masonic sign of distress, and then clutched at the Jupiter talisman around his neck. The talisman was a coveted symbol of personal power for Smith, since Jupiter was the ruling planet of his birth year. He had fashioned it of silver according to instructions in Francis Barrett's 1801 *The Magus*, a manual of magical techniques. Smith believed his talisman gained him both riches and power, including the love of women, all by the invocation of demon intelligences through the use of planetary forces.

Like all temples, the façade of the Nauvoo Temple incorporated symbolic images designed to address and summon supernatural powers. Smith's visions included the erection of thirty "sunstones"—two-and-a-half ton limestone blocks engraved with a radiant sun god—atop temple columns. The sunstones were said by Smith to represent the "Celestial Kingdom" seen in his vision. Thirty moonstones and thirty star-stones topped other temple columns. Eleven large inverted pentagrams adorned doorway lintels. The weather vane atop the temple spire was in the form of a flying angel holding a trumpet in one hand and the open Book of Mormon in the other. Directly above the angel was the Freemasonic compass and square. Smith taught that the temple's astronomical symbols represented the glorious blessings performed within the temple walls. The temple ceremonies, like the symbols outside, were faithful imitations of Freemasonic rituals, which Smith and other Mormon elders had learned as members of the local Lodge. At Nauvoo, the candidate for the temple "endowment" was given a secret sign by the presiding "Saint": as they shook hands, the ball of the thumb was placed between the two upper joints of the forefingers. In Freemasonic ritual this was known as "The Grip of the Entered Apprentice." Two more secret grips followed, corresponding to Freemasonry's "Pass-grip of the Master Mason" and "Sign and Due-Guard of the Master Mason." The candidate then placed his right hand under the left ear and drew it across the throat, after which the left hand was brought to the right shoulder, then quickly drawn across the breast, both gestures symbolic of the mortal penalty the candidate would pay should he reveal the nature of the ceremony.

Those undergoing the Temple Endowment at Nauvoo also were anointed with oil; they were given a special garment—with special stitches sewn into the breasts, navel, and knee—to wear; they were given a secret name, to be told to no one, except female candidates, who were to tell their husbands their secret name; they witnessed an elaborate drama in which a black-clad Lucifer at one point instructs them to don green aprons, symbolic of the planet Venus, the Morning

Star. Along with the ritual grips and tokens, these were all *magical actions*, causing very specific effects on both the candidates and in the spiritual world. Though the Mormon Temple initiation shared characteristics with the white magical activities of alchemy, Rosicrucianism, and other Christian initiatory paths, its character was essentially that of a black magical rite. The inverted pentagrams and stars on the Temple façade were a clue to the perversion of magical ceremonial activity within. The ritual grips were based on ancient knowledge of the body's meridians and pressure points. The pressure applied at the hand flowed back energetically to the nipples, where stitch marks on the Temple garment led to the heart and then down to the navel. The Temple candidate, in performing the "Patriarchal Grip," unknowingly awakened latent sexual energies that produced distinct alchemical changes in his body, soul, and spirit. The third grip, "The Sign of the Nail," was designed to stimulate an individual's hatred and rage, in order to augment the power of black magical action. The exactness required of all initiates assured the proper necromantic effect.

The Temple initiation concluded with the candidate being conducted around the outside of the temple, past the inverted pentagrams and images of the sun god Ba'al, the stars and the phases of the moon. At the Nauvoo Temple, the Moon Goddess Diana was the consort of Lucifer, the sacred god of Mormonism, and the fount of earthly wealth and power. Though the Temple only saw six weeks of use before the Saints were run out of Nauvoo, over five thousand endowments were performed there. Smith's Halloween religion would move west and reach new heights of earthly prosperity; more temples, bigger temples arose throughout the Great American Desert. Back in Concord and Boston (where there had been great success in gaining Mormon converts) the newspapers would continue to report on the Latter Day Saints, but the spiritual politics were always masked by the mundane conflicts. Citizens from the Palmyra area who had known Joseph Smith as a young money-digger and necromancer spoke up about America's fastest growing religion's origins in grave-robbing, animal sacrifice, and demonic invocation, but Joseph's treasure-guarding toad was transformed into a white salamander, the Luciferic demon Moroni into an angel, the pugilistic and pugnacious wanna-be wizard into a Sainted Prophet. No one seemed to notice that "Moorman" was the Scottish term for someone in charge of cattle in waste ground, or that "Mormo" was an archaic name for a spirit who terrified children (antebellum dictionaries gave "Mormo" as "bug bear; false terror"). In the early years after his encounter at Hill Cumorah, Smith referred to the angel messenger interchangeably as both "Moroni" and "Nephe"—the latter meaning "departed spirits called out by Magicians and Necromancers."

The Nauvoo Temple was a horrific caricature of the holy orders Thoreau was conducting at Walden Pond. If America was the site of spiritual warfare, a reflection of a heavenly battle, the dark powers seemed surely to be winning. Concord Transcendentalist Bronson Alcott's Temple School (so-named because it was located in a former Masonic temple in Boston)—where the children circled their chairs round Alcott to have deep heartfelt conversations on the Gospels, and where on one occasion Alcott had a student hit *him* each time that student misbehaved, bringing the boy to remorseful tears and better conduct—had closed after salacious rumors flew about his teachings on the virgin birth. Fruitlands and Brook Farm and dozens of other intentional communities of the idealistic 1840s– all devoted to building temples of Duty, Science, Beauty and Joy—had, by the time the second Mormon Prophet Brigham Young arrived at Salt Lake and church membership approached 50,000, all gone fallow. Transcendentalist fields lay unplowed and their haylofts and silos empty, while the Halloween religion made the Utah desert bloom into a Paradise on Earth.

Sympathy & Somnambulism

By the end of March 1846, as song sparrows and blackbirds were joined by the first robins and the spring rains drove the ice from the pond, Thoreau had finished his first draft of *A Week*, and was largely carrying out the daily communion that supported his ethereal temple. Morning was the most important time of worship: "I get up early and bathe in the pond—that is one of the best things I do–so far the day is well spent." These ablutions were the return blessing for the one that he received each morning upon waking. "The morning brings back the heroic ages. . . . All memorable events in my experience transpire in morning time." The Auroral atmosphere was not confined to dawn, but was available at any moment that one attended to one's Genius. Thoreau expected of himself and wished for all this perpetual dawn, an awakening to the divinity within, even "in our soundest sleep."

Thoreau knew something about sound sleep, having been troubled since his teen years by narcolepsy. His uncle suffered from the illness, falling completely asleep in the midst of shaving or other daytime activity. Thoreau complained of it coming on mainly while he was reading or writing. He also spoke on one occasion of being "somnambulic at least—stirring in my sleep; indeed quite awake."

"Somnambulism" was the most common term used in the 1840s for the state of consciousness produced by animal magnetism, also known as "mesmerism," after its re-discoverer, Franz Anton Mesmer. It had first come to wide public attention in America in the summer of 1837 when Frenchman Charles Poyen and his invalid mesmeric subject Cynthia Gleason made lecture tours in the Northeast, including spectacular successes in Boston and Providence. In his public demonstrations, Poyen found that about half of the audience would succumb quite readily to the somnambulic state, which entailed much more than mere "sleepwalking." Most of the people who came to such demonstrations did so to see their friends and neighbors transformed before their eyes. About ten percent of the subjects attained "sympathetic rapport" with the mesmeric "operator"; it was not uncommon for this group to perform spontaneous feats of clairvoyance, locating lost objects, describing distant events, and telepathically reading the minds of audience members. In the mesmeric state, individuals were carried back into the labyrinth of the Sentient Soul; like the Freemasonic initiator, the mesmerist stole from the mesmerized his precious inheritance of consciousness beyond the magical state of the Sentient Soul. The jettisoning of the Ego brought spectacular feats of escaping the bounds of Space and Time, but also opened the mesmerized person to all manner of influences. Along with the mesmerist, all sorts of harmful spiritual entities had open access to the mind and soul of the spellbound person.

By 1845, hundreds (in 1843 there were estimated to be 200 to 300 in Boston alone) of mesmeric wizards circulated throughout America, and mesmeric demonstrations became an integral part of most stage magic performances. The seeming novelty of the somnambulic state obscured at least thirty years of earlier fascination with the mysteries of sympathetic sleep as it occurred naturally in individual "somnambulists." In 1808, fourteen-year-old Rachel Baker of Marcellus, New York gave lengthy theological lectures while asleep, far beyond her abilities while in a waking state. Most of the adult members in Poyen's audiences recalled Jane C. Rider, a Springfield, Massachusetts domestic who in June of 1833 became a national celebrity through journalistic accounts of her spectacular somnambulism. While completely unconscious, her eyes shut tight, she would set the table, skim milk, slice bread, and cook a full breakfast. She could thread a needle in total darkness, and with her eyes wrapped in bandages, discern the dates of coins held at a distance. During her most acute episodes of somnambulic prowess, Rider wrote beautiful poetry and prose, sang tunefully, and became a gifted mimic. She trounced her physician in backgammon, and for the stream of folks seeking lost treasures, easily pronounced their whereabouts. Rider's and other cases of the 1830s and 1840s, such as Canada's "Stanstead Somnambulist"—challenged all existing theories of human sensory functioning. Physicians were puzzled at the paradoxical eclipse of certain senses while others became so highly developed; they were particularly fascinated by a number of somnambulic subjects who gave exact and effective medical diagnoses and treatments while in trance, for patients who did not even have to be in the same room.

Both physicians and the lay public attributed the miraculous powers of somnambulists to their capacity for "sympathy" with both their own essential selves and with the higher selves of others. The pervasiveness at the time of sympathy as an explanatory concept for a diversity of human relations could be seen in Adam Smith's *Theory of Moral Sentiments* (1759), which held sympathy—the willful emotional identification between individuals—as a fundamental creator of social bonds and a safeguard against self-interested behavior. Just below the surface of this Enlightenment notion lay the older, occult view of sympathy as a powerful primal force of Nature. "Sympathy" denoted the mutual attraction between all manner of bodies—both earthly and celestial. By the affinity coursing through all things, the most distant part of the universe might be drawn together. The astrological relation between zodiacal constellations, the planets, and human beings; the possibilities for alchemical transmutation of the elements; the mysterious relation between body and soul—soon to be collapsed by nineteenth century psychology into "mind"—all operated upon the principle of sympathy. In antebellum America, vitalistic biological theories—which were held as widely by natural philosophers and the earliest professional life scientists as were mechanistic theories—universally rested upon the notion of sympathy. Physical science was equally enamored of sympathetic (and antipathetic) forces, accepting them as operative in the phenomena of gravitation, electromagnetism, and chemical reactions. In his 1838 *The Tongue of Time, and Star of the States: A System of Human Nature, with the Phenomena of Heaven and Earth*, Dr. Joseph Comstock—who attended somnambular patients throughout the 1830s—easily mixed alchemical, astrological, and magical terminology with the Enlightenment language of Bacon and Locke. Prior to 1845, it was still possible for American scientists to blend occult—and hence, non-materialist—and naturalistic explanations in their attempt to explain Nature's most profound mysteries.

The clairvoyance demonstrated by these somnambulists sometimes extended beyond earth to other planets; in 1837 a Rhode Island girl named Loraina Brackett was struck on the head, producing blindness and impaired speech. Treated by a mesmerist, she traveled in trance across Long Island Sound to his home, which she described in perfect detail, down to the pictures on the walls. Miss Brackett then began to narrate while asleep her journeys to the moon, Mars, Saturn, and even the Sun. Such extraterrestrial travel was known to Swedenborgians, who read avidly of the Swedish seer Emmanuel Swedenborg's visits to other planets and the wild descriptions of their inhabitants.

Given their intense interest in connecting heaven and earth, their predilection for ecstatic experience, and their cultivation of sympathetic relations both within society and between society and Nature, the Transcendentalists were fascinated by somnambulic phenomena. Margaret Fuller had gone to Loraina Brackett in Providence seeking—and getting– relief for her migraine headache. Fuller's *Summer on the Lakes, in 1843* (1844) included an entire chapter devoted to a review of the case of Frederica Hauffe, the "Seeress of Prevorst," whose somnambulic state seemed to illustrate the promises and possibilities (and perils) of extracorporeal life. Fuller detailed the extraordinary clairvoyance—for angels, demons, ghosts, as well as humans—and uncanny gifts of this frail peasant woman who died at age twenty-nine. In her trance state, which in her final years of life was much more common than waking consciousness, she: could diagnose her illness and those of others; had intense sympathetic reactions to gems and minerals, flowers, and people, whose moral qualities acted immediately and physically upon her (when completely debilitated, she drew vitality from healthy persons, but lost vigor in the presence of weak or ill persons); saw herself often from a perspective out of her body. All of these phenomena posed a great challenge to "Enlightenment" natural science, which met these mysteries either with stony silence or outright mockery.

Trance phenomena were hard to ignore in mid-nineteenth century America, for they were appearing like mushrooms after an autumnal rain. Not far from Concord, at the Harvard Shaker settlement, much of the community's religious experience centered on trance speaking and dancing. Shakers shared with somnambulists the faculty of prophecy, speaking in unknown tongues, and holding communication with the spiritual world. Mother Ann Lee's founding visionary episodes had been singular and non-somnambulic in character, but in 1837 ecstatic somnambulism became epidemic in Shaker communities. The bulk of the Shaker brethren who fell into trance exhibited classic forms of demonic possession—the sort that in the seventeenth century would have led to accusations of witchcraft. An individual would suddenly be sent spinning like a top, not at all dizzy, continuing for an hour or more. Others would shake violently or skip around the room, wholly involuntarily. After falling to the floor unconscious, they would rise and detail what they had seen and heard while in trance. Some visited with members of a cast of illustrious historical characters: George Washington, General W.H. Harrison, William Penn, the Marquis de Lafayette, Napoleon Bonaparte, and more ancient ones—Saint Patrick, Sampson, Alexander the Great, Nero, Saint John, King David. Then there were native spirits—

Mohicans, Mohawks, Delaware, Shawnee, Seminole, Cherokee, Chickasaw, Choctaw. All assured the Shakers that Americans were a chosen people. Other spinning somnambulists returned to consciousness with instructions for the dances—Winding March, Lively Line, Double Square, Mother's Sister, Celestial March—for which the Shakers were celebrated.

Thoreau's opinion of mesmerism likely squared with that of the German *Naturphilosophes*, who understood the phenomena of magnetic rapport as evidence for their conviction that a vital force permeated Nature, including man. In his notes on J.B. Stallo's *General Principles of the Philosophy of Nature* (1848), Thoreau quotes Stallo: "The magnetized subject has merely been laid to the breast of the telluric parent—has been forced back to the state of impersonality, so that all the channels of direct cosmic emanations, which the waking subject, in distinguishing self from without, closes up, are laid open afresh." Thoreau was always far too immersed in the beauties of life in the body to concern himself with exotic travels out of the body, and yet he was in his own way an experienced astral pilot. A great deal of his enthusiasm for morning came from the ambrosial quality he carried into the waking state from his nighttime dream world. During dreaming sleep, Thoreau felt the heavenly hierarchies close around him, even within him. This communion with the angelic world formed the basis of his theory of dreams:

> A part of me which has reposed in silence all day, goes abroad at night, like the owl, and has its day. At night we recline, and nestle, and in fold ourselves in our being. Each night I go home to rest. Each night I am gathered to my fathers. The soul departs out of the body, and sleeps in God, a divine slumber. As she withdraws herself, the limbs droop and the eyelids fall, and nature reclaims her clay again. Men have always regarded the night as ambrosial or divine. The air is peopled then—fairies come out.

Day or night, sleeping afforded humans commerce with the spiritual world, but that world was peopled with as many baneful as blessed beings. Once the individual ego departed the body, it was open to invasion by deceiving spirits, mischievous elementals intent upon delivering spurious revelations. This demonological knowledge was preserved in a few of modern grimoires, but the "enlightenment" occulting of the spiritual world had by the 1840s especially marginalized the night side of Nature and Man. The Salem witchcraft trials were already seen by enlightened Americans not as a virulent demonic attack but as the supreme example of human gullibility and folly.

Thoreau when asleep—as when awake—seemed always to walk only with angels, never with demons. Joseph Smith, greedy for earthly treasures of gold and silver, sold his soul and thus bound demonic entities to him, while Thoreau, ever hungry for heavenly wealth, drew toward himself only good and guardian spirits. Unbidden but by his pure and lofty thoughts, these spirits left tokens of gratitude for him. All his life his most desired treasures came to him expeditiously, repeating the magic of Tahatawun's arrowhead. Though grateful for the gifts, Thoreau never quite understood from whence they came. In the summer of 1842, intent upon going to Nathaniel Hawthorne's home to borrow his music box, when he arrived, before speaking of it, Hawthorne's wife Sophia offered to lend it to him. A year later, eager to go to hear another neighbor's instrument, a parcel arrived in the mail—a music-box, sent to Thoreau by Richard Fuller as thanks for Thoreau's tutoring and friendship. "I think I must have some Muses in my pay that I know not of, for certain musical wishes of mine are answered as soon as entertained." On earth, there was nothing Thoreau loved better to find than arrowheads, flowers, and melodies; all three flowed to him effortlessly. He intuited that this powerful working of desire operated between men as well: "I know of no rule which holds so true as that we are always paid for our suspicions by finding what we suspect…Our suspicions exercise a demoniacal power over the subject of them. By some obscure law of influence when we are perhaps unconsciously the subject's of another's suspicion, we feel a strong impulse, even when it is contrary to our nature to do that which he expects but reprobates." Suspecting always angels above and the angelic in man below, Thoreau found them. The demons would have to find a foothold elsewhere.

Neptune

In 1846, a week after Henry Thoreau returned from a long canoe trip in Maine with a Penobscot Indian guide, unbeknownst to anyone in America, a new planet was discovered by French astronomer Urbain Leverrier. The discovery was emblematic of the era's magnified scientific reach. Though Neptune was a European discovery, American astronomers quickly joined the discussion about the new planet. In 1846, American science was on the threshold of coalescing into a mature national community. The Smithsonian Institution was founded this year, which would also see the establishment of America's first scientific schools, at Yale and Harvard. American astronomy was just reaching a critical stage, as ten observatories had been established in the previous fifteen years, and the *American Nautical Almanac* would soon begin publication. 1846 was a signal year for seeing more clearly into the Cosmos.

If in 1846 one perused the pages of America's oldest scientific journal, the *American Journal of Science*, one found that the hottest topics of scientific investigation were animal magnetism, galvanism, electricity, and terrestrial magnetism. The same newly discovered powers dominated the columns of the popular periodicals, including the *Concord Freeman*. The previous winter it had carried a report about a Natick, Massachusetts woman who after being mesmerized, described in detail the unsolved murder of a local man five years before, and gave the location of the pond where his body had been disposed of. A month later Concord's Unitarian church hosted L. H. Whiting, "discoverer of the Philosophy of Clairvoyance," for a series of lectures on "Phreno-Magnetism," including a surgical demonstration showing its utility as an anaesthetic. Serial fiction also found mesmerism a useful plot device; in "The Jealous Wife, or Mesmerism Proved," after opening with a mock testimonial hailing mesmerism as "a great science . . . a key to unlock every mystery worth knowing," a charlatan mesmerist is run out of town. The paper's attitude toward mesmerism was flippantly skeptical; noting the last lecture of Whiting's series, the editor promised that "rare sport may be expected."

The mocking of mysteries both scientific and spiritual was common sport in the 1840s, and no mystery came in for as much mockery as mesmerism. A key agent of disenchantment was the popular theater, where magicians quickly incorporated the latest mysteries into their stage routines. Urban opera houses and Masonic temples would frequently host earnest mesmeric lecturers on one evening, and debunking prestidigitators the next. At halls throughout the Northeast, Signor Blitz, Signor Vivaldi, and dozens of other pretend Persian or Hindoo or Egyptian fakirs, along with demonstrating automata and electrical phenomena, invariably made displays of mesmeric fascination part of their acts. In Boston in 1843, while a lecture series on animal magnetism was being conducted at the Masonic Temple, across town at the Boston Museum, "Dr. Guy, Corresponding Secretary of the RMBC, Fellow of the UCS, Member of All Learned Societies East of Bangor and Professor of Everything," was giving a "diffuse lecture" on the same subject. Any occult power that mesmerism might at first have seemed to possess was quickly drained away by the lampooning and sleight-of-hand duplicity, which threw all authentic phenomena into question.

Among the Concord circle, Thoreau was perhaps the least interested in mesmeric revelations. Emerson's notebooks and a number of his essays show that he often read about mesmerism (in *Nature*, Emerson even considered mesmerism as one of a number of hopeful signs of some "in-streaming power"), which he came to believe was entitled "only to a share of attention, and not a large share." Alcott was fascinated by all forms of fascination, and was particularly taken with the somnambulic revelations of Andrew Jackson Davis, the "Poughkeepsie Seer." Margaret Fuller—whom Emerson, Hawthorne, and others were convinced could "magnetize" others — saw mesmerism as a harbinger of "future states of being," and had successful treatments for back pain with a French physician who practiced a form of mesmerism. On one occasion Fuller attempted to get Emerson to attend a demonstration by Anna Parsons, a member of the Brook Farm community who practiced "psychometry," a form of mesmeric trance state in which she would put letters to her forehead and give vivid images of the thoughts and emotions of the writer. The week before inviting Emerson, Fuller had given Parsons a letter to her from Emerson, in which he had enclosed a new poem he had written. In trance, Parsons was able to reveal all manner of information about the writer. Emerson declined the invitation to personally witness Parsons' somnambulic clairvoyance. Yet Emerson knew full well the efficacy of the magnetic relation; his success as a lecturer depended wholly upon it. Discussing Emerson's Boston lecture given the same week as the invitation to hear Parsons, Thoreau voiced his distrust of the charismatic art of the orator, saying "to me it is vegetation, the pullulation and universal budding of the plant Man." Thoreau accurately diagnosed mesmerism's retreat into the labyrinthine arena of the Sentient Soul.

No one distrusted the gravitational pull of the mesmerizer more than Nathaniel Hawthorne. In his novels—*The Scarlet Letter, The House of Seven Gables, The Blithedale Romance, The Marble Faun*—characters meet tragic ends after having fallen under mesmeric spells cast by actual mesmerists or by particularly hypnotic individuals in their lives. As America's master of gothic fiction, and eloquent critic of the Faustian attempt to penetrate nature's secrets, Hawthorne was drawn irresistibly toward mesmerism as an agent of Promethean, but altogether dark and dangerous, power. "It seems to me," thought Hawthorne, "that the sacredness of an individual is violated by it . . . . [It is] an intrusion into the holy of holies." Like the counterfeiters whose crimes were constantly being recounted in the *Concord Freeman* and all American newspapers, the mesmerizer stealthily acquired power over society's open and honest subjects, introducing a note of doubt into all human commerce. Somnambulic clairvoyance collapsed the bounds between "public" and "private," and even the innocent mesmerized subject could enter psychic spaces where he or she had not been invited.

Hawthorne, Emerson and Thoreau intuited that mesmerism was a revolt against the gods, an unholy alliance with a dark power of Nature. Thoreau, with his keen interest in mythology, was aware that before Neptune was chosen as the name of the new planet, many preferred the name "Atlas," the Titan who for his role in the revolt against the gods was obliged to support the heavens with his head and hands. The sea, Neptune's domain, was still in the mid-nineteenth century a dark and mysterious part of Nature, so perhaps it was a fitting name for the new planet, whose discovery coincided with modern man's attempt to see through the murky depths of Mother Nature. The Neptunian decade of the 1840s was a Sargasso Sea of foggy, misty, somnambulic dreaminess, marked by the Opium Wars in the Far East and the Mormon wars in the Midwest. Despite the seeming clarity promised by astronomy, telegraphy, Morse code, and an explosion of fact in the sciences, a thick cloud of illusion hung over America.

Thoreau's remove to Walden was a singular effort from within Neptunian America to see the world true, and the journals he kept while there became gospels instantly because his fellow citizens had fallen so far away from reality. "Shams and delusions are esteemed for soundest truths," Thoreau lamented, "while reality is fabulous. If men would steadily observe realities only, and not allow themselves to be deluded, life, to compare it with such things as we know, would be like a fairy tale and the Arabian Nights' Entertainments." By "the perpetual instilling and drenching of the reality" surrounding him at Walden, Thoreau escaped imprisonment in the hall of mirrors that his fellows erected. While mesmeric revelators, Shaker enthusiasts, and millennial ecstatics peered into a fantastical future, Thoreau set his sights underfoot and found the eternal present. "Men esteem truth remote, in the outskirts of the system, behind the farthest star, before Adam and after the last man. In eternity there is indeed something true and sublime. But all these times and places and occasions are now and here. God himself culminates in the present moment, and will never be more divine in the lapse of all the ages." From his cabin at Walden Pond, Thoreau made a crucial discovery for the Age of the Consciousness Soul: the human being, pulled centrifugally by his new instruments of seeing and hearing, had to hold his own center, and there find both himself and God.

Thoreau was born with Neptune in opposition to the moon, a configuration that seemed to suggest that he was born with the potential to summon the moon forces to overcome and thus redeem the potentially adverse power of the eighth planet. As antebellum America descended into a maelstrom of illusions and humbug, Thoreau saw clearly. He realized that "no method or discipline can supersede the necessity of being forever on the alert." To become a Seer, he told himself, he must keep his eye "constantly on the true and real." As always when articulating his sense of his own personal destiny, he used the language of the stars: "Every mortal sent into this world has a star in [the] heavens appointed to guide him—Its ray he cannot mistake—It has sent its beam to him either through clouds and mists faintly or through a serene heaven."

Manifesting the Dead

The Neptunian mood of illusion in America seemed to culminate on the eve of April Fool's Day in 1848, when Kate and Margaret Fox, two young sisters in Hydesville, New York, decided to respond with telegraphic-style raps to the sounds being made by a poltergeist who had long haunted their family home with rapping, knocking, and dragging sounds. When ten-year-old Kate challenged the "tommyknocker" to echo the snaps of her fingers, it did. Then the girls asked it to tap out the their ages with the correct number of knocks, and again it answered correctly. Drawing on the new technology of the telegraph, the Fox sisters taught the invisible intruder a sort of Morse code where raps could signify yes or no in response to a question, or be used to signify a letter of the alphabet. After becoming fairly fluent in the new percussive language, the rapping entity claimed to be the spirit of a peddler named Charles B. Rosma, who had supposedly been murdered five years earlier and buried in the cellar. Hydesville citizens found out who had formerly lived in the house and accused him of murder; he was shunned by the entire community. Though years later a skeleton was found buried in the wall, records showed no missing person by the name of Rosma. Stories about murdered (or murdering) peddlers were the most common folk tales that circulated for generations of early Americans. The entity, whatever it was, was a ghoulish gossip whose veracity was erratic at best.

Despite being sent away to nearby Rochester because of all the publicity that the raps had caused, Kate and Margaret became famous; their New York séances in 1850 attracted such notables as William Cullen Bryant, Horace Greeley, James Fenimore Cooper, and William Lloyd Garrison. From Hydesville the rapping spread in all directions as quickly as evangelical Christianity had in previous generations. Once again, western New York state became a "burned-over district," this time scorched by the supposed spirits of the dead. The most celebrated case to follow the Fox sisters was in Stratford, Connecticut, where in 1850, Reverend Eliakim Phelps returned with his family from church one Sunday to their sprawling mansion on Elm Street, to find all the doors and windows open. Inside, they found the furniture knocked over, dishes smashed, books, papers and clothing scattered all over. They had not been robbed; Rev. Phelps found his gold watch, silver heirlooms, and even loose cash undisturbed. In an upstairs bedroom, a sheet was spread over a bed, and Mrs. Phelps' nightgown was laid out upon it. At the bottom a pair of stockings were stretched out, and the arms of the gown were folded across the chest, like a corpse.

Later, while the rest of the family returned to church for the afternoon service, Rev. Phelps hid in his study with a pistol, hoping to catch the intruders should they return. After some time he went downstairs, and entering the dining room, found a circle of eleven effigies of women, kneeling or standing in prayer, some holding Bibles. Articles of the family's clothing had been stuffed with rags and other materials from around the house to create the dummies, which had been put in place during the brief period while Phelps was standing guard. Over the next few months, twenty more mock women would appear out of the blue. They would be joined by leaping umbrellas, silverware, books, and other household objects; bedding sailing off of beds; food and clothing dropping out of nowhere onto the breakfast table while the family ate.

Friends and other visitors to the house watched as these objects fell at impossibly slow speeds, or changed course in midair. By the end of April, the disturbances had turned quite nasty: screams and odd sounds were heard each night; silverware was mangled; windows were broken; the children's limbs were jerked about violently and welts appeared on their skin. Rev. Phelps' son was hit with a barrage of small stones. Later, in front of a dozen witnesses, the boy vanished, and was later found tied up and suspended from a tree in the yard.

A week before the odd visitation, Rev. Phelps and a friend had been discussing Spiritualism, and decided to hold a séance, at which they produced knocking and rapping sounds, just as the Fox sisters had in Hydesville. Following their lead, Phelps decided to try communicating with the spirit by raps, and he soon ascertained that his resident poltergeist was a tormented soul in hell. When Phelps asked how he might help, the spirit asked Phelps to bring him a piece of pumpkin pie. Asking again, the invisible trickster asked instead for a glass of gin. When the exasperated minister finally asked why the spirit was making such mischief, it replied: "For fun." It went on to give an elaborate tale of having been a law clerk in Philadelphia who had been convicted and jailed for fraud. Like the Hydesville "spirit," the Stratford spirit's information was frequently false, and yet all were puzzled as to how the disembodied intelligence could exist at all.

Both the Hydesville and the Stratford specters—and thousands of others who manifested throughout America—claimed and were believed to be spirits of the dead, and despite the rude, lewd, and downright demonic nature of much of their communications, became venerated by millions eager for proof of life after death. The faithful turned a blind eye to the fact that Kate Fox's first words to the pioneer poltergeist at Hydesville were "Do as I do, Mr. Splitfoot!" (i.e., the Devil), or that that first manifestation had commenced on the eve of the most favorable day of the year for elfin activity. Clergymen who suggested that the spirits were devils in disguise were ignored or ridiculed. Their congregations—and often they themselves — had long since ceased believing in the active presence of non-human spiritual beings within the spiritual world. They reasoned that these phantasmic folk must be spirits of the dead, and the more physical their manifestations—moving tables, playing musical instruments, oozing ectoplasmic limbs, producing bouquets of flowers and other such corny parlor tricks—the more credence they were given.

The publicity generated by the Hydesville and Stratford poltergeists caused an explosion of mediumistic phenomena from coast to coast. "Experimental" Spiritualist circles formed in Boston (where there was estimated to be over a thousand mediums by 1850), Philadelphia, Providence, all the major cities in New York state, and all the New England states; Cincinnati; Memphis; St. Louis; California, Oregon, Texas. Fittingly, Spiritualism's advent had been prophesied by America's most famous mesmeric somnambulist, Andrew Jackson Davis, who had begun dictating in trance his 800-page compendium, *The Principles of Nature, Her Divine Revelations and a Voice to Mankind* in 1845. Published in 1847 (and going through 34 editions in the next 30 years), it included among its revelations that the truth of a world of spirits would "ere long present itself in the form of a living demonstration. And the world will hail with delight the ushering-in of that era when the interiors of men will be opened, and the spiritual communion will be established." While Davis gave no exact date for the arrival of the event, Shaker somnambulists in the 1830s had made a similar prediction for the year 1848, and also prophesied that

America would see an extraordinary discovery of material wealth to accompany the spiritual wealth. The discovery of gold at Sutter's Mill came only two months before Kate Fox taught Mr. Splitfoot to speak in raps.

Davis's *Principles of Nature* presented a muddy, grandiose-sounding cosmogony in its first section, a damning review of the Old Testament and a rejection of the divinity of Christ in the second, and a program for a Fourierist style socialism in the third. Some of Davis's cosmic pronouncements seemed to come from a true clairvoyance: in advance of the discovery of Neptune and Pluto he spoke of eighth and ninth planets, and his descriptions of Uranus's composition accorded with later findings. He also seemed to know about the Galactic Center long before its discovery. But the bulk of his book delivered wild descriptions of inhabited planets, pop versions of Swedenborg's otherworldly visions. Saturn he described as inhabited by a more advanced race of humanity, while on Venus and Mars the inhabitants were more primitive than on Earth. By 1850, when the Phelps spirit story was grabbing headlines across America, Davis was the most famous authority on Spiritualism in the nation, and he made a visit to Stratford to investigate. Davis lent his authority to the genuineness of the activity, and stated that the outbreak was caused by "vital radiations" from the Phelps children, whose "magnetism" caused objects to be attracted to or repelled from them.

In America, every day of the year became April Fools Day for the liberated sprites and poltergeists. The Stratford shenanigans were just a small sampling of their kaleidoscopic circus of tomfoolery. Puritanical matrons manipulating Ouija boards were made to utter the foulest of oaths. Greedy fortune hunters were promised gold and silver in a thousand secret locales. Would-be prophets were tantalized with authentic tidbits of advantageous foreknowledge, then sucker-punched with ersatz revelations guaranteed to be passed on to the multitudes. Earnest seekers of spiritual truths were hoodwinked with bizarre celestial untruths; the planetary fantasies of Andrew Jackson Davis were repeated in a hundred varieties by unsuspecting Spiritualist mediums. Masquerading poltergeists donned the personas of every historical celebrity imaginable, from George Washington to Alexander the Great, proclaiming all sorts of twaddle as the most sacred scripture.

The Frankenstein monster of Spiritualist manifestations appeared just at the moment when America's national science was maturing into a daylight endeavor capable of penetrating Nature with new power. Transcendentalism, like European Romanticism, was an antidote to the seductive dangers of both Mammon—the materialist mindset—and Lucifer, the unmoored angel of light whose promise of knowledge glimmered blindingly from the temples of Spiritualism, Mormonism, and Freemasonry. Thoreau's martial attitude, his sense that he was doing daily battle with a godless adversary, was as much historical reality as personal myth. His hermitage at Walden Pond was the hallmark of a new era in human consciousness evolution, where each and every individual met his nemesis in the physical world, whose Siren song promised that it would fulfill all his heart's desires. Idealistic young American squires and lads embarking upon their Grail quests could no longer count on joining others in hopeful apprenticeship to sage Knights. The mystery school was now the world, where each individual human heart and mind was compelled to discover Truth amidst a bewildering hall of mirrors.

Magicians have always used mirrors in their efforts to manipulate the laws of Time and Space, and a hidden group of magicians had in the introduction of the physical phenomena of Spiritualism worked "mirror magic" on America and the world. By the early 1840s, within certain secret brotherhoods of the West, a debate was raging as to how to combat the era's rampant materialism. In these brotherhoods, it was widely known that in the year 1841, humanity had reached the "Abyss" of materialism. The debate was among those brothers who believed that they should speak publicly about the secrets of the spiritual world that they knew from firsthand experience in the initiatory orders, and those who feared that making such knowledge public would lead to catastrophe. A compromise was reached: the brothers would use their magical abilities to introduce certain phenomena—*using the elemental beings of Nature.* They believed that once the public witnessed invisible entities rapping, speaking, even moving tables and chairs about, there would follow widespread abandonment of the worldview that denied the existence of invisible spiritual beings. Science would take up the investigation of the phenomena, and thus discover that there were invisible elemental beings of nature who could, under certain circumstances, make their presence known within the material world. Those clairvoyant for the elemental world—like Henry Thoreau—would no longer need to hide their encounters, and might share in conducting the new research effort.

Instead of attributing the manifestations to the activity of elemental beings, however, almost everyone—save the scientists who chalked it all up to sleight-of-hand—interpreted the phenomena as the doings of the dead. America imagined that there were whiskey and cigars on the other side—that life after death was just like life in the physical body. Even before the pervasive culture of mourning produced by the Civil War's massive death toll, America was seized by a collective desire to communicate with the dead, and Spiritualist mediums seemed to offer that possibility. Wed to America's democratic spirit, the whole nation soon discovered its own mediumistic abilities. For the members of the brotherhoods who favored divulging occult secrets, the plan had totally backfired. They ceased their magical activity with mediums, but the genie was already out of the bottle; mischievous elementals—like the ones at the Phelps and Fox homes—were unleashed wherever people turned their thoughts to attempting communication through mediumistic means. The lowering of consciousness at each séance gave them free access to American parlors and the psyches of those gathered there.

Once the well-meaning occultists had withdrawn their efforts, it provided an open field for the so-called "Brothers of the Left," occult organizations that used ceremonial magic for strictly selfish means. It was in the interest of these occultists that as many souls as possible went through the gate of death with a materialist understanding about what lay beyond, since these souls then became a source of occult power fully in their control. It is important to realize that the most powerful of these brotherhoods were truly "secret societies," that is, unlike Freemasonry or Skull & Bones and similar fraternal organizations, they were completely veiled from public view. But even in the more well-known lodges, there was a possibility for magical manipulation of the membership, via the system of ceremonial "degrees." Lower degree Freemasons who worked earnestly toward higher degrees were ignorant of the magical control exercised over them by unknown individuals at the top. Here was the real reason for William Morgan's murder and for the binding oaths against divulging ceremonial secrets that were routine in these groups—the occult elite worried that the public would discover their method of exercising control over their own membership.

This is perhaps the cruelest aspect of these "Neptunian" phenomena—somnambulism, mesmerism, Spiritualism. At a crucial moment in the development of the Consciousness Soul, when a small circle of Grail knights gathered in true friendship and community in Concord and a few other American places to fashion a philosophy and science of true freedom, the dark Klingsor knights in the occult brotherhoods plotted against the Grail, using the old Sentient Soul labyrinthine binding of ceremonial magic. The black brotherhoods succeeded to the degree that they seduced America backwards to Titurel, not forward to continue to mature Parzival's path of the Consciousness Soul.

When Thoreau was young, he enjoyed reading tales about Fortunatus, the young man who finds a purse that cannot be emptied and a hat that carries him anywhere he wishes to be. Thoreau always felt himself as lucky as Fortunatus; "I was born in the most estimable place in the world, and in the nick of time, too," he boasted. Though divinely favored, Thoreau clearly brought such luck as was his in his direction. Like Parzival, he persevered through his share of trials; the trial of Neptunian illusion that seized America at mid-century was one he passed easily, because of his fidelity to the truth of his own senses.

During his first winter at Walden Thoreau anchored himself in the real by conducting a survey of the pond with compass, chain, and sounding line. Local folklore held Walden Pond to be bottomless, a convenient myth for Thoreau simultaneously to debunk—physically—and prove—philosophically. With the solid, sixteen-inch thick ice beneath his boots, he could easily sound any spot below from the ice roof above, sometimes dropping his pound-and-a-half stone and attached cod line down through holes made by ice fishermen, and more often through cuts he had made with his axe. Thoreau—whose techniques permitted him such accuracy that he could calculate the variation of the bottom depth over each hundred feet within three or four inches—delighted to find a fractal symmetry in the submerged topography. Mapping out his data, he discovered a "remarkable coincidence"—the pond's greatest depth (at 102 feet, the deepest pond in Massachusetts, even if not bottomless) lay at the exact intersection of the lines of greatest length and breadth. Other topographic laws and formulas disclosed themselves—such as how coves come to have bars at their mouths—and these rippled out under Thoreau's attention to become laws by which the human being could also be mapped and measured:

Such a rule of the two diameters not only guides us toward the sun in the system and the heart in man, but draw lines through the length and breadth of the aggregate of a man's particular daily behaviors and waves of life into his coves and inlets, and where they intersect will be the height and depth of his character.

Amen.

8: Kaspar Hauser's Path of Sacrifice

In the vast desert of our time, where the blazing sun of selfish passion parches and turns dry our hearts, to have finally found a true human being is one of the most beautiful and unforgettable experiences I have had in the evening of my life.

—Anselm von Feuerbach, *A Case of a Crime*
Against the Soul of a Human Being (1832)

The face of Kaspar Hauser's gravestone in Ansbach, Germany, bears the inscription:

Hic jacet Casparus Hauser
Aenigma sui temporis
ignota nativitas
occulta mors.

There have been more than 3000 books and at least 14,000 articles written about Kaspar Hauser, and yet, his death is still a mystery (*occulta mors*), his origin is still unknown (*ignota nativitas*), and he is still a riddle for our age (*aenigma sui temporis*). You have now read Anselm von Feuerbach's account of Kaspar Hauser (*A Case of a Crime Against the Soul of a Human Being*): you have pondered Kaspar's odd abilities, explored the significance of his captors' having suppressed his *Ich*/Ego, and listened to the rumors of his royal birth. For you, as for the many generations of students of Kaspar Hauser's life, it all remains a perplexing riddle. And there may be rising up before you another riddle—how is it that I have chosen to spend so much time on this one strange story, within a course that is meant to cover 500 years of the entire planet's history?!

Perhaps you have noticed the subterranean theme that runs through our journey so far—the bringing in of new impulses *by a youth*. Think back on all of these young characters—Prince Georgy and Parsifal; Joan and John; Genghis Khan and Marco Polo; the Youth in Goethe's fairy tale; Henry Thoreau; even the brief glimpse of Mark Twain chasing that stray but fateful piece of paper…—and now think also of Kaspar Hauser, an individual who is kept not only from becoming a mature adult, but from even becoming a youth! His development has been cruelly frozen in time, and then, as he miraculously unfolds his "I," he is brutally murdered, at age 21.

So often when we are left with a mystery, it is because we are asking the wrong question. Whodunits ask the obvious question; is there perhaps another question that we could ask to help us get to the bottom of this mystery? Rather than asking who killed Kaspar Hauser or even who *is* Kaspar Hauser, let us begin with this question: *Where did Kaspar Hauser come from and what was to have been achieved by him?* Asking this question leads one in a very different direction from where "It Matters" inquiries have led these last two centuries. The most stunning result is that this question leads us once again to contemplate the Grail, Parsifal, and our own moment in history with new eyes, and a new consciousness.

A Favored Place

In 1555, half a century before the Rosicrucians were heard of in Europe, the Provençal astrologer Nostradamus wrote:

> *A new sect of Philosophers shall arise,*
> Despising death, gold, honours and riches,
> They shall be near the mountains of Germany,
> They shall have abundance of others to support and follow them.

The German Rosicrucians who made a furor in the opening decades of the 1600s with their calls for utopian reform did renounce earthly wealth and fame, but they certainly did not have much support. Though rumors abounded of magical Rosicrucian masters, they were wholly out of the public eye. Nostradamus clearly was pointing to some officially sanctioned—rather than scorned—philosophical movement, one that took hold of the larger society. At the turn of the nineteenth century, in the region of Germany's Black Forest Range, the new sect of philosophers would seem to have been the circle of "Idealists"—the descendants of Germany's 17th century Rosicrucians—around Georg Friedrich Wilhelm Hegel and Friedrich Wilhelm Joseph von Schelling. But the Idealists, for all of their influence, hardly transformed German culture.

In the Middle Ages, the Black Forest region—then called "Swabia"—was renowned as the home of the *minnesingers*, whose songs celebrated their land as a uniquely favored place. Running along the east bank of the Rhine River, the region was rich in timber, minerals, and wildlife, and was the favored hunting place of royalty.

In 1715, Karl III Wilhelm, Margrave of Baden, the state comprising most of the Black Forest, established a palace where he could rest after hunting in the nearby forest. Around the palace he created the town of Karlsruhe (Karl's Rest); to attract immigrants from all over Central Europe he granted a series of benefits to settlers—serfdom and statute labor were prohibited; no taxes were due for 20 years; settlers were given free land and wood; religious freedom was guaranteed. Karl Wilhelm made Karlsruhe his official residence in order to persuade the new citizens to move there; the wide variety of immigrants—Prussians, Poles, Saxons, Bavarians, Swabians and Alsatians—gave rise to a new dialect—*Brigandendeutsch*. Modeling himself after the late Sun

King Louis XIV of France, Karl Wilhelm built his new capital with streets radiating out like sunbeams from the palace. "Karl's Rest" was truly a favored place associated with images of sun and peace.

The Baden region was in the early 19th century a place where myth was being enacted on the physical plane, for Wolfram's tale of a future Grail Castle seemed within reach there, seven centuries after the epic was first written down. In 1806, after the dissolution of the Holy Roman Empire, Baden pioneered new, liberal forms of government and administrative organization. Its legislature became an incubator for the Liberal-Nationalist movement. In 1831, two years before Kaspar Hauser was murdered, Baden expressed sympathy and support for the Polish rebellion against Imperial Russia. As the Revolutions of 1848 swept across Germany, Baden joined in the rebellion; Baden was the most liberal German state, providing 26 of the 51 liberal delegates to the Frankfurt all-German Parliament. But it was also in Baden that the last revolutionaries were crushed when in June 1849 Prussian crown prince Wilhelm (later Emperor Wilhelm I of Germany in 1871) marched to Baden at the head of 50,000 soldiers and suppressed the Baden radicals.

This was not the way it was supposed to happen, had Kaspar Hauser's mission unfolded rightfully. In 1848 he would have been the Grand Duke of Baden, and would have provided the "abundance" and "support" that Nostradamus had foreseen. The importance of the Baden region can be seen in the fact that it came under the thumb of Napoleon, who in 1806 finally destroyed the old Holy Roman Empire, in his quest to create a new Rome. It was as if the tyrannical imperial spirit that Joan had once fought off from England, now possessed Joan's nation, in the form of Napoleon, who attempted to dominate Germany and central Europe completely. 1806 was the year that Napoleon arranged the marriage of his adopted daughter Stephanie Beauharnais (indeed, she *was* the beautiful *harnais*—harness—by which Napoleon linked France and this favored and influential region of Germany) to Duke Karl of Baden. Six years later, in 1812, a male heir—who would have been in power at the time of the Revolutions of 1848—was born to the royal couple. *This child was "Kaspar Hauser."*

A "Counterfactual" History

Historians are fond of creating what they term "counterfactual" narratives, as a sort of thought experiment to envision what might have occurred as alternative historical paths. Let us stop a moment and engage in such a counterfactual experiment. In 1831, as Kaspar turned 18, he was living under the care of Baron von Tucher; a year earlier, the Grand Duke Ludwig had died and was succeeded by Leopold, the eldest son of the Countess Hochberg. This would have been the point at which Kaspar would have become the Grand Duke. His own father Grand Duke Karl I had died in 1818 when Kaspar was just six years old. Karl's brother Ludwig then became Grand Duke, but had no children. On May 26, 1831—exactly three years to the day after Kaspar's appearance in Nuremberg—the well-connected English Earl Philip Henry, Lord Stanhope, arrived in Nuremberg and insisted on seeing Kaspar. By December, he had both won Kaspar's favor and succeeded in being appointed Kaspar's guardian.

In 1833, Kaspar's beloved teacher Friedrich Daumer—the "last Rosicrucian" as he was known to later generations—turned 33. Because of Stanhope's intervention, Kaspar was living in Ansbach with the sadistic teacher Meyer, employed by Stanhope. On the 20th of May Kaspar was confirmed in the Swan Knights' chapel of the Ansbach church. The Order of the Swan, founded on Michaelmas day in the year 1440 by Friedrich II, Prince of Brandenburg, dedicated themselves to the service of the Grail. These Swan Knights were known as *lebendigen Toten* ("living dead"), in the sense that their sacrifice for the spiritual world was so total that their own life was eclipsed.

On September 29, Kaspar turned 21—the beginning of his "Sun period," which would have lasted to 1861. The Sun period is the stage of life when an individual's ego is fully developed, and he can exercise his talents and purpose most effectively. Knowing this, Kaspar's hidden enemies, who had gone to such extraordinary lengths to keep him alive but *without an ego*, feared his belatedly seizing upon his mission, and laid out the plot against his life. On December 14 came the assassination attack upon Kaspar in the Ansbach garden.

The 1830s marked a turning point in European politics and society; beginning with the July Revolution in 1830 in Paris, continuing with the Polish uprising against the Russians and the Greek revolt against the Turks, a wave of democratic fervor crested in Germany in the May 1832 Hambacher Fest, where 30,000 citizens, led by students, gathered to demand a liberal, unified Germany; freedom of the press; the lifting of feudal burdens; religious tolerance; and ultimately, a German republic. As Grand Duke, Kaspar would have supported the democratic impulse. In England, that impulse was manifesting in dramatic ways—the Reform Act of 1832 extended voting rights and sought to end patronage and corruption; the Slavery Abolition Act of 1833; the 1833 Factory Act, which ended child labor; the rise in 1836 of the Chartist movement, which campaigned for universal suffrage and a better life for the working class.

In 1847 Kaspar would have begun his final septennial of the 21-year Sun period, a time which in modern individuals sees the flowering of the Consciousness Soul. Kaspar would have been 35. A year later, during the 1848 Revolutions, the Grand Duke of Baden would have received the crown of a united Germany from the Frankfurt parliament; absent Kaspar, the crown was offered instead to the arch-reactionary Friedrich Wilhelm IV of Prussia, whose troops later squashed the last efforts of the Baden revolutionaries. As leader of the new liberal German monarchy, Kaspar would have been able to guide Germany onto a different path than the one it ultimately followed.

Seven years further on, in 1854, the Crimean War broke out over the protection of the Holy places in Palestine. As in the year of Kaspar's birth in 1812, the West—Britain and France—invaded the East—Russia—while Central Europe looked on helplessly. Two years later, the Second Opium War—another attack by the West upon the East—began. Kaspar might have been able to use his position as a Central European leader to balance these forces of East and West, preventing war.

In 1861 Kaspar would have been 49; this was the moment of humanity's first "'Moon Node," when, as with each individual, humanity could cast a glance over its past and future, and take steps toward new growth and development. The 1860s instead saw the Civil War in America; an unsuccessful effort (1864-67) by the Austrian House of Habsburg to establish an empire in Mexico under Maximilian, son of the Austrian Emperor; Otto von Bismarck's "Iron Chancellorship" began in earnest in 1862 and Germany went to war against Denmark (1864) and Austria (1866). In 1867, the Austro-Hungarian Empire was founded. Germany was thus experiencing its own civil war, and Kaspar Hauser might have been able to resolve these tensions—although they might never have arisen had he successfully guided the Revolution of 1848. By this time, German art, science, and humanities would have flourished under Kaspar's stewardship, contributing to the unfolding of a Grail culture right where Nostradamus had predicted it would.

The Attack on the Grail

But none of this was to be. The establishment of a "Grail culture"—an expressive, humane, open culture within a truly democratic central European polity, where the triumph of the individual "I" did not come at the expense of the community—was forestalled because of a sustained attack focused on a single individual, Kaspar Hauser, the so-called "Child of Europe." To effectively carry out that attack, many more people than Kaspar were killed. It is now clear that the first person murdered was Johann Jakob Ernst Blochmann, the infant son of a couple who were servants of Countess Luise von Hochberg. Johann Jakob was born three days before Kaspar Hauser, on September 26, 1812. A German researcher discovered in the Karlsruhe death register that while the other nine children had their death dates recorded next to their baptismal registration dates, "Kaspar Ernst Blochmann"—his profession given as a soldier in the Bavarian army—was entered in the death register as having died in Munich on November 27, 1833. In Munich, the researcher found that in both the death register and the funeral register of the grave committee, the individual's name was given as "Ernst Blochmann"; only in the Karlsruhe register did the name "Kaspar" appear.

In the records of the Bavarian army, it was found that no soldier by that name had served. This bogus death register entry points to an extraordinary fact that will surface again and again—the murderers continued to attempt to erase all evidence that *the Blochmann child, not Kaspar Hauser, was the infant who died in the Grand Duke and Duchess's palace on October 16, 1812.* The Blochmanns had ten children, a number of others who died in infancy, and it is likely that "Ernst" was also ill during infancy. In 1875, when rumors about Kaspar Hauser's royal birth continued to circulate, the infant prince's birth, illness, and death certificates were published, and they made clear that no proper identification was ever made of the dead hereditary Prince— by Stephanie, Karl, or a wet nurse, which would have been the usual procedure. There was also never a proper autopsy. And yet there was a doctor's report stating that the newborn on September 29 was in perfect health, while on October 16 the child suffered from a number of ailments. One final fact points to the Blochmann child: his father, a gardener at the Hochberg estate, was suddenly promoted not long after the death of the impostor child.

In 1817, Stephanie and Karl lost another son, Alexander, just before his first birthday. At least one other male heir died in infancy, and it is almost certain that these boys were murdered. In 1818, at age 33, Grand Duke Karl, Kaspar Hauser's father, was poisoned. On May 29, 1833, Anselm von Feuerbach died, and he his son publicly declared that his father had been poisoned. Two other members of the Feuerbach family—both of whom knew of their father's suspicions about Kaspar Hauser's fate, as well as the murder of their father—died under mysterious circumstances. But that is not all: a series of people intimately associated with Kaspar Hauser in one way or another—Mayor Binder, Johann Biberbach—a wealthy Nuremberg merchant in whose home Kaspar had lived for 6 months in 1830; Dr. Preu, the city physician who first examined Kaspar; Dr. Osterhausen, another doctor who made a thorough medical examination of Kaspar shortly after he was jailed in Nuremberg; and Dr. Albert, who performed the autopsy—all died between 1833 to 1835. This brings to a total of eight the number of individuals, outside of the Blochmann child, Kaspar, and his two would-be-prince brothers, who were killed.

We can now compose a revised biographical sketch for the kidnapped Prince who was given the name Kaspar Hauser: sometime between the day of his birth on September 29, 1812 and October 16, 1812, the day the substitute Blochmann child died or was killed, Kaspar was abducted from the palace at Karlsruhe. At first he was well cared for, and even vaccinated. He grew up in isolation, but normally at first. The captors' plan was to allow Kaspar to learn to stand and also to walk—to become "stabilized" in his body. They even let him develop speech and thought to a very primitive level. What was critical was the age from which he would be able to form his first lasting memories. This is when Kaspar's treatment changes radically; sometime between the age of 2 and 3—the age when a child's ego ("I") comes in—Kaspar was imprisoned in a small, dark dungeon room. He would be kept there for the next 12 or 13 years.

By keeping him in what was essentially a cage, his captors prevented Kaspar from an upright position, once again holding back the development of speaking and thinking. His dimmed state of consciousness was such that it became impossible for him to know how long his imprisonment lasted. In the spring of 1828 Kaspar was quite literally "set on his feet." Taught about 40 words, and instructed how to write "Kaspar Hauser," he was then thrust out into the world. The plan went astray when the riding master, instead of making Kaspar a stable boy, sent him off to the police, but they too did not know what to do with him, and he was put under the care of the prison keeper of Nuremberg Castle, Andreas Hiltel. Hiltel was a man of heart who had a gift for observing and judging human beings. Despite his long contact with scoundrels of all types, Hiltel was no cynic, and saw clearly Kaspar Hauser's pure, innocent, childlike soul qualities.

The next two important individuals for Kaspar are Doctors Preu and Osterhausen, both of whom were keen phenomenologists, and both of whom pronounced Kaspar as genuine, in the sense of their diagnosis of his physical impairments caused by long incarceration. Their opinion so impresses Mayor Binder, that as the Chief of Police, he personally takes over the interrogation, which creates a deep sympathy in him, and leads to the publication of a long public proclamation, which finds its way to a much wider European audience, thereby making Kaspar a great sensation all over Europe. This was quite out of the ordinary, and led to his being reprimanded by his superior officers.

Only a few days after he appeared in Nuremberg, Georg Friedrich Daumer visited Kaspar, and without hesitation, took hold of instructing him. Mayor Binder puts Kaspar in Daumer's care, and he goes to live with Daumer and his sister and mother; this is Kaspar's first real home.

In addition, both Feuerbach and Baron von Tucher—Kaspar's first legal guardian—seem to have been destined to encounter Kaspar. Finally, Pastor Fuhrmann, the Protestant minister in Ansbach, who confirmed Kaspar, becomes the seventh in the circle around Kaspar Hauser; Fuhrmann witnesses his conversion to Christianity, and also stands at Kaspar's bedside, where Kaspar's final words are prayers for his murderer. All of these individuals were critical to Kaspar's well being after he comes to Nuremberg; without their aid, Kaspar would no doubt have languished as an ill-treated, anonymous stable boy whose story would never have come into such wide public view.

The Dynastic Crime and the Occult Crime

Kaspar Hauser's story is a riddle, an "unsolved mystery," solely because the contemporary world's own materialist mindset obscures the truth of this "offense against the human soul." Though the dynastic crime may be understood, the whole mystery goes completely unsolved. This is another example of how critical it is to bring an "It Spirits" perspective to this event. Just as with the question of Aztec heart sacrifice, we are left with an enormous question that transcends all of the smaller, more immediate questions that we might ask or answer. In the case of "the child of Europe," Kaspar Hauser, what deep-seated motives can lead to a child—and later, a young man—being treated so horrifically? The entire episode was a very dangerous procedure which necessitated a long, drawn-out course of action—more than twenty years! A whole series of people must have been engaged in preparing these events long in advance, and considerable means were employed. There were clearly two crimes against Kaspar Hauser: a dynastic crime and an occult crime.

The dynastic crime strikes us as wholly imaginable—even expected, given the world's long history of such crimes. "Cruella" von Hochberg is a sort of stock character, determined to see her own sons gain the throne over the rightful heir. But the dynastic crime only serves to obscure a much more important event. The abduction and the very particular way in which the imprisonment was carried out (not to mention that this same method was never followed for the other heirs) hint at a wider crime, but until recently, not one of the thousands of books and articles approached a solution. For Anselm von Feuerbach even, the only explanation he could give for the abduction was that some unknown benefactor was seeking to protect Kaspar—but this hardly accounts for the prodigious cruelty inflicted upon him.

While the dynastic crime favored the outright murder of Kaspar and his brothers, the "occult"—i.e., hidden—crime *depended upon the living Kaspar Hauser*. This crime sought above all to keep Kaspar away from his earthly task. The criminals knew that if they had killed Kaspar, he would have incarnated again, for they were aware of the esoteric law that a child carrying with it a certain destiny—especially a world historic destiny—can and would quickly reincarnate.

As soon as Kaspar began to develop memory, he was transferred to his underground prison. His captors knew well in advance that this time would come, and had made plans for it. They thus placed Kaspar in a condition between life and death; between waking and sleeping. They made it so that it was impossible for Kaspar to develop as a human being, but also kept him from returning to the spiritual world by means of death. As Kaspar himself describes, he sank into a dreamy state—not unlike the dreamy state that soon would envelop millions of Chinese opium fiends, thanks to the greed of the East India Company and the New England opium merchants. Kaspar's bodily development was arrested, and so were his intellectual and soul development. He became not only a physical prisoner, but a spiritual prisoner. This state of imprisonment is a sort of negative apotheosis of the development of the "Consciousness Soul."

It was in some way fitting that in such a fairy tale land as the Black Forest region, the Kaspar Hauser story has all the markings of a fairy tale, *but a fairy tale that is simultaneously actual history.* In the story of Kaspar Hauser, time and again, one finds that myth has turned into history, and history into myth. In the image of Kaspar Hauser caged and walled up below the earth, inside an opulent castle, surrounded by a grand and gracious green landscape just beyond his imprisoned reach, we have an archetypal picture of the modern human being. Today, the human being is rammed down below the level of his destiny, which is to develop fully the Consciousness Soul, to stand upright and assert fully his individuality. Modern man is hamstrung, caged, kept from freely roaming the capacious cosmic landscape to realize his destiny.

Kaspar Hauser's fate was at least in part, to experience in advance the destiny of modern humanity. I wonder if you have sensed this as you have become familiar with Kaspar's story. Since our first classroom meeting, I have seen and felt and heard the invisible cages around each one of you. You were thrust into that cage perhaps within minutes of your entry into this green, growing world; go and look at the maternity ward up at the Plattsburgh hospital and you will see exactly what I mean. Despite the best intentions of your parents, and then of your teachers, your schooling has fettered and enfeebled you, coming repeatedly between you and your destiny. I say "you," but surely I mean myself as well, and I participated in this fettering as I raised my own daughter. I believe that our deep empathy for Kaspar's plight is in some way an acknowledgement that *we share in his fate.*

Each of us has the potential to rise above this fettering, to break free of the chains. Like Kaspar, we receive aid from just the right places, at just the right moments along our way. But Kaspar faced a continued assault upon his destiny, from two powerful groups—the Freemasons and the Jesuits. How is it possible that these two groups, which were perpetually at war with each other, came to cooperate in the attack upon Kaspar Hauser? At the highest level of both Jesuitism and Freemasonry, a select group of individuals are possessed of significant spiritual knowledge. One can say that the elite individuals standing behind the occult crime had a rank, but not morality, that was akin to that of the Three Holy Kings—Kaspar, Melchior, and Balthazar. Like the Magi, these Unholy Kings used star wisdom—knowledge of reincarnation and karma– to see Kaspar's star rising, and used their secret knowledge to prevent that.

I've spoken a bit about the manipulation within Freemasonic circles through the practice of ceremonial magic; in the Jesuit training, magical action is accomplished through the practice of Ignatius Loyola's "spiritual exercises," which consisted of a series of intense visualizations designed to bring certain spiritual beings to one's aid. As with other episodes we have encountered, the question is *which spiritual beings were being supplicated.*

In the Jesuit training, the candidate was meant to be secluded for a period of 30 days, during which time he would carry out with the most intense effort possible, a series of meditations, prayers, and mental exercises, all oriented to imaginary pictures of Jesus. The first step for the candidate was to imagine a person who has committed sin, and awaits a terrible punishment. Once the guilt is so great that he feels that indeed he has committed these sins, he imagines Christ whose sacrifice has atoned for men's errors. The goal as stated by Loyola is to reach a place where there is contempt for earthly existence, due to one's despair at having sinned. These pictures are meant to work directly upon the will, and to bypass any normal thought process.

Then the pupil focuses his attention on the image of Jesus, instead of Christ, in a position of dominion over the whole world; this is what would have transpired had Jesus not resisted the temptation in the wilderness. Then, the pupil was to form an imagination of Babylon and its surrounding plain, with Lucifer above it, bearing his banner, seated on a throne amongst flames and smoke. The soul was to be entirely engrossed in the Imagination of the danger which issues from the banner of Lucifer and the hosts of fallen angels surrounding him. The candidate was instructed to feel that the greatest danger facing the world was Lucifer and this fallen host. In his mind's eye, he next visualized King Jesus as victor, scattering the hosts of Lucifer, thus becoming himself the ruler of the earth. The Jesuit came to the powerful conclusion that he was himself a member of the hosts of Jesus, and that as a soldier for King Jesus, he must never betray his banner.

As a result of these exercises, the Jesuit gained the ability to work his will directly upon that of another, in the way that mesmerists were able to do. In this Jesuit initiation, Lucifer was put in place of the Christ, and thus Ahriman in Lucifer's place. This was essentially the same substitution that Tlacaellel's Huitzilopochtli cult effected among the Aztec. Now reflect a moment upon the diabolical deeds that surrounded Kaspar Hauser. At the level of the dynastic crime, one can imagine bribes and threats working to cause individuals to take unscrupulous actions—even murder. But there must have been instances which called for more direct manipulation—by the occult power of the will. That will could even be brought to dominate the wills of their Freemasonic brethren.

Both Jesuits and Freemasons were active in the Nuremberg and Ansbach region at the time of Kaspar Hauser's incarceration and murder. Remembering how effective the real puppet-masters of the occult brotherhoods are at concealing their own role, we can look to the person of Lord Stanhope, the false friend and guardian of Kaspar Hauser. Stanhope—a down-on-his-luck disinherited aristocrat—was in the employ of the Grand Duchess Sophie of Baden, whose weak-willed husband Grand Duke Leopold, only became Grand Duke when his mother, the Countess Hochberg, aided by her lover, Grand Duke Ludwig, had arranged the kidnapping of Kaspar and the substitution of the Blochmann child. None of these individuals had any clue as to why Kaspar was important, beyond their own personal ambitions for power. The real villains lay farther afield, in London, Vienna, and Munich, within the upper echelons of the secret brotherhoods.

By the time that he became involved in the Kaspar Hauser affair, Stanhope had worked as a British spy in Italy. The sadistic schoolteacher Meyer and other adversaries were paid by Stanhope, who was himself (as shown by documents in Baden and in England) paid by Baden banks. But beyond these villains lay even more sinister figures—writer, publicist, Prussian royal advisor and high-ranking Freemason Friedrich von Gentz, and Prince Clemens von Metternich, Chancellor of Austria, and staunch friend of the Jesuits in Germany. Gentz wrote propaganda tracts celebrating a future dominated by England and America. While this vision may have been the product of actual occult vision, it is more likely that it derived from his pocketbook; he was the highest paid propagandist in Europe. From 1800 onwards, Gentz wrote numerous tracts urging Austrians and Prussians to unite against Napoleon and France. Known as "The Pen of Europe," Gentz served as Metternich's secretary, criticizing liberal democratic movements and helping Metternich to preserve the old European oligarchical order. Both Napoleon's political tyranny and England's rapacious mercantilism were updated versions of ancient Roman tyranny, strangling central Europe at the moment when she was meant to achieve Grail consciousness and culture.

The alliance between Gentz, a Freemason, and Metternich, who publicly condemned the Jesuits but privately worked with them to advance their interests, was symbolic of the method of the anti-Grail forces. At the highest levels, Freemasonry and Jesuitism cooperated closely to achieve their perennial goal of stymieing the progress of the Consciousness Soul. Their apparent animosity toward one another served to provide cover for their crimes against humanity.

These political intrigues seem far removed from the occult intrigues that took the freedom and then the life of Kaspar Hauser, and yet there are telltales all along the way. It is now known that between 1815 and the fall of 1816, Kaspar was held at Beuggen Castle on the River Rhine near Basel. The interior walls of the castle chapel were decorated with the skull and crossbones—a symbol that was common in several of the crusading orders, including the Knights Templar. After the destruction of the Templars in the 14th century, the symbol was taken over by various Freemasonic groups and also criminal gangs (e.g., the Jolly Roger of Caribbean pirates) and pseudo-Masonic secret societies (like Yale University's infamous Skull and Bones fraternity, which was founded in 1832-3). The dagger that was used to kill Kaspar Hauser bore on its blade the skull and crossbones symbol, suggesting a link to Freemasonry—or perhaps someone trying to make it appear that the murderer was a Freemason. Kaspar Hauser's other known place of incarceration—Schloss Pilsach, a manor house outside Nuremberg –was located in Bavaria, where the Jesuits had always had an influential presence.

A True Fairy Tale

When we are caught up in trying to solve a riddle, in our earnest attempts to look far and wide for answers, we can often miss important clues right in front of us. I have always been amazed to see, when we are playing detective together as a class, how rarely anyone ever raises this question: who gave Kaspar Hauser his name, and what does it mean? (Another question that rarely comes up: how could Stephanie, Kaspar's mother, have let him be abducted? Sing out if you know the answer to that one!) According to Kaspar himself, "the man with whom he had always been" taught him to write his name a few days before his release. It was almost as if he had no name up until this point, and that the name was given for no purpose other than to make him a little less conspicuous than he already was. Kaspar clearly did not relate to the name in any emotional way; without an "I," it was impossible for him to actually connect the name to himself.

In the Gospel of Matthew, "Kaspar" is the Black King, who represents the human will. The will is the part of us that is directed toward the future; all three kings, in their journey to see Jesus, were looking toward the future. Kaspar's black skin suggests something hidden or held back, and his gift—myrrh—similarly has a quality of hidden potency that will come forth in the future. "Hauser" is appropriate both for Kaspar's outer and inner situations; he is a *hauser*, i.e., a house-dweller, in that he is locked in a dungeon and he is imprisoned in his own autistic consciousness, because of his having been deprived of any social contact.

Surely this was not the name given by his parents Stephanie and Karl, nor even by his jailer, but by the mysterious one or ones who plotted everything. A Jesuit would be well-versed in the Gospels, and so acquainted with the name Kaspar and its significance. I imagine that the villain who chose the name Kaspar was playing a cruel joke on the world, thumbing his nose at everyone. He would have known that the magi were Zoroastrian astronomer-priests, and that the star they followed was no outer one, but an inner one, related to their master Zarathustra, who had prophesied that he would return one day, and might be tracked "in the stars." The Jesuit initiates had done just such tracking to determine Kaspar's path of incarnation. These Jesuits were the consummate dark initiates of the will, and would also have gotten sadistic pleasure in choosing a name that reflected that *their will, not God's will, had been done.*

Kaspar Hauser appeared in Nuremberg at 4 pm on Whit Monday, May 26, 1828. He had been imprisoned for 12 years—a Jupiter cycle. In esoteric terms Europe is especially associated with Jupiter, and Kaspar was widely known in his own lifetime as "the Child of Europe". For those 12 years he had been kept at Schloss Pilsach near Nuremberg, a city at the crossroads of Europe; Nuremberg was an ancient trading centre that connected the Baltic and the Mediterranean, Iberia and Russia. Whitsun is a festival of light celebrating the descent of the Holy Spirit upon the Apostles at Pentecost. Both in the case of the original Whitsun, and in 1828, on that day the illuminating fire of a new social impulse came down to a darkened earth from the spiritual world. Just as the disciples were enabled by the Whitsun fire to go abroad and spread a new social impulse, Kaspar—despite his being crippled in normal human functions—was destined to achieve this same end. The place as well as the time of Kaspar's appearance has the ring of fairy tale about it; he was first found in the place in Nuremberg known as the *Unschlittplatz*, which means Tallow (or Candlewax) Square. Kaspar was himself a candle, bringing a great light into the darkness of 19th century Europe as it approached the abyss of its philosophical materialism, its violent nationalism, and estrangement from the Grail path.

The Grail! Kaspar Hauser was to gather round himself the heirs of Germany's rich spiritual and cultural tradition of Idealism, Romanticism, and *Naturphilosophie*, and create a renewed chivalric "round table" whose influence would be felt throughout central Europe. Such a prospect terrified the enemies of the Grail, the Freemasons and Jesuits, and more importantly, the dark spiritual powers that inspired and supported them. Southern Germany, with its introspective, almost mystical tendencies, was the perfect cradle for this new Grail culture, which was meant to foster the cultivation of new powers of clairvoyance in the human being. The anti-Grail brotherhoods had always jealously guarded their secrets of seeing into the spiritual world, and would do anything to prevent such clairvoyance from becoming the inheritance of the general public. All of their power was predicated upon knowing more than their contemporaries about the wondrous workings of the cosmos.

The cosmic powers had arranged that on Michaelmas Day in 1812, an exceptional spirit would come to earth to build a Grail castle in the heart of central Europe, the place upon the Earth that was clearly leading human evolution into the future. The timing of Kaspar's birth at the festival of the Archangel Michael allies him with this mighty spiritual being, whose mission was ever the protection of humanity from the Dragon. Remember that Joan of Arc had been born on January 6, Epiphany; it is 266 days—the gestation period for human beings—from Epiphany to Michaelmas Day, meaning that Kaspar Hauser was likely conceived on Epiphany, Three Kings' Day. Joan and Kaspar were both rightful "kings" in the Age of the Consciousness Soul; allied with both Christ and Michael—as so beautifully demonstrated *before their birth*, in their choice of when to come to earth—their lives were dedicated to overcoming the adversaries of the Grail.

The great Nuremberg jurist Anselm von Feuerbach described Kaspar Hauser as "a true human being," meaning that Kaspar had qualities that made him in some sense primeval. Claiming that Kaspar was "a living refutation of the doctrine of original sin," Feuerbach pointed to Kaspar's "innocence and goodness of heart," even though he had no concepts of right and wrong, or good and evil. Almost everyone who met him commented on this. Mayor Binder spoke of "the most exalted innocence of his nature…his indescribable gentleness, his…tenderness even towards his oppressors…his care for the tiniest insect." The jailor Hiltel swore to Kaspar's innocence "even if God himself had said the opposite." Georg Friedrich Daumer felt Kaspar was a "paradisal archetypal human being." Kaspar's guardian Baron von Tucher described Kaspar as "man before the Fall." Daumer concluded that Kaspar "died with a lie, but it was the lie of an angel."

In their choice of such exalted language to characterize him, these friends of Kaspar Hauser were closer than they realized to solving the question of where Kaspar came from, and what he was meant to achieve, for *on Michaelmas Day in 1812 an angelic being had indeed entered the world, in the infant prince of the House of Baden.* This angelic being, named Vidar, had been the guardian angel of Siddhartha Gautama, and at Gautama's ascent to Buddhahood, Vidar was freed to ascend to the rank of Archangel. He had instead made a great sacrifice, and renounced this rank for 2500 years; in 1879, Vidar took the place of the Archangel Michael, who had himself ascended to the rank of the Archai, of Folk Spirits. And if this is not mysterious enough, Vidar was also the angel who appeared before the shepherds, as told in the Gospel of Luke, and he was the angel who appeared to Christ in the Garden of Gethsemane. Kaspar's qualities of love and compassion we can understand as a humble echo of the Buddha's gift to humanity, since as Gautama Buddha's guardian angel, Vidar both inspired and received these gifts. Perhaps now you can see how it is that the occult brotherhoods were aware of the angel's impending incarnation, and were able to "track" it in the spiritual world. Vidar was the angelic equivalent of the Millennium Falcon, come to annihilate the Death Star. The black brothers, by watching the stars—that is, by clairvoyantly observing the zodiacal and planetary forces that prepared Vidar's incarnation into a human being—launched a pre-emptive strike on Vidar, whose entry into the world would assuredly have been feared by them. As Grand Duke of Baden, Vidar would have been the founder of a Grail castle in central Europe, and put the anti-Grail forces into hasty retreat.

Can one really speak of such mysteries? We must, for *the time is at hand!* All I can do is to lay these mysteries before you, and invite you to contemplate them. You are completely free to ignore them, scorn them, or take them into your heart, as a true fairy tale which can shine like the ferryman's beacon across the fog-shrouded river of our time. Think of the level after level of freedom that is operative in this true fairy tale: an angel freely gave up becoming an Archangel, *to patiently wait for 2500 years*; just before being granted his new rank, this same angel freely descended into the body of a human being, in order to help all humanity find the Grail; captured by black brotherhoods, Klingsors who would deny humanity's rightful evolution, and put in a state of soul limbo to blot out his destiny, the angel—and the entire spiritual world—refrained from any magical intervention to salvage the Grail mission, and allowed events to take their course in full freedom.

In German/Scandinavian myth, which preserves a living memory of ancient clairvoyance, when humanity was able to *see and hear* the gods, Vidar—whose name means "The Silent One"—was the son of Wotan/Odin. While we think of Odin as a god of war, the Eddas speak of Vidar as abstaining from war; his "silence" is a ritual form of denying vengeance. Here again we have a true fairy tale, an enactment of myth upon the plane of history, for what is Kaspar's most stunning trait but his abstention from vengeance—even the thought of vengeance—against those who have so grievously wronged him?

Odin was associated with the planet Mercury (and is the origin of our "Wednesday," i.e., "Woden's Day"; *en Français, "Mercredi"*), and by extension, so is his son Vidar. While Kaspar was living with Professor Daumer, Daumer discovered that Kaspar could distinguish various metals through his hands and fingers, and was most sensitive to quicksilver (mercury). Even in this small detail there is the mark of the true fairy tale. In myth, Mercury/Hermes/Odin is the messenger, the go between, the supreme communicator, who gets things stirred up and moving. In alchemy, the element mercury was seen as a mediator between heaven and earth. Vidar/Kaspar certainly was such a mediator, but more importantly, in the role that he was to play as Grail King, Kaspar was to be the quicksilver mediator for the German people, who were themselves the quicksilver nation of Europe. Goethe's Rosicrucian training had taught him that the cultural impulse of Germany was meant to flow like a healing homeopathic elixir into central Europe, *to spiritualize 19th century thinking*. As Grand Duke, Kaspar would have given the support to this impulse, promoting Rosicrucian-inspired arts and sciences.

Kaspar's Quicksilver Trick

The quicksilver trick of Mercury is that even in defeat and retreat, he wins. From Loki, Kokopelli, Coyote, and Karagöz (the outrageous character of Turkish shadow play) to Charlie Chaplin, Bugs Bunny, the Pink Panther, Bart Simpson, and Michael Moore, the shape-shifting trickster Mercury performs a great deed for humanity, saving him from stasis and petrifaction. His unexpected, small gestures of authenticity shine a light upon evil, and upend it. Kaspar astounded Daumer one day when he said he preferred not to think back on his time in the dungeon, because it made him think of the intense anxiety that his jailer experienced. Kaspar assumed that his jailer always hoped that he would die, and now that he was free, it caused him real physical pain to think about how much more anxious the man must be.

Kaspar's entire existence was marked by the spirit of "Not my will, but Thy will be done," by Buddha and Christ's unmistakable attitude of non-attachment and acceptance. Quicksilver/ Mercury moves in these words of Kaspar:

> Contentment is the greatest worker of miracles. It transforms water into wine, grains of sand into pearls, raindrops into balsam, poverty into wealth, the smallest into the greatest, the most common to the most noble, earth into paradise. Beautiful is the heart with all its stirrings, which remains in purest harmony with itself. Beautiful is that life where deeds agree most perfectly one with the other.

Looking at the outer events in the biography and destiny of Kaspar Hauser, there is an unmistakable sense of something incomplete, inferior, defeated. What Kaspar Hauser accomplished outwardly is quite insignificant—it doesn't MATTER. But what "It Matters" history tells us about Kaspar does not reveal the possibilities of his individuality. In this way, there is no compulsion exerted by him; one is completely free to make one's own judgment about him. *His essence is accessible only from an "It Spirits" perspective.*

This sense grows even stronger if one looks at the venom directed at Kaspar in the wake of his death. For decades after his murder, Meyer, Stanhope and others spread vicious lies about Kaspar. The effort to suppress the truth continues apace; take a look at the Wikipedia entry for Kaspar Hauser, and you will hear the echo of the vile Lord Stanhope in every sentence. It is as if Kaspar Hauser is still being crucified! And yet, if one shifts one's view just slightly, that same set of events become a story of supreme sacrifice. Kaspar Hauser's entire existence upon earth was a path of torture and self-sacrifice. Kaspar lived in the acceptance of his destiny, transforming his suffering into a *free deed of sacrifice. When a person accepts a destiny imposed upon him, as Kaspar did, it brings about a situation which the black powers opposing human evolution are not able to foresee. Their plans are frustrated; the limits of their insight are made visible, and their power is curtailed.*

9: Zwischenspiel

A Forgotten Fundamental Theme Necessary to Our History

On November 12, 1880, King Ludwig II of Bavaria, sitting alone in the Court Theater in Munich, was treated to the first performance of the *Vorspiel*—prelude—from Richard Wagner's new opera, *Parsifal*, conducted by Wagner himself. As Wagner raised his baton, the King heard the *Grundthema*, the fundamental theme from which Wagner built the entire opera. Three times over the course of the prelude, Ludwig was transported by the small but sublime melody—a rising tonic arpeggio, followed by the sixth. Modulating from the tonic key to the mediant and back again, the prelude did indeed, as Wagner later described, "unfold like a flower from its bud." Each time the *Grundthema* sounded, there rose up before Ludwig's vision luminous, swirling clouds of glory, into which the King felt lifted. When Wagner finished the opera early in 1882, he would close it with this same motif, as a chorus of Knights sang *"Erlösung dem Erlöser!"*—"Redemption to the Redeemer!"—while Parsifal waved the radiant Grail cup over the heads of the worshipful Knights.

The theme of redemption was a principle leitmotif in the lives of both Wagner and Ludwig, for both had individually suffered periods of sin in their lives, and as friends, had seen dark, troubled episodes. Wagner's composition of Parsifal was both the crowning achievement of his musical career, and the culmination of his 16-year relationship with the King. As a boy Ludwig had spent summers at his father's Hohenschwangau ("The Highland of the Swans") Castle, which had been associated in the 13th century with the Swan Knights of the Holy Grail. Wandering the castle, whose walls were covered with frescoes depicting the story of Lohengrin, the son of Parzival in Wolfram von Eschenbach's tale, the young prince developed a profound love of the Swan Knights and of Lohengrin. At age 15, Ludwig had seen a performance of Wagner's opera *Lohengrin*, and had been deeply moved by it, as he identified so completely with the Swan Knight. Ludwig asked for a copy of the libretto, and soon knew the entire work by heart. In 1861, Ludwig heard a performance of *Lohengrin*; the climax of the opera comes when the Swan Knight reveals his identity, which has been kept secret. Lohengrin became Ludwig's alter ego; after his coronation in 1864 he was known as the "Swan King."

Within days of his ascension to the throne, the 18-year-old King sent an envoy to bring Wagner to Munich; the envoy was given a portrait of the King and a ruby ring, to be delivered with the words: "As this ruby glows, so King Ludwig glows passionately with desire to see the poet-musi-cian who wrote *Lohengrin*." This passion was both particular to Ludwig's feelings for Wagner, but also characteristic of his romantic manner. The King wished to install Wagner as court composer, to renew German cultural life through Wagner's epic music dramas. Wagner was deep in debt, and without Ludwig's patronage, it is almost certain that his musical career would have been over. (Wagner wrote of this first meeting: "Alas, he is so handsome and wise, soulful and lovely, that I fear that his life must melt away in this vulgar world like a fleeting dream of the gods.") Ludwig paid Wagner's debts; provided him with a lavish home; and planned a large festival theater in Munich for the performance of Wagner's epic works. The two men became inseparable. But the vast amounts of money Ludwig lent to Wagner and lavished on his productions upset his sub-jects, who were also alienated by Wagner's arrogance and jealous of Wagner's influence on the King. Ludwig sent Wagner away to Switzerland; Ludwig fled to Hohenschwangau Castle.

The early years of Ludwig's reign were a disaster for him and for Bavaria. In 1866, when war broke out between Austria and Prussia, the most powerful German state, Ludwig sided with Austria. Prussia was victorious, and Ludwig signed a secret treaty putting the Bavarian army at the command of Prussian generals. Prussian expansionism led to the Franco-Prussian War, and after Prussia's victory, Ludwig wrote a letter in 1870 to Prussian President Otto von Bismarck endorsing the creation of the German Empire. Ludwig had sacrificed Bavaria's independence; he was now a mere figurehead in a constitutional monarchy.

Even before the war had ended, Ludwig had withdrawn from court and state affairs, into a reclusive, solipsistic fantasy world. He spent all his time in the mountains, at Hohenschwangau, and planned the construction of extravagant new castles at Neuschwanstein and Linderhof. Ludwig commissioned plays to take place in exotic settings—the Himalayas; Louis XIV's court; Tibet; imperial China—which he designed. He frequently attended plays, concerts, and operas staged for him alone.

Ludwig's Neuschwanstein ("New Swan Stone"—the model for the castle at Disneyland) was in a sense a caricature of the Grail castle that the Parsifal legend and Nostradamus' prophecy had pointed to. Instead of a flourishing Grail culture that would lift up the German people and provide a model for other European nations, this fabled and favored region saw the rise of Prus-sian militarism and a concurrent cultural malaise, while precious royal resources went into Lud-wig's extravagant private collection of art inside his fantastical castles. Wagner's operatic citadel at Bayreuth was only partially what it could have been had Kaspar lived, and given the necessary direction to balance Wagner's volatile personality. Both King Ludwig and Bismarck "needed" Kaspar Hauser to balance and guide their missions; absent him, both swung to destructive one-sidedness. In Ludwig's case the endpoint was merely a personal tragedy, with his disenthrone-ment (really a carefully planned coup d'état—approved by Bismarck—effected by declaring Ludwig officially insane) and mysterious death (most likely he was murdered) in 1886; had there been a King Kaspar of a united Germany or even with a Grand Duke Kaspar of Baden, Bismarck would not have led Germany into its sustained national tragedy from 1879 to 1945. Without Kas-par to temper Bismarck's tendency toward muscular nationalism, he increasingly coveted Great Britain's military and industrial power.

Kaspar as King?! After the 1848 Revolutions, given Baden's stature within the Frankfurt Parliament, it is very likely that the Grand Duke of Baden—rather than the reactionary Frederick William IV of Prussia—would have been the one offered the crown of Germany. King Kaspar could then have helped bring about the reconciliation of Bismarck with the Prussian Jewish labor leader Ferdinand Lassalle, helping the two men to work together for social healing through a new constitution. From the new Grail Centre in southern Germany, King Kaspar would have inspired impulses for both the German people and all of central Europe. Southwestern Germany's mystical affinity, so long incubated by the minnesingers and Swan Knights, would have provided a fruitful path for the Consciousness Soul in the late 19th century.

One of the impulses that King Kaspar would have nurtured was knowledge of karma and reincarnation. The Vidar being who descended into the Baden prince would have brought vast wisdom regarding the mysteries of human birth, death, and destiny. Richard Wagner was fascinated by reincarnation, but had to turn to Hindu and Buddhist ideas—principally as interpreted by the philosopher Arthur Schopenhauer. In August 1860, in a letter to a friend that is mainly an outline of his ideas for the composition of the dramatic element of *Parzival*, Wagner states:

> Only a profound acceptance of the doctrine of metempsychosis [i.e., reincarnation] has been able to console me by revealing the point at which all things finally converge at the same level of redemption, after the various individual existences—which run alongside each other in time—have come together in a meaningful way outside time.

In *Parzival*, Wagner says in this letter, when he refers to Parsifal's "purity" he means the hero's karma as acquired in previous lives.

* * *

Before the fateful day of May 4, 1864, when Richard Wagner first met King Ludwig in the Royal Palace in Munich, they had actually met before—the last time on the evening of November 28, 1581. At that time, the individuality we know as Richard Wagner was the Carmelite nun St. Teresa of Avila; King Ludwig was the Spanish mystic St. John of the Cross. Teresa's first meeting with John of the Cross took place in September 1567, when John made the decision to enter the Carmelite Order. Their relationship would last until the end of Teresa's life.

In 1572, when Teresa became prioress at the Convent of the Incarnation in Avila, near Madrid, she requested that John be appointed confessor of the convent. Collaborating, they brought great improvements to the convent, both spiritually and materially; St. Teresa called St. John "a divine, heavenly man," unlike any in Castile, one who "inspires souls with such fervor to journey to Heaven." In December 1577, his partnership with St. Teresa ended when friars from an order hostile to the Carmelites abducted him, and imprisoned him at Toledo.

Not long after his first meeting with King Ludwig, Wagner had written:

Daily he sends [for me] either once or twice. Then I fly as to a sweetheart. 'Tis a fascinating interview. This thirst for instruction, this comprehension, this quiver and glow, I have never encountered in such splendid unrestraint. And then this charming care for me, this winning chastity of heart, of every feature, when assures me of his happiness in possessing me; thus do we often sit for hours together, lost in each other's gaze.

When Wagner addressed Ludwig, he called him "my most worshipful, angelic friend"; Ludwig wrote back: "Oh saint, I worship thee." As their relationship developed, the King would address Wagner as "most inwardly beloved"; "source of the light of my life"; "bliss of life"; "highest good"; "majestic, divine Friend." Wagner had taken to calling the King "Parsifal."

In all of these phrases one can hear the sounding of the intense spiritual marriage of St. Teresa of Avila and St. John of the Cross. And it is in their mystical communion with God and each other that one finds the key to the fascination of both Ludwig and Wagner for the Holy Grail. While outwardly the two were occupied with the reform of the Carmelite order, inwardly they made extraordinary journeys in which they met with the Risen Christ. As might be expected, the writings of both St. Teresa and St. John of the Cross are now often seen as documenting their mental illness! Both then and now, their experiences *were* abnormal, but their accounts of the mystical communion reveal a picture of experiences that will become common in the future.

St. Teresa's *The Interior Castle* describes the path taken by the soul through 7 stages of initiation to reach union with Christ. This "interior castle" is the *Castle of the Grail*—the innermost sanctuary of the Divine within us. St. John of the Cross describes the same path as the "Ascent of Mount Carmel," which he calls *Monsalvaesche* ("Mount of Salvation"), the same term that Wolfram gave to the place of the Grail Castle. Their dedication to the Grail remained strong enough that upon their incarnation in 19th century Germany, both worked to advance the Grail path— now, in the more influential sphere of cultural life rather than a cloistered religious order. In music and poetic drama—above all in his opera *Parsifal*—Richard Wagner achieved a renewed path to the Grail, though he only barely recognized it.

Like Leonardo da Vinci, Wagner was *inspired* by spiritual beings of which he was barely conscious, and so he imbued his operas with knowledge of which he himself was not conscious. In the Grail mysteries of the late Middle Ages, candidates had to pass through three stages: the first stage, of *simple-mindedness*, where he was to turn away from all of the world's accepted views, and rely only upon his own power of love, which would light up his being; the second stage was that of profound *doubt* (think back on the opening lines of Wolfram's poem: "When indecision's in the heart/ The soul is bound to grieve and smart"); the third stage, *Saelde* (*blessedness*), brought the candidate into conscious relationship with the gods. Once he passed through these three stages, he achieved the title of "Parsifal"—literally "through the vale."

In the figure of Klingsor, Wagner presented an image of all the degenerate mystery traditions of the Middle Ages. Just as Mesoamerica and Asia saw ancient white magical traditions degenerate into black magic, in Europe the Grail tradition was similarly tainted. The figure of Kundry in the opera symbolized the force of unrestrained reproduction in nature; that same force was purified in the Grail initiation. Parsifal releases and redeems Kundry, and in so doing, he released the listener from hidden forces. Wagner magically wove into his music tones that could act within the listener's etheric body to purify it and ready it to receive the mysteries of the Holy Grail.

* * *

Four years after his first encounter with King Ludwig, Wagner met another man who would play an enormous role in his life—Friedrich Nietzsche. Nietzsche had gone to hear a performance of the preludes of Wagner's *Tristan & Isolde* and *Die Meistersinger*, just weeks after his 24th birthday. The effect on him was immediate: "I am quivering in every fiber, every nerve, and I have never experienced such a lasting feeling of ecstasy as I did when listening to the [*Meistersinger*] overture." In 1869, after the young Friedrich Nietzsche assumed the chair of classical philology at Basel University, just 50 miles from Tribschen, where Wagner had settled in 1866. Just as had happened with King Ludwig, an immediate and intense friendship developed between Wagner and Nietzsche. Wagner entrusted to Nietzsche the proofreading and printing of his autobiography. He became a member of the Wagner household, the children treating him like an elder brother.

A state of *Saelde* settled over the two men; Nietzsche described these idyllic times:

At no price would I relinquish from my life the Tribschen days, those days of mutual confidence, of cheerfulness, of sublime incidents—of PROFOUND moments. I do not know what others may have experienced with Wagner: over OUR sky no cloud ever passed.

Wagner poured forth praise for Wagner's musical genius in a series of books, and Wagner fully enjoyed the adulation; in 1877, his *Richard Wagner in Bayreuth* drew from Wagner the response: "Friend! Your book is prodigious! However did you learn to know me so well?"

Nietzsche's early admiration for Wagner's compositions faded, however, and eventually turned to outright hostility. In 1888, Nietzsche published *The Wagner Case*, which characterized Wagner's music and Wagner himself as "neurotic" and "decadent." He attacked *Parsifal* mercilessly:

In the art of seduction, *Parsifal* will always retain its rank—as the stroke of genius in seduction. . . . Here the cunning in his alliance of beauty and sickness goes so far that, as it were, it casts a shadow over Wagner's earlier art—which now seems too bright, too healthy. . . . Drink, O my friends, the philtres of this art! Nowhere will you find a more agreeable way of enervating your spirit, of forgetting your manhood under a rosebush. Ah, this old magician! This Klingsor of all Klingsors! How he thus wages war against us! us, the free spirits! How he indulges every cowardice of the modern soul with the tones of magic maidens! Never before has there been such a deadly hatred of the search for knowledge! One has to be a cynic in order not to be seduced here; one has to be able to bite in order not to worship here. Well, then, you old seducer, the cynic warns you.

Such criticism of course completely soured the relationship between Nietzsche and his former idol.

Both phases of intensity between the two men reflected a previous relationship—Nietzsche had in an earlier incarnation been the Franciscan monk St. Peter of Alcantara. In 1559, Fray Pedro de Alcantara—renowned in Spain for his great piety (he was known to practice severe self-mortification; in forty years of prayer, he had only allowed himself one hour's sleep each night)—arrived in Avila, and among the many people who came to see the monk was Teresa, who shared with Peter the experience of regular mystical visions and ecstasies.

Like Wagner and Nietzsche, Peter and Teresa felt an immediate affinity. While many in the church criticized Teresa's visions as diabolical, Peter supported her, declaring that "the things which this woman sees are of divine origin." Teresa was at the time seeking to reform the Carmelite Order, and turn it toward the austerity known as "discalced"—bare-footed Peter was himself a discalced Franciscan, who, like both Teresa and John of the Cross, devoted his life to the search for the Holy Grail, or union with Christ.

On January 3, 1889, Nietzsche was in Turin, his favorite city, when he witnessed a livery driver whipping his horse; Nietzsche rushed into the street, throwing his arms around the horse to protect it. In the wake of this, he suffered a complete mental collapse, from which he never recovered. Nietzsche sent letters to a number of friends in which he clearly demonstrated his madness. To his former colleague, historian Jakob Burckhardt, Nietzsche wrote: "I have had Caiaphas put in fetters. Also, last year I was crucified by the German doctors in a very drawn-out manner. Wilhelm, Bismarck, and all anti-Semites abolished." In another letter he commanded the German emperor to go to Rome in order to be shot and summoned the European powers to take military action against Germany. He signed a number of his letters, "The Crucified One."

Nietzsche often raved about crucifixion; *however, it was not Nietzsche himself who was speaking, but Ahriman.* If one examines closely the invective against Wagner, then the tirades that make up his other works all written in 1888—*Twilight of the Idols, or How One Philosophizes with a Hammer*; *The Anti-christ, Curse on Christianity*; and *Ecce Homo, How One Becomes What One Is*—one begins to hear a familiar, bone-chilling voice. In *Twilight of the Idols*, Nietzsche argues that no one can estimate the value of life. He calls the great Greek philosophers "decadents," while applauding Caesar and Napoleon. Nietzsche champions Rome over Greece, in a foreshadowing of his philosophy of the "will to power." In *The Anti-christ*, his sarcastic voice savages Christianity, accusing it of corrupting the noble values of ancient Rome. Finding Jesus Christ, the Gospels, Paul, the martyrs, priests and the Crusades unhealthy, weakling influences, Nietzsche proposes a universal and transcendental anti-Christian morality. Ahriman speaks in the first person in *Ecce Homo*; the mock autobiography has sections entitled "Why I Am So Clever," "Why I Am So Wise," "Why I Write Such Good Books." The unbridled egotism combined with the hatred of Christ unmistakably identify the true author of Nietzsche's books—Ahriman.

At age 33, Nietzsche's body and soul began to be possessed by Ahriman; the 1889 breakdown and subsequent full-blown madness was the final stage in that possession. Nietzsche had brought about the conditions for both his madness and his possession through his actions in his previous lifetime as the ascetic monk Peter. Having in his past life regularly flagellated himself with a leather whip, it was as if the sight of the horse being whipped triggered a memory of his earlier life. Nietzsche had already shown the consequences of this treatment, in his having been constantly wracked by psychosomatic illness—headaches, vomiting, eye ailments, and upset stomach. The pain he caused himself as Peter returned to cause a new and uninvited suffering. All could be traced back to the physical torture he inflicted upon himself. All torture—including self-torture—drives the soul from the body; in Peter the soul's flight had produced mystical visions, but it also left a karmic effect that in Nietzsche had to be overcome. Failing that, the soul's flight was a dangerous condition that allowed the entry of malevolent spiritual beings. St. Peter of Alcantara's soul encounters had been with Christ, and this attracted the ever-jealous Ahriman toward Nietzsche.

I probably do not need to point out that if one accepts the doctrine of reincarnation, one must radically rethink the way one studies history. Almost every single aspect even of a single biography demands a fresh investigation. One need only contemplate these three individuals, Wagner, Leopold, and Nietzsche, in their individual biographies, apart from their karmic interactions, to see this. The scholarly and medical consensus about Nietzsche's madness has long been that it was due to a case of syphilis. Even the most recent studies of Leopold explain him as just one more eccentric in a line of royal eccentrics. Richard Wagner described how the vision of his opera *Parsifal* came to him at Villa Wesendonk on the shores of the Lake of Zurich on Good Friday in 1857; historians routinely dismiss Wagner's story as poetic invention or merely ignore the significance that the great modern work of the story of Christian redemption came to him on the anniversary day of Christ's resurrection. "It Matters" history cannot begin to touch on the mysteries within mysteries necessitated by recognition of the truth of karma and reincarnation.

Imagine for a moment how different might have been the lives of these three former 16th century Christian allies from Castile, if they had grown up within a culture that respected and nurtured knowledge of reincarnation. If this is difficult for you to imagine, just think of your own life, and of your closest relationships. How might your actions toward your friends and family shift if you were aware that you knew each other from an incarnation four or five centuries before?

So often our greatest strengths and our greatest weaknesses are but a hair's breadth apart, and the more wisdom we can bring into our actions, the more that we can act from out of our strength, and not fall prey to our weaknesses. Each of these three personalities gave great expression to magnificent forces that were living inside of them, and yet, they were also limited from developing these forces further because their own karmic pasts were veiled to them. Ludwig's Neuschwanstein Castle is a spectacular sign of the Grail impulse that was living inside him, metamorphosed from his previous incarnation as St. John of the Cross. So was his faithful support of Richard Wagner, who could magically bring the Grail impulse to expression through music.

Ludwig's tragic end was a metamorphosis of the abduction and imprisonment that he had suffered as John of the Cross. While St. John of the Cross was able to draw upon his mystical relationship with Christ and the Virgin Mary (he reported that one night the Virgin appeared to him and told him he would soon be free) in order to withstand the trial of eight months of solitary confinement, Ludwig, with no inner spiritual path, had not developed the inner strength by which he might have resisted the attack upon him.

In their 16th century incarnations as St. Teresa of Avila and St. Peter of Alcantara, these individualities had put themselves fully in the service of the Grail—i.e., Christ—but in their 19th-century incarnations both came unmistakably in their own names, not in the name of the Father or the Son. While Wagner's egotism often took precedence over his devotion to high spiritual ideals, in his play *Parsifal* he reunited with the Christ. Nietzsche, on the other hand, broke completely with the impulse toward Christ that had sustained him as a monk. He became the most vehemently anti-Christian philosopher of his age and perhaps any age since. Instead of becoming the philosopher of a new kind of Christianity based on knowledge rather than faith, Nietzsche succumbed entirely to the worst materialism. In his concepts of both the "superman"—a highly intelligent human produced by Darwinian evolution—and the "eternal return," one can clearly see Ahrimanic caricatures of the higher spiritual self, and of reincarnation.

The Grail in the Stars

Though the theft of Kaspar Hauser's destiny prevented a science of karma and reincarnation from developing in a broad, socially sanctioned sense, there have been a handful of individuals who have advanced this much-needed Grail science. In the 1980s, English mathematician Robert Powell discovered two "laws" of reincarnation, both of which can be seen in the horoscopes of St. Teresa of Avila and Richard Wagner. The first "law" (the quotation marks indicate that this relationship is not found in all cases, but the majority of them) states that the angular relationship between the Sun and Saturn at an individual's birth is the same or is the complement of (with respect to 180 degrees) that angle at death in the previous incarnation. Richard Wagner was born with a Sun-Saturn angle of 132 degrees; the planetary configuration at the death of St. Teresa of Avila shows an angle of 134 degrees.

The second reincarnation "law" is fulfilled by the fact that the heliocentric position of Mercury at Wagner's birth (7½° Capricorn) aligns opposite to the heliocentric position of Venus at St. Teresa's death (6° Cancer). The orb of difference from exact alignment is only 1½°.

If we examine the birth and death charts for other relationships, we find:

—Venus and the Sun, conjunct on the Ascendant at Richard Wagner's birth, are aligned with the zodiacal location of the Moon at St. Teresa's death;

—the conjunction of Mars and Jupiter in the geocentric chart at St. Teresa's birth metamorphose into an exact opposition between the two planets in the geocentric chart of Wagner's birth;

—in Richard Wagner's heliocentric birth chart, there is an opposition between the Moon and Jupiter along the axis of the Moon's nodes.

This last relationship has a great deal to do with the inspiration behind Wagner's music. The importance of the relationship is emphasized if we look at their positions in St. Teresa's birth and death charts, where in both the Moon is square to Jupiter. The heliocentric or "hermetic" chart gives a picture of a person's mission, since it portrays the structure of the person's spiritual organism as it is organized in the system of lotus flowers. The "hermetic man" depicts the correspondence between the lotus flowers (or *chakras*)—the microcosm—and the planets—the macrocosm.

The Moon corresponds to the 4-petalled lotus flower (or root chakra) and Jupiter to the 2-petalled lotus flower (or brow chakra); their positions on opposite sides of the 12-petalled lotus flower (the heart chakra) mirrors the position of the Moon and Jupiter in the heavens, since the heart chakra corresponds to the Sun. The opposition between Jupiter and the Moon at Wagner's birth indicates that he sought a cooperative relationship between the organ of higher thought (the brow chakra, corresponding to Jupiter) and the organ of will (the root chakra, corresponding to the Moon).

At almost every moment in Richard Wagner's biography, one can recognize the stamp of both his driving will and his intelligence, but in a spiritual sense the cooperation between these two typically manifests as an intense pursuit of supersensible cognition, that is, clairvoyance. Though Wagner was not consciously clairvoyant, he did bring down into his time significant spiritual knowledge through his music dramas. In *Parsifal*, his final opera, the higher realm— the Grail Castle—for which he had his whole life been unconsciously striving, came into full view.

St. Teresa was born with the Moon square Jupiter, that is, at a 90° angle. This configuration represents dynamic interaction between the intelligence and the will; in St. Teresa this manifested in the way that she could move with great facility between the pole of higher thought or contemplation (Jupiter), as expressed in her intense mystical life, and the pole of action or will (Moon), as reflected in her work as reformer of the Carmelite Order. While Wagner drove forward through his life without cultivating any relationships to the spiritual world, St. Teresa from an early age looked to spiritual beings for guidance, and thus put both her thoughts and deeds in the service of a higher realm. Her entire life said "*Thy* will be done."

The struggle between the mind and the will is perhaps *the* archetypal struggle of the age of the Consciousness Soul, and no individual biography demonstrates that struggle more poignantly than Friedrich Nietzsche. Like Wagner, Nietzsche was born when the Moon was in its node (the Moon's nodes are gateways or openings to the cosmos), signifying an openness of the will to cosmic influences. Both Wagner and Nietzsche were enthusiastic students of the philosophy of Arthur Schopenhauer, whose philosophy was founded upon the principle that the will is the primary force of life. Nietzsche went beyond Schopenhauer to develop a radical philosophy that held the will to power to be the basic human drive. Mankind's goal, according to Nietzsche, was to develop into an amoral but creative "superman." Instead of a selfless, sacrificial ideal—

like Buddha or Christ—Nietzsche put at the center of his philosophy a caricature of the modern, self-interested striver after power through the domination of others. His explicitly anti-Christian attitude represented a Promethean failure to properly bring to expression the higher potential given by his chosen horoscope. Nietzsche's implicit injunction of "*My* will be done" presaged the 20th century, for it was an invitation to Ahriman to take possession of *all* humanity.

10: *The Right Place at the Right Time*

Face to Face with Ahriman

ON THE AFTERNOON of January 22, 1896, in Naumburg, Germany, seven years after Friedrich Nietzsche's breakdown in Turin, his sister Elisabeth Förster-Nietzsche ushered into Nietzsche's darkened room a young Austrian philosopher and literary editor named Rudolf Steiner. Steiner, who had for the past seven years served as archivist and editor of Goethe's scientific works, was being courted to oversee the organization of Nietzsche's archive. During those years, Steiner had written two epistemological studies (epistemology is the branch of philosophy that explores theories of knowledge, i.e., that asks 'How do we know what we know?') of Goethe's philosophy, as well as a major philosophical work of his own, *Der Philosophie Der Freiheit* (*The Philosophy of Freedom*, 1894). In that book he had championed a path that he called "ethical individualism," which he suggested could liberate the human will from its bondage by instinctual drives. "To be free," Steiner stated, "is to be capable of thinking one's own thoughts—not the thoughts merely of the body or of society, but thoughts generated by one's deepest, most original, most essential and spiritual self, one's individuality." With this work and these words, Rudolf Steiner clearly voiced the ultimate aspiration of the Age of the Consciousness Soul; in formulating this aspiration, he himself *realized*—made real—the Consciousness Soul.

But consciousness was absent from Friedrich Nietzsche that afternoon, as it had been for seven years. Looking into Nietzsche's eyes, Steiner shuddered when he beheld there only empty space. Before this first and only meeting of the two philosophers, Steiner had greatly admired the fiery brilliance of Nietzsche's thought. Calling Nietzsche's work "of a boldness hardly to be surpassed," Steiner was particularly captivated by Nietzsche's critique of modern culture. He was drawn to Nietzsche's contrast of Dionysian—passionate, freedom-loving, life-affirming—and Apollonian—cold, controlling, life-hating—man. Though a Ph.D. who frequently was in the company of academics, Steiner agreed with Nietzsche's dismissal of professors as "dissatisfied, proud, disagreeable creatures…clever, secretive, anemic vampires." When, in his 1882 book *The Gay Science*, Nietzsche imagines a madman running into the middle of a marketplace, shouting "Whither is God? I will tell you. We have killed him—you and I. All of us are his murderers," Steiner could see the truth in Nietzsche's rant, given the lackluster Christianity of the Edwardian era church, when compared to the dominance of materialist natural science. Steiner was irresistibly drawn to Nietzsche's fidelity to freedom, especially to his style of expression that left readers free to form their own opinions. Steiner found in Nietzsche a heroic "adversary of his age," who was willing to topple all the false gods of modern man.

By the time of their meeting, Steiner had come to see the limitations of Nietzsche's thought. Recognizing Nietzsche's "intellectual lust for destruction," his former admiration turned to horror, as he increasingly came to see Nietzsche as having been "crucified" by the materialistic impulse of the age. Steiner saw that Nietzsche embodied the tragedy of the human "I"; having in the mid-19th century descended to the deepest level of enmeshment in matter, and endowed with all the faculties to raise himself out of the abyss, Nietzsche succumbed to materialism. His theory of "eternal recurrence" was a horrible caricature of the lofty truth of reincarnation. The "superman" was an equally twisted misunderstanding of the higher spiritual self, which Steiner's own major philosophical work had fully elaborated and embraced.

Rudolf Steiner could see that Nietzsche's philosophy was spoken by Ahriman, who, having met Nietzsche at the crossroads of Time, emerged victorious. Nietzsche's hateful, anti-Christian works of the 1880s were but the first step of that victory; the descent into madness was the final step. Indeed, sitting that afternoon looking into the vacuum of Nietzsche's eyes, Rudolf Steiner clairvoyantly beheld Ahriman's possession of the broad-browed, broken fighter for freedom:

> Spiritually seen, there were present only a physical body and an etheric body, especially in respect of the upper parts of the organism, for the being of soul-and-spirit was already outside, attached to the body as it were by a stubborn thread only. In reality a kind of death had already set in, but a death that could not be complete because the physical organization was so healthy. The astral body and the ego that would fain escape were still held by the extraordinarily healthy metabolic and rhythmic organizations, while a completely ruined nerves-and-senses system was no longer able to hold the astral body and the ego. So one had the wonderful impression that the true Nietzsche was hovering above the head. There he was. And down below was something that from the vantage-point of the soul might well have been a corpse, and was only not a corpse because it still held on with might and main to the soul. . . .

From this one encounter, Steiner was able to diagnose the karmic cause of Nietzsche's possession and madness. He had already detected in Nietzsche's writing a sense that Nietzsche "had always been a little outside his body," and acknowledged that this was partly due to Nietzsche's use of chloral hydrate as a sedative and painkiller. After meeting Nietzsche, Steiner could inwardly meditate upon Nietzsche's most characteristic gestures, and *discover his previous incarnation as St. Peter of Alcantara*:

> Now we have the key to the riddle. The gaze falls upon a man in the characteristic Franciscan habit, lying for hours at a time in front of the altar, praying until his knees are bruised and sore, beseeching grace, mortifying his flesh with severest penances—with the result that through the self-inflicted pain he knits himself very strongly with his

physical body. Pain makes one intensely aware of the physical body because the astral body yearns after the body that is in pain, wants to penetrate it through and through. The effect of this concentration upon making the body fit for salvation in the one incarnation was that, in the next, the soul had no desire to be in the body at all.

The encounter between Friedrich Nietzsche and Rudolf Steiner was truly a world historical event, for on that January afternoon, one tragic representative of the highest possibility for humanity in the age of the Consciousness Soul met with his victorious counterpart. His soul driven out by the pincer-like attack from Lucifer in Nietzsche's prior incarnation, and Ahriman in his current one, Nietzsche could not see that before him stood the true "superman," the true representative of the highest achievement of the Consciousness Soul era. Steiner too had been attacked by Lucifer and Ahriman. In his mid-20s he had lived in Vienna, where he moved in and out of various circles—Theosophists, Symbolists, neo-Buddhists, admirers of medieval Christianity—that were prey to Luciferic inflation. His work with Goethe's natural science grounded him and protected him from Lucifer.

When the confrontation came with Ahriman, it was direct and personal; Steiner immersed himself in the ideas of Ernst Haeckel, the great embryologist who was the German champion of Darwinian evolution. Coming to know Haeckel (and many other German natural scientists) personally, Steiner even dedicated his book *Thoughts on the World and on Life in the 19th Century* to Haeckel, and wrote a sympathetic treatment of Haeckel in *Haeckel and His Opponents*. Called the "Pope of Monism," Haeckel was perhaps the first well-respected natural scientist to stridently call for a universal materialism as the highest pinnacle of human thought. "There is no God, no immortality, and no freedom of the human soul," cried Haeckel. Despite such a seemingly contradictory philosophy to his own, Steiner saw "no better foundation for occultism" than Haeckel's evolutionary theory. Haeckel was the finest expositor of Darwinian materialism; Nietzsche was the most eloquent spokesperson for nihilism—the philosophy of "nothingness." Steiner stepped into the skin of both, understanding and interpreting them more coherently than they could do themselves.

In 1879, Steiner's parents had moved near Vienna, and the eighteen-year-old student commuted to school by train. He became friends with a "simple man of the people" who rode the same train, to sell herbs he had gathered to pharmacists in Vienna. This man, Felix Koguzki, was like Steiner, clairvoyant, and shared with the young student his profound knowledge of the elemental beings of nature. This was the first time in Rudolf Steiner's life that he could speak about his inner experiences, which had begun at age 8, when, while sitting in a railway station, the boy saw a recently deceased relative who approached him for help. Before this, his clairvoyance had caused him profound loneliness, since he could not speak of it with anyone.

The herb-gatherer introduced Rudolf Steiner to someone to whom he would only refer as "Teacher," and it was from this individual that he had confirmed his own inner sense that his life's mission was to "crawl into the skin of the Dragon," to conquer it. In his deep engagement with Haeckel and Nietzsche, Steiner had conquered the Dragon—Ahriman—with his own weapons. The result was that he found that he could now grasp the physical world more firmly than had ever been possible up until that point. In Steiner, "It Matters" met "It Spirits," and rather than a triumph of one over the other, there occurred a fruitful marriage of the two paths of knowledge, into a yet higher path. Rudolf Steiner was the first "self-initiated" individual in human history, who, by virtue of his own thinking, was able to penetrate into the hidden spiritual essence of the material world. Like Parsifal, Steiner had formed a question out of his own experience, and informed by compassion and love, he had received an answer. He, rather than Kaspar Hauser, became the one to enter the Grail Castle and heal Amfortas.

The Time is at Hand!

In his autobiography, Steiner spoke of the two-year period following the encounter with Nietzsche as a "severe test." The battle he waged was one in which he attempted with all of his thoughts, to penetrate through Nature to Spirit. While for anyone who was not clairvoyant, this would hardly be thought of as a battle, for someone as highly clairvoyant for the spiritual world as Steiner was, this opened him to attack by Ahrimanic beings, which he described as relentlessly working to turn his thoughts toward a materialistic world conception, in which "the world must be a machine." In the process of persevering through this "soul's probation" period, Steiner discovered an entirely new form of spiritual knowledge. As we saw in Chapter 3, earlier peoples had an "instinctive" knowledge of the spiritual world, one that came to them through their "subtle body," particularly through the *chakras*, which act within the subtle body similarly to the way the senses act in the physical body. Though dormant in most people today, they can be awakened through bodily postures, the control of breathing, or through physical or mental exercises which work upon the solar plexus and the sympathetic nervous system.

In working always from the pole of pure thinking, rather than the *chakras*, Steiner created an entirely new *yoga*, a yoga of thinking. He actually put *kraft*—force—into his own thinking, to the point where it became independent of the body. To do so, he found, was akin to pushing off in a little raft into a raging sea, since, freed of the body, one was adrift in the titanic ocean of cosmic thought, without even the life raft of one's own identity. Gradually, however, the waves subsided, and Steiner discovered that *thinking itself was the life raft*, and that he had awakened his chakras from above, just as in the old mystery traditions, they had been awakened from below. As he continued to unfold this new meditative path, he eventually penetrated into the sphere of spiritual beings; sometime between the fall of 1898 and the summer of 1899, this culminated when Rudolf Steiner had a first-hand experience of Christ and His active presence in the evolution of the world. In his own words, he stood "in a solemn festival of knowledge before the Mystery of Golgotha."

The first public indication that Rudolf Steiner had experienced this Christian initiation was an essay—"The Character of Goethe's Spirit as Shown in the Fairy Tale of the Green Snake and the Beautiful Lily"—that he published in his own *Magazine for Literature*, in August 1899, in honor of the 150th anniversary of Goethe's birth. The fairy tale showed not just Goethe's spirit but his own, for in the wake of his initiation experience, he could now describe exactly the spiritual realities that Goethe had hidden within the tale. As surely as he was actually the "superman" anticipated by Nietzsche, *Rudolf Steiner was the Green Snake who built the bridge between the world of the senses and the world of the spirit.* A single human being in the Age of the Consciousness Soul, out of his hard-won spiritual capacities, was able to build a bridge for all people of good will to freely cross. That this was signaled with a fairy tale should make us all stop in our tracks, and give thanks for the spiritual world's whimsical sense of play.

Think of it! At the turn of the twentieth century, as the spiritual world held its breath, wondering whether humanity would turn away completely from its destiny, Rudolf Steiner appears, to tell the world about the bridge that he has himself built toward our rightful destiny. A year after his essay was published, Friedrich Nietzsche died, and Steiner was invited to give a memorial address to a small circle of Theosophists in Berlin; the audience was so moved that they asked him to lecture again on a subject of his choice. On September 29, 1900, Michaelmas Day, Rudolf Steiner spoke on the fairy tale, under the title "Goethe's Secret Revelation." It was his first esoteric lecture; over the next 25 years, he would give over 6,000 more lectures, and through them he would reveal secrets to which only the gods had previously been privy.

The fairy tale quality that we experienced in Kaspar Hauser's biography seems already to loom up before us in the life of Rudolf Steiner. This man, virtually unknown to the world today outside of the circle of his devoted followers, seems to be like Superman (the Clark Kent Superman, not Nietzsche's!), in the way that he is always *at the right place at the right time.* In 1879, just as the Archangel Michael is being given the 354-year regency over human evolution, Steiner meets his Teacher; in 1899, just as the Kali Yuga, the 5,000-year the Dark Age in the Hindu reckoning of history, ends, Steiner has his Christ-experience; in 1900, the first year of the "New Age," Steiner comes forth as an esoteric teacher, *on Michaelmas Day.*

This uncanny timing began with Steiner's birth, on February 27, 1861, in Kraljevic (King's Village), Austria, on the western outskirts of the vast Hungarian plain, the Puszta. As mentioned in the previous chapter, the lunar nodes—the points where the orbit of the Moon crosses the plane of the ecliptic (the apparent path of the Sun across the heavens against the background stars)—precess so that they cross the ecliptic again at the same point after 18.61 years. The ascending node (the place where the moon crosses to the north of the ecliptic) and the descending node (where it crosses to the south) in each individual's biography signal places where key decisions are made for one's life's purpose. At that time, one is afforded a brief view of one's prenatal intentions, inscribed into the Moon sphere before descending to earth. Steiner's birth in 1861 is an extraordinary instance of being in the right place at the right time; it was the year that humanity as a whole passed through its first lunar node.

Though I have said little about it, one of the key ideas behind eurythmy—the "dancing" that we have been doing from time to time this semester—is the ancient Hermetic adage "As above, so below," which means that the macrocosm is mirrored in the microcosm. This is especially true of the rhythmic dimension of Time, and its microcosmic reflection in human biography. With this in mind we can compare humanity and the individual human being. We know that the life of the individual human being unfolds in periods of approximately seven years. In each of these periods, a different part of the human spiritual and physical organism unfolds. In the first 7 years the child develops its own physical body, independent of that of its mother; this period ends with the change of teeth at approximately 7 years old, perhaps slightly younger today as a result of the accelerated development which has been one of the features of the 20th century. Then by age 14, the end of the development of the human life body is marked by the more subtle change of puberty. At around age 21, the individual's capacity of feeling and thinking has developed and this is marked by the less physical social rites of passage such as graduating from college, getting a job, perhaps even marriage.

Even more subtle changes in the psyche and spirit occur at 7-year intervals after this, but with this complete development of the physical body in the first three seven-year intervals, the person's life—the feeling and thinking capacities, the house, so to speak—has been prepared, and the master or mistress of the house then fully arrives to take up residence. This is the beginning of the unfolding of the Ego at age 21, when the individual becomes truly responsible for himself or herself in the eyes of society. Having carefully shepherded and stewarded your talents and capacities, at age 21 you can step forth into your "Sun Period" of 21 years, in which you are at your full creative and destiny-manifesting powers. In our own country, that this extraordinary moment is marked merely by the ritual of having your first legal drink of alcohol speaks volumes about the divorce of the modern human being from the great cosmic rhythms.

Keeping with this esoteric law of "as above, so below," one can envision human history as bearing the imprint of these same rhythms, writ large. Indeed, one can follow the biography of humanity as a whole if one realizes that a year in the life of the individual human being is analogous to 100 years in human history. Thus the 4th century corresponds to the child at age 3; the 9th century to the 8-year-old; the 1500s would correspond to the child in his 16th year; the 19th century to the 18 year-old; and mankind at age 20 reached its "21st birthday." We thus see that the centuries leading up to humanity's "21st birthday"—the year 2000—are extremely important, *and the year 1861 (100 x 18.61) is the moment when a brief window opened for humanity to glimpse and seize its destiny.* As he prepared to incarnate, Rudolf Steiner made a pre-birth commitment to serving humanity by building a bridge between the world of "It Matters" and "It Spirits," and thus, his birth in 1861 represented a window for mankind as a whole—an opportunity to know once again its own origins and destiny.

The Mirroring Rule in History

In 1861 Kaspar Hauser would have turned 49, and entered his "Jupiter period" (49–56), when his accumulated wisdom would have found its fullest power. Absent his building the bridge to the spiritual world, it became Rudolf Steiner's task. Rudolf Steiner experienced his own Moon node *in 1879, as the Michael Age began.* In fact, the three important dates in both Rudolf Steiner's life and the life of humanity—1861; 1879; 1897—are linked by a rhythm that was discovered by Rudolf Steiner. This discovery could revolutionize the study of history, but, as with so much of the bridge building done by the "Green Snake," it has gone almost completely unnoticed:

> Things go in cycles or periods. Anything which happens in the physical world is really a kind of projection, or shadow, of what happens in the spiritual world, except that it would have happened earlier in the spiritual world.

Steiner showed that every cycle is brought to completion on earth after equal intervals of time. In the case of his own biography, we see that in 1861 he made a promise to dedicate himself to overcoming the Dragon, Ahriman, and to find the Grail. In the spiritual world, 18½ years later, in the autumn of 1879, Michael was victorious over the Dragon, and cast the Ahrimanic demons down into the earth realm, where, it was expected that the newly free human beings would be capable of conquering them. Nietzsche's experience suggested that humanity was not quite ready; if Kaspar Hauser had lived, the outcome might have been very different. Another 18.6 years on from the fall of 1879 leads to the summer of 1898, the time when Rudolf Steiner was single-handedly battling the Ahrimanic demons on the inner plane, as he forged a path to sense-free thinking. When Steiner experienced the "festival of knowledge before the Mystery of Golgotha," it was the mirror event to his pre-birth pact in 1861, *and signaled his successful entry into the Grail Castle. Rudolf Steiner performed this deed for all humanity, and so it remains present as a seed impulse in the spiritual life of humanity and the earth.*

Let us examine another example of the mirroring rule, centering once again on the year 1879, the advent of Michael's reign as ruling Archangel (although remember that Michael has actually passed on to the next rank, allowing the Angel Vidar to take his place). The year 1859, twenty years before 1879, was another milestone in the life of humanity. That year had long been anticipated among the brothers of the Rosy Cross, who were taught centuries before by Christian Rosenkreutz that their order was to prepare for a time in the 19th century when natural science would have found the solution to three problems: (1) the material constitution of the Cosmos—"solved" with the discovery of spectral analysis by German physicist Gustav Kirchhoff and chemist Robert Bunsen; (2) the material process of organic evolution—"solved" by Charles Darwin's *Origin of Species*; and (3) the question of differing states of consciousness—"solved" through G.T. Fechner's mathematical treatment of sensation and thought. All three of these developments came around 1859: Kirchhoff and Bunsen published their findings on the spectra of metals in 1860; Darwin's *Origin of Species* was published in 1859; Fechner's *Elements of Psychophysics* appeared in 1860. As you might imagine, such events will not be exact, given the length of time that scientific discoveries need to unfold, but clearly these three revolutionary developments in modern science cluster around the year 1859.

All three of these "solutions" (the quotation marks are to suggest that they are only solutions within the framework of 19th century "It Matters" thought, and are at best only partial truths waiting for spiritual scientific explanation) further reified the scientific materialism of the era, and cried out for a counter-impulse—the very impulse that the Rosicrucians had been preparing. As the supreme bearer of the Rosicrucian impulse in the late 19th century, Rudolf Steiner's Christ experience in 1899 was the "answer" to the events of 1859. From that experience, he would go on to develop fully elaborated sciences of physical matter, of organic evolution, and of psychology, which would, if taken up by humanity, quickly consign Kirchoff and Bunsen; Darwin; and Fechner to the archive of outmoded materialist theories of the late Kali Yuga.

In a lecture in the fall of 1917, Rudolf Steiner gave as an example of the mirroring rule the years 1841—1879—1917. From his own journey through the spiritual world before his birth in 1861, he knew that in 1841 a battle had begun there, between Michael and the Dragon, and that this battle had ended in 1879. 1841 found its echo in the horrible events of 1917, when World War I, which had already been raging across Europe for three years, escalated with the entry of the United States. In Russia, 1917 saw the beginning of the Bolshevik Revolution, which would bring—even with Russia's withdrawal from the war—its own carnage.

Both of these world tragedies, as complex as they were in their proximal causes, had their ultimate origin in the spiritual battle begun in 1841. They also were fueled by a whole constellation of false dichotomies or polarities created by highly restricted, polarized thinking. As a Grail deed in response to these catastrophes, Rudolf Steiner not only revealed the mysteries of History, but worked tirelessly to foster the impulse of *threefoldness*, as an antidote to the destructiveness of black-white polarization. In *Riddles of the Soul* (1917) he described how the nerve-sense system, rhythmic system, and metabolic-limb system were the foundation of human thinking, feeling, and willing. From this trinity he then unfolded a radical program of "social threefolding," which he attempted to bring to the highest levels of German policy-making, in hopes of staving off the impending catastrophe of war.

From Christmas to Easter: The 33-Year Rhythm of History

More often than not, some rhythmic logic ran through Steiner's public lectures. Two months after he revealed the mirroring rule in history, Rudolf Steiner gave another, even more remarkable, lecture about cycles in history. The lecture was given on December 23rd, the eve of Christmas Eve:

> All of the actions of former generations, all the impulses and the deeds connected with them, pour into historical evolution and have a life cycle of 33 years. Then comes the Easter time of these deeds and impulses, the time of resurrection. . . . All things in historical evolution are transfigured after 33 years, arise as from the grave, by virtue of a power connected with the holiest of all redemptions, the Mystery of Golgotha. . . . Just as we calculate the cyclic rotations of celestial bodies so we must learn to calculate historic events by means of a true science of history. . . .

"33" was Rudolf Steiner's shorthand for 33⅓, for the historical law that Steiner suggests here is a consequence of the actual biography of Jesus Christ, whose life—from the birth of Jesus of Nazareth on the night of December 6/7, 2 BC, to the Resurrection at sunrise on Easter Sunday morning, April 5, AD 33—lasted 12,173½ days, or 33.329 years, which is 33⅓ years less 1 _ days. This "Christ rhythm" was like a new planet, joining the one-year rhythm of the Sun; 29½-year rhythm of Saturn; 12-year rhythm of Jupiter, and so on). Since the moment of Christ's resurrection, the 33⅓-year rhythm of the life of Christ Jesus is impressed forever into the earth's destiny, and becomes of signal importance to the unfolding of human history. One can cast one's eye across the centuries since the year AD 33, and think of countless events as "Christmas" births whose "Easter" resurrection—the coming to fruition or completion—takes place 33 years later.

Unlike the planetary and solar rhythms pulsing eternally through time, this rhythm was "won" for humanity by a god becoming a human being, and was forever after inscribed into the cosmos only after Christ's death on the cross at Golgotha. The planetary rhythms manifest in space as the orbital periods moving against the background of the zodiac, but the Christ rhythm has no spatial signifier, being a purely temporal rhythm, measured out by the duration of the life of Jesus Christ. Since AD 33, three times a century that pulse has echoed through human history.

Though our Western habit of reckoning time and anniversaries in 100-year increments is a wholly arbitrary artifact of a human mathematical system, there is hidden within it an intuition of the century's significance as the sum of three 33⅓-year periods. Since the rhythm is a day and a half less than 33⅓ years, the "commemoration" of any event migrates slightly backwards in time. If one follows this rhythm, the third cycle—the second since Christ's death and resurrection—completes at sunset on December 1, AD 99. Following this rhythm through the centuries, one arrives at the threshold of the twentieth century at the completion of the 57th cycle, on September 10, 1899. This rhythm was intuited by the millennia-old Hindu historical calendar that set the end of the 5000-year-long Kali Yuga in 1899.

The 33-year rhythm manifests most dramatically in Grail knights, that is, in individuals who serve the Sun Spirit, Christ, and so it is not surprising that the lives of both Rudolf Steiner and Kaspar Hauser show the 33-year-rhythm. 33 years after Kaspar Hauser's appearance in Nuremberg, Rudolf Steiner was born. From the 4th of October until the 15th of October in 1911—exactly 99 years after the infant who would become known to the world as "Kaspar Hauser" lay in his mother's cradle in the castle at Karlsruhe—Steiner gave a series of lectures in Karlsruhe, entitled "From Jesus to Christ." Steiner's appearance at Karlsruhe is one of countless examples during his life when he was both carrying on his "day job", his readily visible, everyday responsibilities as a teacher, and simultaneously answering deeply mysterious currents within the spiritual world. At Karlsruhe in 1911, Steiner was defending and supporting Kaspar Hauser and his destiny. Without making reference to Kaspar in these lectures, they were clearly intended to point in the direction of his enemies, the ones who directed the occult crime, as they focused on the Jesuit initiation of the will.

Rudolf Steiner's deed of exposing the Jesuits, coming 99 years after Kaspar Hauser's birth at Michaelmas, 1812, was extremely courageous, for it opened him to attack by the Society of Jesus. The truest mark of Swan Knights—high initiates of the Holy Grail—is this willingness for sacrifice, which has its archetype and ideal in Christ's sacrifice on the cross. In these individuals, one can almost always find that the 33rd year of their life brings some extraordinary deed. At age 33, in 1894, Rudolf Steiner published his *Philosophy of Freedom*, which demonstrated how the threefold unity of human cognition, observation, and thinking can restore the primal unity of the world, setting man free. This work had as another "Christmas" birth impulse the deeds of J. W. Goethe and Friedrich Schiller a century (3 x 33⅓ years) earlier. The two men had become friends in the spring of 1794, after Goethe had shared with Schiller his theory of the "archetypal plant," a pioneering example of the sort of spiritual scientific investigation that Rudolf Steiner would perfect a century later. Goethe's theory of plant metamorphosis—and also his theory of color—was an important step toward freeing man's powers of observation from the stranglehold of Ahriman, who wishes always that human beings see only "It Matters" explanations for phenomena which all have their origins in the realm of "It Spirits."

In 1795, in a magazine he had founded called *Die Horen*, Goethe published both his fairy tale and his friend Schiller's pivotal work, *On the Aesthetic Education of Man*. Inspired by the disenchantment Schiller felt about the failure of the French Revolution to create a truly democratic republic, he wrote the book as a philosophical inquiry into what had gone wrong, and how to prevent such tragedies in the future. In asserting that it is possible to elevate the moral character of a people by touching their souls with beauty, Schiller performed a deed of overcoming Lucifer.

Goethe and Schiller's publications were just the sort of bridges to the spiritual world that the fairy tale described, and they were also simultaneously a "one-two" punch against the twin adversaries of Lucifer and Ahriman; Schiller gave humanity a path for treading healthily through Lucifer's realm, while Goethe's fairy tale was a salvo directly against Ahriman, since it established the reality of the spiritual world as an alternative to Ahriman's denial of that world. In the spirit of the "true fairy tale," one can see the release of Kaspar Hauser from his dark prison cell at Whitsuntide, 1828, as the consequence of this dual deed of bridge building by Goethe and Schiller in 1795, *33 years earlier*. The spiritual force created by their friendship entered the stream of time to become an "ally" to Kaspar Hauser. This is a deeply mysterious process that future historians will have the obligation—and the delight!—of investigating.

It is a spiritual law that all great impulses for humanity enter history when a single individual has won through to that impulse out of his own forces—Rudolf Steiner's life is perhaps the most spectacular example of this in the last 500 years. The friendship between Goethe and Schiller is just such a deed, the winning through to a true human community of the spirit, which will increasingly become the path of *all* humanity. The significance of this single human friendship for the future is hinted by the first 33-year echo of their deed—the liberation of Kaspar Hauser—but it also appears at the second rhythm, 1861, *the year of Rudolf Steiner's birth*, and in the third echo in 1894, with the publication of Steiner's major philosophical work, *The Philosophy of Freedom*. By mapping a middle path between the spiritual excess of pure aestheticism and the dry, abstract desert of modern materialist natural science, Steiner's *Philosophy of Freedom* completed these deeds of Goethe and Schiller in 1795.

One of the most wonderful things that I have experienced as a teacher is to observe the friendships between my students. Some of these friendships exist before I meet them, but from time to time, I get to witness a friendship that develops between people who meet in my class. A good friendship lifts all of us up, does it not? In Goethe and Schiller's friendship we have an example from history that can lift up our ideal of friendship even further. Perhaps you know of other such creative friendships in history, or in your own experience. Think now that each of these is a *spiritual force for the good, that ripples through time in 33-year waves*. Indeed, your own freely performed deeds, especially when they are done for the good, against the stultifying judgment of the status quo, are also a spiritual force. I hope that as you come to see this, you can see that what happens in history is not a matter of predetermined fate, but of ever-open *possibility*. Each and every one of us can, by our deeds, create tremendous spiritual forces to stem the growing tide of evil in the world.

Kaspar Hauser would have turned 33 in 1845, and because he was not on earth to shape events, there arose around that year significant counter-deeds. One can interpret both the publication by Karl Marx of the *Communist Manifesto*, and the revolutions of 1848 as such counter-deeds. 33 years later, in the summer of 1878, Kaspar Hauser's absence allowed another counter-deed to be performed, when, at the Congress of Berlin, Chancellor Otto von Bismarck brokered agreements between Russia and the European powers that would, in its breakup of the Balkans, lead directly to World War I, *33 years later*.

Following this 33-year rhythm one more cycle from the year of Kaspar's birth, we come to 1911, the year that Rudolf Steiner gave his lecture series "From Jesus to Christ" in Karlsruhe. Taking as its central impulse the counter-deed of the Jesuit attack on Kaspar Hauser, Steiner was with these lectures combating the *ongoing* crimes of the Jesuits, which were about to bear fruit in the strife poised to rip across central and eastern Europe. Steiner's focus on hypnotic manipulation of the will did not just point back to Stanhope and other enemies of Kaspar Hauser, but to the enemies of the entire world who were working behind the scenes to create World War I. By exposing the secret black magical activities of the Jesuits, Steiner redeemed the "ghost" of Kaspar Hauser, whose absence had allowed the continued destructive machinations of the Society of Jesus. Steiner's crystal clear annunciation of the evil methods of secret orders was balanced by his description of the healing potential in attuning to the deeds of Christ.

1911/1912 saw two other deeds of healing performed by Rudolf Steiner. His *Calendar of the Soul* bore on its title page the inscription: "1879 years after the birth of the ego." Here again Steiner was pointing to the 33-year rhythm—both how it began in AD 33, and its fruition with the advent of Michael in 1879. The *Calendar* consisted of 52 weekly verses which were arranged in a mysterious lemniscatory (figure eight) structure, designed out of Steiner's clairvoyance to address the rhythms contained in the human subtle body. About this same time Steiner developed eurythmy, a new art of movement which could provide a healthy training of the will, as opposed to the demonic training of the will pursued by the Jesuits. In eurythmy, Steiner showed humanity how it could put back into movement the supersensible powers that had once been the instinctive inheritance of earlier ages. Taken together, these two innovations provided a bridge for human beings to regain their connection to the life-giving etheric forces, at a time when these same forces were being used against humanity by the secret brotherhoods.

A "Record of My Love"

Let us step away for a moment from the deeds and counter-deeds springing from the lives of Kaspar Hauser and Rudolf Steiner, and consider another Grail knight whose connection to the Christ impulse and the 33-year rhythm has never been recognized. The practice of historical study employing the 33-year rhythm is universally applicable, but is easiest to do when we have a well-chronicled biography. Henry Thoreau's 2-million word journal, with its focus on chronicling nature's cyclic rhythms, offers just such an ideal source for tracking the 33-year rhythm.

Thoreau had begun his journal in 1837, at age 21, in response to a simple question from his mentor Ralph Waldo Emerson: "What are you doing now? Do you keep a journal?" "So I make my first entry to-day," Thoreau replied, and thus began his life's task. But anyone wishing to chronicle Thoreau's thoughts and actions on a daily basis for the next dozen years would be frustrated by the journal, which is full of missing pages and dates. Indeed, Thoreau rarely gave date headings to his entries, until November 16, 1850. After this date, Thoreau almost never missed a daily entry, and assumed the habitual practice of heading each day's journal entry with the date. Beginning with this November 16 entry, Thoreau's journaling practice transforms entirely, becoming a laboratory for phenomenological perception and description. Whereas previously he had on dated days typically taken up individual questions, told single discrete stories, or noted particular places or people, and in undated entries separated subjects from one another slightly, now a single day's reflections would come cascading one upon another, alternating between diurnal or seasonal arcana and perennial philosophical discussions.

November 16 opens with Thoreau's report that he has found three arrowheads while out walking, then declares that he regards the tiniest tributary brook with the same awe he would feel for the Orinoco or Mississippi; his next paragraph claims that it is always the wild element in literature that is most compelling; he discovers that cranberries are fine fare as one crosses meadows; wonders what alarm a blue jay is sounding in some birch grove; muses on how he chooses his bearing when setting out on a walk; wrestles with his antipathy and sympathy toward friends; confesses that the scream of a cat whose tail was caught by a closing door drove off celestial thoughts; asks why shrub oaks keep their leaves all winter; observes black walnut trees heavy with nuts, and birches bare but for their catkins; notes the late autumn burst of blossoming by spring herbs; hears cows running scared in the woods; asks what salvation there might be for men who are afraid of the dark, since "God is silent and mysterious"; discovers that some of our brightest days are ones when the sun is not shining; comments that land where trees have been cut off and are rejuvenating is called "sprout land"; questions whether the partridge-berry should not be called "checker-berry"; laments the loss of wild apple trees; and closes with this extraordinary—though for Thoreau altogether ordinary—declaration:

> My Journal should be a record of my love. I would write in it only the things I love, my affection for any aspect of the world, what I love to think of. I have no more distinctness or pointedness in my yearnings than an expanding bud, which does indeed point to flower and fruit, to summer and autumn, but is aware of the warm sun and spring influences only. I feel ripe for something, yet do nothing, can't discover what that things is. I feel fertile merely. It is seedtime with me. I have lain fallow long enough. . . . Notwithstanding a sense of unworthiness which possesses me, not without reason, notwithstanding that I regard myself as a good deal of a scamp, yet for the most part the spirit of the universe is unaccountably kind to me, and I enjoy perhaps an unusual share of happiness.

With this entry, Thoreau already began to practice his intended goal for his journal: the string of reflections is punctuated with "I love to pause in mid-passage" (crossing fences); "I love my friends"; "I love nature, I love the landscape." "I love" hereafter becomes one of the journal's most characteristic expressions.

November 16, 1850 was three years, four months and four days after Henry Thoreau's thirtieth birthday, almost to the day the exact length of the 33⅓-year Christ rhythm. Thoreau left his home in the stars with a sure eye for his place and time on Earth, having chosen to ally himself with a cohort of Grail knights—Emerson, Alcott, Fuller, Brownson and their fellow Transcendentalists—who could only dimly recall the pact they made before birth. Having crossed the Lethean river of forgetfulness, there was no guarantee that they would carry out their missions. Each individual, between the ages of thirty and thirty-three, chooses to follow or forget his spiritual patrimony. At the culmination of his Christ period, Thoreau entered all the more deeply into his own destiny, and marked the moment with an outburst of love.

Perhaps with this small example you can understand more fully why I have chosen, in a course on world history, to favor biographical study, and to go so deeply into the lives of a small set of individuals, particularly Rudolf Steiner. All along I have hoped to emulate the Green Snake, and build bridges for you, out of the parched land of materialism in which we dwell, to the land of the Will-o'-the-Wisps and the Garden of the Beautiful Lily and the 3 Maidens and the Risen Temple—the land of the Supersensible. Following the Green Snake, we can recover the deep mysteries that lie within the single human biography, as a reminder to ourselves that *we too participate in these mysteries*. These cosmic rhythms and karmic patterns play into each of our lives, and the time is at hand for us to come to know these mysteries ourselves, to become Green Snakes who can shed the constricting old skin of conventional thinking, and win our way through to the cognition that would begin to make a textbook like this unnecessary, for we would begin to know these realities for ourselves.

"Thinking Outside the Box"

It is completely possible that at this point in the course, you think of Dr. Dann's "It Spirits" approach as meaning "imagination," and "It Matters" as "fact." In fact, I would wager that this is the case for *most* of you. I want to leave you absolutely free to do what you wish with the stories that I tell in this course, but I also feel compelled to whisper something in your ear: *To think of these stories as imaginary, and the history that you have learned in the past as "fact," would be a great mistake.* At the end of each semester, I wait months before I read the course evaluations, because I am so afraid to read student comments like "I learned absolutely nothing from this course. It was all about fairies and angels" or "What a crock! How do they let this kook teach in a university?!"

OUCH! But sometimes we can learn something from the people whose criticism hurts us. One of the reasons that I wrote this book is to see if, by setting these stories down in print, it worked the magic of getting some of you who hate this course to take it more seriously. College students—and most adults who have left college—tend to think that if something is said in a textbook, it must be true. Even in this age when we get the majority of our knowledge about the wider world from digital media, we still consider print as authoritative, definitive, *true*.

College textbooks are almost always conservative in their presentation of knowledge. In subjects like biology, chemistry, physics, sociology, psychology, and many other realms of study, these introductions and summaries of information tend to leave out whatever theoretical or factual controversies might be raging at the moment between scholars in those fields. Publishers and textbook authors (and unfortunately, the teachers and students who use these textbooks) end up building walls to keep new ideas and knowledge out, rather than doors and windows to let new truths in. Textbooks are a tangible picture of the "status quo," the received truth, which, history itself (the process of change over time, not the body of official knowledge) always shows us, is at best only partially true, and more often, downright false.

At your youthful age, "history" probably means the body of official knowledge, a subject taught in school, and one that you will be happy to leave behind once you have filled your college requirements. What a shame! *History is mystery. History is a fantastic story. History is a vast, rhythmic unfolding whose mysteries can and must be penetrated by us in this age of the Consciousness Soul.*

Every semester, a handful of those course evaluations say: "I like that this course taught me to think outside the box." I don't use that "outside the box" expression, but I am so glad that my students have found it useful as a way to characterize their experience, since it is doubly descriptive, in that *most schools are boxes.* In the long centuries before most people on the planet went to schools—I mean those big, ugly, sterile *boxes* that spread across the landscape of the West in the 19th century, not "schools" in the sense of groups of people organizing to impart wisdom to the next generation—the status quo, the accepted truths, *the frames through which people saw the world,* lived in the atmosphere, in everyday lived experience. In periods of rapid change, those frames, or "boxes," become readily visible, in the way that society reacts to new ideas. The centuries that we have been studying are the most dynamic, revolutionary ones in human history, and are marked by successive overthrows of old ways of thinking and doing. Think of Copernicus, Galileo, Kepler, Giordano Bruno—their observations of the heavens were at first scorned, and they themselves were vilified. Some were imprisoned, a few executed, for their public proclamation of new knowledge.

As a rule, *no new truth wins widespread approval without considerable resistance, even anguish.* Just cast your glance across your own present, and you will find countless examples of firmly established "truths" that only became accepted after a long struggle. This is exactly what we can be alerted to through the study of history, and yet historians themselves are likely to forget this when it comes to their own discipline. Ever ready to point out the boxes in which other disciplines live, they are oblivious to their own boxes, and the most pervasive box is materialism. "It Matters" is the ruling dogma of the historical profession, and where there is dogma, there are vast invisible networks of fear, ignorance, and intimidation.

By your own efforts in previous lifetimes, you have won the great privilege to be born again into the age of the Consciousness Soul, where your task is to overcome dullness and doubt, and to achieve freedom in your thinking. It is a very dangerous task, fraught with unseen peril—just think of Nietzsche's fate!—but to shrink from it will surely bring tragic consequences. If you haven't done so yet, I invite you to peek over the wall, outside the box, and see if something there doesn't have a gift for you.

A New Mystery Center

Was I exaggerating when I said that achieving sense-free thinking was "dangerous"? Think of what happened to Kaspar Hauser! The dangers were even greater for Rudolf Steiner. The encounter with Nietzsche gives us that picture. By the end of the Kali Yuga, in 1899, Steiner had vanquished the host of Ahrimanic beings who attacked him, but there were still other enemies who wished not just to poison his thinking, but to destroy him. These enemies became especially determined after Steiner's lecture in Karlsruhe in October 1911, but a year earlier he had been in Karlsruhe and had given another lecture that rattled them deeply as well. It began by noting that reincarnation only makes sense if each time we come into incarnation, the conditions on earth are much different from before, which gives each person the chance to add to his own soul development. He explained that Christ's physical appearance in the age of the Kali Yuga was necessitated by humanity's having lost its ancient clairvoyance, and said that if there had been at the time of Christ's physical incarnation no human beings capable of establishing an active soul connection with Christ, all human connection with the spiritual world would have been gradually lost.

Today, just two years shy of a full century after these words were spoken, we can hopefully appreciate them even more than his audience in 1910 did. Steiner tells us that: 1) reincarnation and karma are fundamental supersensible experiences that must be understood, and that the path of wisdom that he brought—Anthroposophy, or as he also termed it, "Spiritual Science"—gives this possibility; and 2) Ahriman—embodied principally in the opposing materialistic currents—fights against spiritual science so as to make an understanding of these newly awakened faculties impossible.

With this in mind, we can shed new light on the events of the early twentieth century. Kaspar Hauser was the one who knew about the newly arising experiences of how karma is formed, and was predestined to prepare for it. The ideology of National Socialism could never have gained any great importance in Germany if there in the new Grail culture of Baden and beyond, people had learned that each human being incarnates in various nations and races in the course of evolution. (Picture for yourself George W. Bush—or Pope Benedict—going to Iraq or Turkey knowing that they have themselves been a worshiper of Mohammed in a previous incarnation!) It is thus clear that Rudolf Steiner, by his solitary and mostly misunderstood efforts to teach about reincarnation and karma between 1900 and his death in 1925, took up the broken mission of Kaspar Hauser. Indeed, it was just after his 1910 lecture that occult attacks began upon him, because the Jesuits and Freemasons knew the truth of these previously esoteric secrets. It was not so much the fear of his identifying Kaspar Hauser's murderers as it was their fear of the 33-year rhythm in history becoming known, since this also pointed to Kaspar Hauser as a real spiritual being.

The anti-Grail brotherhoods usually act only at a distance, allowing others (since the 19th century, this has mostly been politicians, since politics has become quite clearly the realm of untruth) to do their work for them. Only when an initiate—a spiritually awakened human being like Rudolf Steiner or Kaspar Hauser—begins to work concretely on the physical plane, do they sense great enough danger to pick up knife or gun themselves. It was above all the *truth* of Steiner's revelations in 1910 that frightened the adversaries.

Unlike comic book or cinema superheroes, who, when they are in danger, use their super-powers to save themselves, Grail heroes consistently withhold the use of their powers, *because doing so leaves all parties free to act.* Christ knew exactly what fate lay in waiting for him: "One of you shall betray me," he told the disciples at the Last Supper, and then identified Judas by dipping the bread in the bowl. Imagine for a moment having the ability to know the future at every step of your life, or at least, at the most critical, and dangerous moments. Such foreknowledge was available to Christ, and to Kaspar Hauser, and yet they walked through their destiny with the "Ah" gesture of "Thy will be done," and left the future wide open. Rudolf Steiner had lesser, but quite profound faculties of foreknowledge, and constantly refrained from taking actions that would have saved himself from suffering, pain, and even death.

In the autumn of 1912, on his way from Basle, Switzerland to Alsace after a lecture series on the Gospel of St. Mark, he stopped overnight in Dornach, a small village nearby Basle. The Dornach region was a crossroads of ancient spiritual traditions: the Druids had a sacred shrine there, and centuries later Irish monks settled there and spread Irish Christianity. Parsifal—the real Parsifal, who lived in the 9th century—had been in the region on his search for the Holy Grail. In 1499, Dornach was the scene of a battle that was decisive for the preservation of Switzerland's—the European state which was the crucible of some of the purest impulses of the Consciousness Soul era—political and social freedom. In the 16th century, the great Swiss alchemist Paracelsus, who was inspired by Rosicrucian wisdom, worked in Basle. A Capuchin monastery in Dornach had been a pastoral and religious center for over two centuries. On this overnight visit, Rudolf Steiner quickly sensed these past events in the etheric atmosphere, and the next morning he announced to friends that he would found there a new spiritual center, a temple for the future. This brief visit was another example of being in the right place at the right time; Steiner's visit came on Michaelmas Day; Michael, who had worked with and through Rudolf Steiner all along, would come into even closer collaboration with the building of the new mystery center at Dornach.

One of the people with Steiner at the time described his appearance on that morning:

> The next morning Rudolf Steiner awoke as never before. He was haggard, as though crushed; a dark shadow hung over him. There was no apparent reason for this, such things never happened to him—to him who, despite continual activity and hurry, lived in eternal harmony . . . in that night he foresaw a great deal which he had to forbid himself to think about.

"Basle has a favorable karma," Steiner told his friends, never hinting to them that he had that night witnessed a horrible personal and collective tragedy that lay only a decade away.

Exactly a year later, on September 20th, 1913, Rudolf Steiner laid into the earth of the Dornach hill a foundation stone for a remarkable building that he had designed, the "Goetheanum." Named after J.W. von Goethe, construction began that very day, and later the international cadre of workers continued the construction even as the battles of World War I were being fought all around them. At the ceremony for the laying of the foundation stone, Rudolf Steiner said:

> We must have the strength of consciousness to gaze out into far distant cycles of time to become aware of how the mission, whose distinctive symbol this building is to become, will be included among the great missions of humanity on our Earth.

Rudolf Steiner's laying of this stone was a profound mystery deed intended to support the great event of the twentieth century—the return of the Grail to earth, i.e., the coming of Christ into the etheric aura of the Earth. The mystery dimension of this deed is that *he gave up the forces of his own etheric body to weave a spiritual aura around the Dornach hill.*

In ancient times, priests had always performed similar deeds; this is why the crop circles appear in locations where there were ancient mystery centers, whose spiritual aura lingers into the present, allowing spiritual beings to work with the nature spirits to weave the crops into a living symbolic language. Though today we see only the massive stone ruins of these centers, in the invisible realm there are beautiful etheric structures which, like the cereal crops in which the magnificent circles appear, are life-giving, radiant sources. The flowing, twin-domed Goetheanum that rose from the Dornach hill was clearly not built out of the laws of the dead mineral world, but out of the living laws of the etheric world. The massive building was more like a plant, a picture in timber and glass and shingle of the world of dynamic metamorphosis.

May Human Beings Hear It!

On New Year's Eve in 1922, the tragedy foreseen by Rudolf Steiner in 1912 struck—the Goetheanum burned to the ground; most members of the anthroposophical community believed an arsonist started the fire. The destruction of the Goetheanum was not aimed at disrupting the activities of the anthroposophists, *but was an assassination attempt directed at Rudolf Steiner, whose life forces the attackers knew were united with the building.* Like the imprisonment and murder of Kaspar Hauser, the fire was an occult crime, a criminal act against humanity's destiny, focused upon a great initiate of the Grail.

The very next morning, Rudolf Steiner spoke to the members of the Dornach anthroposophical community, declaring that they would begin rebuilding the Goetheanum—in concrete this time—that very day. The year 1923 saw incredible activity at the Dornach hill; while volunteers worked to rebuild the Goetheanum, Steiner, after creating a new building design, poured forth an increasing stream of esoteric knowledge.

The true tragedy of the Goetheanum fire, the one he had foreseen that first night in Dornach, was that the fire could only have happened due to the failure of the members of the community. Not outer failures, for, ever since the outbreak of World War I, the building had been guarded day and night. The inner plane, however, received no such watchfulness. The Anthroposophical Society was split by personality clashes and factional differences, and the members, though mostly aware of the demonic forces that would constantly attack the new mystery temple, did little to actively protect it from those forces. The Goetheanum—a temple not just for the age of the Consciousness Soul, but for the next epoch, the 6th post-Atlantean—needed no gargoyles. These were the spiritual protective devices of the 4th post-Atlantean. The Goetheanum needed *consciousness*, consciousness by the Anthroposophical Society members that their inner forces were needed to unite with the etheric web laid into the building by Rudolf Steiner.

Within months of the fire, one faction of the Society split off; it was the final manifestation of the true cause of the fire. The Goetheanum had been founded and built according to purely occult spiritual laws, and as such, it could never be destroyed by any external means. It could only be attacked when there was a weakening of the inner, spiritual defense by the Society's members. Rudolf Steiner could not speak openly about this danger, for in doing so, he would violate the fundamental law of the epoch of human freedom—to never directly influence the will of the human being. Bound by the exact opposite tenet and practice, the Jesuits could work with demonic forces to black magically ignite the conflagration that destroyed the building.

These demonic forces wished ultimately to destroy the Society itself, by seeding social conflict whenever and wherever they could. Knowing this, Steiner made sure that on New Year's Day in 1923, while the smoke still rose from the ashes of the Goetheanum, all of the day's planned activities were carried out. He would not allow the spiritual work to be interrupted for even an instant, since such a break would give fuller entry to the demons.

At the end of January, Steiner began a series of lectures aimed at awakening anthroposophists to a deeper understanding of their tasks, and of the true essence of their spiritual movement. In mid-July, three lecture cycles—"The Evolution of Consciousness," "Man as Symphony of the Creative Word," and "Supersensible Man"—addressed the long-forgotten connections between the human being and the Cosmos. Meanwhile, he had laid the groundwork for the total reorganization of the Society. Steiner's year of titanic exertion culminated in a lecture cycle on "Mystery Knowledge and Mystery Centers," in which, for the first time in history, the secrets of the principal Western Mysteries were revealed. Though he did not say so at the time, Steiner brought this knowledge directly from the supersensible school of the Archangel Michael, and delivered it into the hearts and thoughts of the small group gathered to hear the lecture:

> This [vision] has been left to us: we cast our gaze on the secrets into which the initiates of the Mysteries were once initiated. Let us bring them to our consciousness! Let us bring them to the consciousness of those spiritual beings around me who were never in an earthly body but live in an etheric form. Let us bring it to the consciousness also of those who were often on the Earth in earthly bodies, but who are now present and belong to the community of Michael—let us bring it to the consciousness of these human souls. Let us outline the teaching of the great initiates that once streamed down to the Earth in the old form through the Mysteries. . . .

To formally anchor the new mysteries, Steiner organized a conference for the week of Christmas 1923, where he would assume the official leadership of the Society. This was an unprecedented act; up until this moment, Rudolf Steiner had never even been a member of the society which he himself had founded, in order to maintain the complete independence of his spiritual work. When he accepted the leadership of the earthly affairs of the Society, it was completely possible—and probable, given previously held occult laws—that the spiritual powers who had guided and guarded the movement through Rudolf Steiner would withdraw. Once again, Rudolf Steiner had to perform a deed whose consequences even he, a great initiate, did not know.

A couple of years ago, when I was first struggling with how I might integrate the biography of Rudolf Steiner into a course on world history, I asked my students to read a single lecture by Steiner, choosing, just by the title, from a list of dozens. In class, as we were having a discussion about what the students had found, one wonderful student named Matt Mulson blurted out: "Man, this cat Steiner knew *everything!*" Matt recognized this because he was in the nursing program, and was midway through the intensive course of study of human anatomy, physiology, endocrinology, embryology, epidemiology, genetics, immunology, neuroscience, nutrition, pharmacology.... I'm sure I've left out some subjects. Within Steiner's arena of knowledge, those fields are just the microcosm; he had equally commanding knowledge of the macrocosm—astronomy and astrology to zoology.

Given that Rudolf Steiner's clairvoyance permitted him to know *everything* (including, very often, the future), how could he not have known what the consequences would be of his decision to join himself to the earthly activity of the Anthroposophical Society? He gave the answer to this question years before, in his book *Philosophy of Freedom*, where he states that when a person performs actions solely out of moral intuition, he brings something completely new into the world through these actions. Every human being at that moment *creates something out of nothing*, something that has never existed anywhere, and so there is no being in the cosmos or on earth—even an initiate—who can know of the consequences beforehand. Indeed, this impossibility of prediction is the easiest way to distinguish whether a deed has been truly performed out of moral intuition. In his book *An Outline of Esoteric Science*, Rudolf Steiner spoke about how in the far future human beings would actually create a New Earth, and a new Cosmos of Love; this would come about through just such deeds of moral intuition.

In this deed, Rudolf Steiner was a forerunner who took upon himself the karma of every single individual, past and present, involved with the Anthroposophical Society. Their destinies would bear fully upon his own. *What Christ did for the whole of mankind upon Golgotha, Rudolf Steiner did for the members of the Anthroposophical Society at the Christmas Conference.* By virtue of his sacrifice, the Ahrimanic demons were silenced, and could no longer keep Steiner from revealing to humanity the very deepest secrets of the spiritual world, of which Michael was the guardian. In the 9 months following the Christmas Conference, Rudolf Steiner gave 338 lectures and 69 talks in almost every branch of human knowledge, transforming them into seeds for the future.

But the affirmation of the spiritual world had come immediately. At 10 AM on Christmas Day, in the carpentry shop of the Goetheanum, before 700 members of the Society, Steiner laid the foundation stone of the General Anthroposophical Society with these words:

Human Soul!
Thou livest in the Limbs
Which bear thee through the
World of space
Into the spirit's ocean-being.
Practice *Spirit-Recollection*
In depths of soul,
Where in the Wielding Will
Of World-Creating
Thine own I
Comes to being
Within God's I.
And thou wilt truly *live*
In Human-World-Being.

For the Father-Spirit of the
Heights holds sway
In Depths of Worlds begetting Being:
Seraphim, Cherubim, Thrones!
Let there ring out from the Heights
What in the Depths is echoed.

This Speaks:
Ex Deo Nascimur.

The Spirits of the Elements hear it
In East, West, North, South,
May human beings hear it.

Every person present felt the power of these words, and realized that they came through Rudolf Steiner from the Sun Spirit himself. One participant, Arvia MacKaye, the daughter of the American poet and playwright Percy MacKaye, watched from a perch on the metal slab of a saw-ing machine:

Never had I seen Rudolf Steiner as he appeared then. There was a light from his eyes, a power and majesty about him, which gave the impression that he had grown to a great size. There was an intensity and activity, united with a cosmic calm, that was breathtak-ing, and indicative of what was to come.

He opened this event by giving three strong, incisive, measured raps with a gavel upon the speaker's stand, such as those given in the temple in the Mystery Plays. It was as though the room became thronged with unseen spectators. Then as he spoke, giving for the first time the words of the Christmas Foundation Mantra ["Human Soul…"], it was as though, in this little carpentry shop, he spoke not only to the whole earth but to the assembled heavens; as though he became like a sun, light-outpouring, his voice like gold, a Michaelic fire infusing his words. Something poured forth of such a magnitude, and in a realm of such awakened consciousness, on this Christmas morning that it can only be likened to a spiritual birth.

Those gathered understood that Rudolf Steiner was performing a Mystery deed, one that took place on earth, but was enacted on the highest possible spiritual plane, a deed for all eternity. Calling this meditation the "Foundation Stone of Love," Rudolf Steiner thereby gave a new name to what had traditionally been called the "Holy Grail."

This verse was just the first; he gave six more over the next week, opening each day with their stepwise recitation. These seven verses, like the Goetheanum, were a living power, built up out of an architecture that addressed the human willing, feeling, and thinking. The last verse carried humanity's answer to the spiritual world:

> O Light Divine!
> O Sun of Christ!
> Warm Thou our Hearts,
> Enlighten Thou our Heads,
> That good may become
> What from our Hearts we would found
> And from our Heads direct
> With single purpose.

This was something entirely new in human history—a purely spiritual esoteric stream joined with an altogether earthly exoteric association of individuals, and by doing so, made it possible for spiritual forces to flow directly into human society. There is a great paradox here; *the step toward openness taken in the Christmas Conference made it all the more esoteric.* Since that day, any spiritual movement founded on secrets reserved for a small circle of initiates runs counter to the rightful flow of human evolution. *The time of secrets had passed forever.*

The events of the Christmas Conference of 1923–4 show that not only does mankind depend on the Gods, *but the Gods also depend on mankind.* To the extent that humanity does not take up its assigned tasks, the adversarial spiritual beings are fed and strengthened, and this means real trouble for the gods who wish for our proper development—and for us. The greatest adversary for humanity at this moment is Ahriman, and humanity is Ahriman's greatest ally in his battle with the Sun Spirit, Michael, and the host of Grail knights both here on Earth and in the spiritual world. How can we fight Ahriman? *The only way to combat Ahriman is to consciously win for our own individual development something that by its nature does not belong to his domain.* Ahriman is the "Prince of this World," and thus the whole of the content of contemporary civilization—from Hollywood to the World Wide Web—belongs to him. What each of us must win for ourselves is something outside of his domain—Love—that then must be practiced faith-fully and relentlessly in community.

Rudolf Steiner did more than any 20th century individual to describe the starry script—the patterns written into the heavens, that shape each person's life, and the course of history. He also suggested that human beings, *by their deeds, could write in the starry script, influencing it to serve the continued development of humanity.* In a meditative verse he once gave, Steiner said that "in the deepening silence/There grows and ripens/What humanity speaks to the stars." Certainly this is true of Rudolf Steiner's inspiring biography. Why not ours?

11: The War of the Worlds

Omens of Things to Come

BY THE BEGINNING OF SUMMER in the year 1898, from Maine to California, the upper peninsula of Michigan to the Gulf coast of Texas, in big cities and little towns and even out on the far-
flung farms, one song was being sung by Americans. Well, not quite one song, for in that pre-
radio age, it was impossible for a single song to sweep the whole nation. But there were a dozen
or so songs—with titles like *Before the Maine Went Down*; *Brass Buttons on the Naval Cadet*; *After
the War Is Over*; *Brave Dewey and His Men*; *The Charge of the Roosevelt Rough Riders*—that were
sung, whistled, or played on pianos in parlors across the nation. Patriotic marches or saccharine
ballads that lauded war heroes, sentimentalized soldiers' struggles, and romanticized America's
glorious imperial adventure in Cuba and the Philippines, they all sang "War."

More than the sensationalized stories penned by yellow journalists, the rhythms of these
songs stirred America into a patriotic frenzy. William Randolph Hearst's *New York Journal* published the sheet music to half a dozen such songs: *It Takes a Man to Be a Soldier*; *For Old Glory*;
The Gallant 71st (commissioned expressly for the *Journal*). When the music to *The Ill-Fated
Maine*—made popular by the international music hall superstar Bessie Bonehill—was published, the cover sheet bore an engraving of the battleship USS *Maine* sinking in Havana Harbor,
under which a banner read: "Gather up the bodies, and take them to the camp/And as you move
your solemn march,/Be dumb—or if you speak be it but a word;/and be that word Revenge!"

Revenge. On the very eve of the Kali Yuga's end, the threshold of the 20th century and the
new Age of Light, darkness closed in with a vengeance. Since the sinking of the *Maine* in mid-
February, the headlines had blared a steady stream of triumphal notes of American military victories. While the songs were mostly sentimental ballads in the vaudeville style, set in triple
meter, the tap-tap-tap of the newspaper stories sounded an ominous backbeat of imperialist
violence. No one pretended *not* to be vengeful. 284 sailors and marines were killed in the blast,
and few doubted that America's full fury should be directed at the perpetrator nation. "Remember the *Maine*! The hell with Spain!" went the vengeful refrain.

An official U.S. investigation agreed with the songs and the newspaper stories. On April 25,
1898, Congress formally declared war on Spain. By summer's end, Spain had ceded Cuba, along
with the Philippines, Puerto Rico and Guam, to the United States. No reliable evidence was ever
produced linking Spain to the explosion, and it is now widely believed that the event was caused

by a fire in a coal bunker that detonated a reserve powder magazine. This was the conclusion reached by a 1976 investigation headed by Admiral Hyman Rickover.[1]

In the Philippines, a guerrilla war of resistance to the American invasion and occupation lasted officially until 1902, but remnants of the Philippine Army and other resistance groups continued hostilities against American rule until 1913. Before the start of the war with Spain, American newspapers had calculatedly stirred up hatred for the Spanish by running stories about the horrors of Cuban life under oppressive Spanish rule. Headlines screamed about "death camps," Spanish cannibalism, and torture. By the end of the Philippine War, the United States was engaged in all of the same brutality that the Spanish had been—concentration camps, scorched earth campaigns against civilians, mass murder. American soldiers had committed widespread atrocities—including the "water cure," i.e., waterboarding, the torture technique widely used by the CIA under the Bush administration—which were ignored and minimized by the press, and whitewashed by an investigation by the War Department. The conflicts on either side of the world transformed the United States into a maritime empire, a world power, full of all the illusion and hubris and propensity to violence that comes with empire.

Europe's imperial violence had inspired English writer H.G. Wells' novel, *The War of the Worlds*, which appeared in American bookstores just as the Spanish-American War began. Written in semi-documentary fashion, the book's story of an invasion from Mars was a thinly veiled cautionary tale of what England might expect if continental Europe's late 19th century imperial wars came home to British soil. The novel made Wells famous as a prophet, for in it he described a variety of military technology that had not yet been invented—tanks, aerial bombing, nuclear war, gas warfare, laser-like weapons, and industrial robots. But Wells' depictions of the Martian tripods—fast-moving and equipped with heat-rays—were not that far from what British and German military inventors were trying to develop, and that would soon see action in World War I.

Wells was an enthusiastic Darwinian who saw every species as being engaged in a constant, brutal struggle for survival. The battle between the Martians and mankind in *The War of the Worlds* is just such a Darwinian struggle, writ large. Both a reformer and a fatalist, Wells envisioned a twentieth century of destructive, worldwide warfare, but his story was aimed at waking mankind into forestalling this tragedy. In the novel's first chapter he speaks in his own voice:

> And before we judge them [the Martians] too harshly, we must remember what ruthless and utter destruction our own species has wrought, not only upon animals, such as the vanished Bison and the Dodo, but upon its own inferior races. The Tasmanians, in spite of their human likeness, were entirely swept out of existence in a war of extermination waged by European immigrants, in the space of fifty years. Are we such apostles of mercy as to complain if the Martians warred in the same spirit?

Another source of inspiration for Wells' novel was Boston astronomer Percival Lowell's writings about the "canals on Mars." Lowell had mistranslated Italian astronomer Giovanni

---

1. A less common explanation is that the explosion was caused by a mine, set to create a "false flag" incident, that is, to provoke war with Spain.

Schiaparelli's *canali*—lines—for human-constructed "canals," and had written a number of bestselling books that made popular the idea of life on Mars. For Americans and Canadians in 1898, there was a much more dramatic possible inspiration for Wells' story of visitors from another planet. In North American skies from Vancouver and California east to Chicago, and Texas north to Minnesota and Manitoba, from July 1896 to April 1897, thousands of people saw strange, unknown craft that they called "airships." Airships were variously explained as kites, balloons, the planet Venus, the star Sirius, or just plain hoaxes or fakes. Many explained what they saw as ships from an abandoned civilization on Mars. True to form, William Randolph Hearst tried to use the sightings as another means of promoting war between the United States and Spain. "Airship to Bomb Havana" read one Hearst newspaper headline.

The people who saw the mysterious airships also saw and heard the ship's "pilots" and/or passengers. During the first American sighting in Sacramento, several people reported hearing voices from the ship, including one that said: "Well, we ought to reach San Francisco by tomorrow noon." Others heard laughter. Within a week or so, the airships were seen in San Francisco, by even more observers, and on December 2nd, two Italian fishermen offshore from Pacific Grove, watched a craft swoop down and land on the beach. When they saw three occupants emerge and carry their ship into the woods, the fishermen headed into shore to speak with them. One of the aeronauts stopped and argued with the fishermen, and then allowed them to approach. Coming closer, they saw a 60-foot long cigar shaped object with retractable wings. The next night, in Twin Peaks California, a similar craft crashed. Witnesses noticed a foul-smelling gas coming from the structure. A man calling himself "J. D. DeGear" emerged and said that this was the airship's initial flight, and was not connected with any of the other ships sighted.

After a few months quiet, on April Fool's Day in 1897, the airships started to appear again, this time in Kansas City, Missouri. Around 8 PM a powerful searchlight swept the air, the streets, the housetops and bluffs around the town, attracting attention, and the streets were soon filled with people watching the show. For more than an hour it hovered and wobbled, flashing its light beam along the horizon, then finally it lifted off, growing smaller as it climbed swiftly and vanished to the Northwest. Minutes later it was sighted 60 miles away over Everest, Kansas. Thousands of witnesses—including the governor and other officials, professionals, and ordinary citizens—saw the Kansas City airships, and they all agreed that the strange vehicle could make abrupt changes in direction and other skilled maneuvers. At one point it had extinguished its light and hung over the city, then vanished.

Suddenly, it seemed as if the heartland of the nation was under siege by an aerial armada of searchlight-equipped airships. The first week of April saw hundreds of reported sightings in Kansas, Nebraska and Missouri, then the phenomenon spread northeastward to Burlington, Iowa. The airships then turned east through Illinois, appearing in Chicago on April 10. People watched the flickering green and red lights from the top of a downtown skyscraper. On April 14, in Glenboro, Manitoba, among the many airship witnesses was the Honorable James Colebrooke Patterson, Lieutenant-Governor of the province, who had just completed a term as federal Minister of Defense.

Again, there were reports of "close encounters." In Springfield, Missouri, a traveling salesman named William Hopkins was driving his wagon when he suddenly saw an airship on the ground—and two creatures "dressed in nature's garb." Hopkins described to his local newspaper how the odd naked couple had communicated with him telepathically, inviting him into the airship, which then began to rise. Hopkins panicked and jumped off before it got far off of the ground.

Mysterious spacecraft equipped with advanced technology; naked, mind-reading aliens; the smell of fire and brimstone; nonsensical stories; April Fool's Day—all in 1897, nearly fifty years *before* what is regarded as the official beginning of the "UFO era," in 1945, and centuries *after* demons and fairies were meant to exist. The battle with these powers and principalities—demonic denizens of an unseen world—has been going on for millennia, but the 20th century, especially in America, saw the demons, the *jinn*, increasingly make themselves temporarily at home in our world. In 1897 it was only telegraph lines that went haywire when the airships appeared; today, UFO sightings routinely see: cell phones and television sets and computers go dead; car alarms sound; hundreds of electronic door locks in shopping mall parking lots all seize up simultaneously. A few cattle, sheep, and chickens disappeared from Midwest farms in 1897; in recent decades, livestock and domestic pets have been found mutilated in ways that baffle both seasoned ranchers and wildlife biologists, but not exorcists and demonologists. The turn of the century episode saw a few fishermen and farmers who encountered fairly friendly spectral airship pilots. The last half-century has seen millions of Americans claim that when they were lifted aboard spaceships, the occupants performed horrific acts upon them, akin to what prisoners at Abu Ghairab and Guantanamo have suffered at the hands of their captors.

Whether "patriotic" war-mongering incitement by the media, visions of impending total war, or enigmatic aerial visitors, the closing moments of the Kali Yuga were strange and ominous glimpses of the century to come. The Kali Yuga was meant to be followed by the Satya (or Krita) Yuga, the "Yuga (Age or Era) of Truth", during which mankind once again—this time, by his own efforts—speaks with the gods, and hears the gods speak back. As the new age opened, the first gods to speak—these proto-aliens in their speedy, mercurial airships—were fickle, feeble, *faux* gods. At the same time, an easy falsehood, refined to an art by the yellow press, was increasingly characteristic of the modern civic sphere as the Age of Truth dawned.

Thanks to the spread of Theosophical ideas in Europe and America, there was widespread expectation that the "New Age" would see a whole new range of clairvoyance develop among moderns. What had been hidden from view for centuries and millennia would come into view once more. The airship wave was a "coming into view" of long-hidden beings, but rather than an expression of clairvoyance, it was an indication of a new level of materialism. Human thoughts were literally making possible the physical manifestation of non-physical beings.

The episode of media manipulation that accompanied the Spanish-American War seemed to suggest just the reverse. Physical facts, discernible to the critical mind and eye, were being "occulted," or hidden, in increasingly sophisticated ways, using the new technologies of communication. The modern world was becoming an arena of grey magic, of propaganda and lies and mental manipulation unprecedented in human history.

The Karma of Untruthfulness

In his writings and lectures, Rudolf Steiner had often described how the first level of clairvoyance, which he called "Imagination," can be cultivated through meditation, and that this would be the form of clairvoyance that would begin to appear in the 20th century. Often he referred particularly to Goethe as the premier example of someone who had reached this faculty of Imagination, and pointed particularly to Goethe's work on color, anatomy, and the metamorphosis of plants as embodying qualities of living thought which must become more widespread in the modern world.

Steiner warned that if humanity did not cultivate this new faculty, a counter-image of true Imagination would seize hold of the life of human thinking—*fabrication*. More so than at any other point in his career, Steiner in December of 1916 and January of 1917 repeatedly called for clarity of thinking:

> Sharply delineated thoughts are needed, thoughts which are imbued with the will to pursue reality in an objective way. . . . Above all, what is needed are not fleeting thoughts, but a certain quietness of thought. We must work toward achieving this kind of thinking. We must strive unremittingly to force ourselves to think thoughts with clear contours and not wallow in sympathies and antipathies. . . . We must seek for the foundation, the basis, of what we maintain—otherwise we shall never penetrate in the right way into the realm of spiritual science…We must be fully aware of the fact that at the present time every human being who longs for the evolution of the earth to proceed in a healthy way must seek conscientiously and honestly for objectivity of thinking. . . . This is the task of the human soul today.

In the absence of such clear thinking, Steiner warned that a "poison" would develop within the human being. Indeed, the poison was already working, causing "all the sickness of civilization." Steiner was hardly alone in his diagnosis of turn-of-the-century European culture as sick. For decades, cultural critics had been proclaiming the "degeneration" of the modern European, just as Theosophists and Spiritualists were announcing the advent of the New Age of Light. Authors like Max Nordau (*Degeneration*, 1895) and Irving Babbitt (*The New Laokoön*, 1910) saw widespread decadence in their generation's art and literature, and employed the new language of Darwinism to claim that modern humanity was degenerating *biologically*. They drew upon the studies of psychologists for support, citing cases of individuals who experienced various visionary—synaesthesia, eideticism (popularly known as "photographic memory"), hallucinations, etc.—or psychic—precognitive dreams, automatic writing, apparitions of the dying or dead, telepathy—phenomena. In fact, these were the very same phenomena that fin de siécle Romantics interpreted as harbingers of humankind's new clairvoyance for the spiritual world. Visual artists like Wassily Kandinsky, producing the first modern abstract paintings, argued that all future art would represent the spiritual world. Symbolist poets and avant-garde composers like Alexander Scriabin and Arnold Schoenberg also aimed at abstraction, believing it would lead to a spiritual renaissance. All of these artists championed the sensory capacity of "colored hearers"—rare individuals who saw fantastic patterns of bright colors in response to sounds. The more rarefied, anomalous, or eccentric one's sensibilities, the "higher" one's spiritual constitution, according to these thinkers.

Early 20th century scientists, on the other hand, saw all these visionary phenomena as caused by disruptions of the nervous system. "Nervousness" or "neurasthenia" was the characteristic malady of late 19th and early 20th century Western society. Urban, modern life had produced a permanent condition of enfeeblement, and a rash of would-be healers rushed in with remedies, from patent medicines to rest cures to a bewildering variety of "electrical" treatments. Seeing all these ills of modernity out of an "It Spirits" perspective, Rudolf Steiner felt they were symptoms of a "poison" that had been deposited in modern humanity due to its inability to take up the impulse toward Imaginative cognition. "Cultural decadence, emptiness of soul, the states of hypochondria, the eccentricities, the dissatisfactions, the crankiness" were all caused by people refusing to develop etheric clairvoyance. He noted how in the languages of Central Europe, many dialects used their word for "poison" to express anger. In Austria, someone irascible was said to be *gachgiftig*, meaning "quick to grow poisonous."

Rather than merely condemn modernity as decadent and degenerate, Steiner saw this poison—essentially created by excessive "It Matters" thinking—as a necessary stimulus to human spiritual evolution. He likened contemporary culture to Judas; just as Christianity needed Judas's betrayal—the poison of the Scorpion kiss—to unfold the events of Golgotha, modern culture needed the poison of materialism to unfold its higher spiritual possibilities. But this did not mean succumbing to the poison, but *resisting* it, and this meant particularly resisting the fog of lies and propaganda enveloping the West.

A year and a half after World War I had started, Steiner sought particularly to dispel the fog of untruth surrounding the causes of World War I. Before this time, Steiner had said little about the war, as he busied himself with developing practical work in eurythmy, speech, and drama, and with the construction of the Goetheanum. On June 28, 1914, the day of Austrian Archduke Franz Ferdinand's assassination, Steiner was at the Goetheanum, lecturing on "Ways to a New Style of Architecture." As the crisis grew toward war, he lectured on architecture, color, and the relationship between anthroposophy and Christianity. On September 1, 1914, as the catastrophic Battle of Marne was about to begin, Steiner gave his first lecture about the war, "The Destinies of Individuals and of Nations." The unfinished Goetheanum looked down across the Swiss border into Upper Alsace, where it was possible to not only hear but see flashes of cannon fire. Before the lecture, Steiner said a prayer for those on the front, directing it to the guardian angels of the soldiers:

> Spirits of your souls, guardian guides,
> On your wings let there be borne
> The prayer of love from our souls
> To those whom you guard here on earth.
> Thus, united with your might,
> A ray of help our prayer shall be
> For the souls it seeks out there in love.

His remarks continued in this vein, stressing inner solidarity with all involved in the conflict, and the power of prayer to aid those in danger. Over the next year, he opened every lecture by reciting this same mantram, and asking the audience to remember the living and the dead, but he said nothing at all about the details of the war.

1916 saw Europe descend into the bloodiest slaughter ever seen on the continent. In February began the Battle of Verdun, which lasted most of the year and sapped the strength of the French army. In late summer, the Russian army fell back in exhaustion. A British offensive on the Somme on July 1 led to 60,000 British casualties (including nearly 20,000 deaths) on that single day; by September, there had been 620,000 Allied casualties, and 465,000 German.

Lecturing at the Goetheanum on the 20th of December, Steiner received news that the Entente—Great Britain and France—had rejected Germany's peace proposals. The lecture that day stated unequivocally that Germany's initial provocative act—the entering of Belgium on August 1, 1914—would never have taken place if Sir Edward Grey had been honest with Germany, and warned the Kaiser that England would declare war if Belgian sovereignty was violated. Steiner, while never absolving Germany of its share of blame, examined British imperial policy, focusing on the Opium Wars with China, clearly implying that WW I continued Great Britain's aggressive attempt to dominate world trade.

> If you want to judge the yield of the Opium War you must look at it as a whole. Then you will see that what has grown out of those millions—after all, this has been going on for a century—is something which is preparing to rule the world, to overrun the world; this is what may be found in what was won at that time!

More important, however, was the continuation of the present war; Steiner saw clearly and told his audience that America's entry into the war, and the rejection of Germany's peace proposal would bring "the most terrible destiny for the whole of mankind."

On the very day that the peace proposal was rejected, Rasputin, the Russian mystic and advisor to Tsar Nicholas II, was murdered—with the help of the British Secret Service—by Prince Yussopov, who had been initiated into a Freemasonic order in Oxford, England. The secret brotherhoods of Great Britain were the real instigators of the war; Steiner's December 1916/January 1917 lectures, though ranging over a subjects from Sir Thomas More's *Utopia* to Norse mythology to the Opium Wars, continually kept British Freemasonry in their crosshairs. In the very first lecture, Steiner spoke of how these secret brotherhoods had as early as 1890 drawn up maps that showed how Europe would be divided after a world war. He said that Sir Edward Grey was a puppet in the control of these brotherhoods.

A key to the unmasking of these brotherhoods and their aims was to realize that they reckoned with long stretches of time, and that they made extensive use of intermediaries to accomplish their aims. Steiner obliquely but unmistakably stated that the brotherhoods used hypnotism to control the thoughts and actions of key political players. "All he need do is form his sentences in a certain way, use certain expressions, and other means which I shall not describe, and he succeeds in turning the other's mind in the desired direction." They also knew the black magical secret of mass hypnosis; Steiner elaborated the history of the forged "Testament of Peter the Great" as an example. Finally, he showed how the brotherhoods rarely worked from one direction, instead confusing the public and covering their tracks by enlisting the activity of other groups—particularly the Jesuits. "Don't believe that there can be no individuals who are both Jesuit and Freemason," warned Steiner.

In the early years of his work as an esoteric teacher, Steiner had sought—from within German Freemasonic orders—to reform Freemasonry, to rescue it from the dark political interests that had taken it over everywhere in Europe. Long before the outbreak of the war, he abandoned these efforts, and after the war began, he never again said anything positive about Freemasonry. At the heart of the Western brotherhoods, asserted Steiner, was the conviction that the English-speaking peoples—essentially Great Britain and America—were to assume for the Age of the Consciousness Soul the position that Rome held in the previous epoch. This meant that the brotherhoods should do all within their power to assure the disintegration of the "Latin element," and the triumph of Anglo-American culture.

The entire sequence of historical events leading up to and during the war take on new meaning in light of the activity of the occult brotherhoods of the West. "It Matters" historians almost universally explain the event that precipitated World War I—the assassination, on June 28, 1914, in Sarajevo, of Austrian Archduke Franz Ferdinand—as the political act of the Black Hand (their Serbian name, *Ujedeinjenje ili smrt*, literally means "Unification or Death"), a Serbian secret society dedicated to Pan-Slavic union. Scholars today assume that the assassination—like dozens of others in late 19th/early 20th century Europe—was purely an act of terrorism designed to intimidate the Austro-Hungarian Empire, and that the aim of the assassins was the independence of the Slavic peoples of Austro-Hungary. The scholarly debates usually center upon the degree to which the assassin Gavrilo Princip and the Black Hand were tools of the Serbian military intelligence, and whether Serbian ambassadors had warned Austria-Hungary of the impending assassination. All agree that this act was of the gravest consequence for the twentieth century, since it led to World War I, the punitive Treaty of Versailles, and thus Hitler's rise to power and World War II, and ultimately the creation of the US and Soviet Union as the polarized world superpowers.

Steiner knew from both outer reports and his spiritual research that Franz Ferdinand was deeply sympathetic to the desires of the southern European Slavic peoples for independence, and that he intended to bring about a triadic structure in Austro-Hungary which would foster that independence. The British brotherhoods feared this, since their long-term goal of imperial rule was to be accomplished by augmenting Russian power, and diminishing German power. For them, any triad—be it Central Europe between East and West, or a free Slavic confederation independent of both Austro-Hungary and Russia—was a threat to their goal of world economic domination. The world war, by damaging both Germany and the other Central Powers (Austro-Hungary, the Ottoman Empire, and Bulgaria) and Russia, fulfilled their imperial designs. Above all, the Western brotherhoods were intent on creating a map of Europe with a "Danube confederation"—their term for a southern Slav confederation that consisted of the Slavic peoples of the Balkans, Austria, and Romania—independent of Austria, but under the control of Russia.

In his descriptions of the conspiratorial doings of the British lodges, Steiner frequently used the metaphor of the electric spark, or of pushing a button. Without speaking of it directly, he was trying to alert his audiences to the brotherhoods' practice of ceremonial magic, which literally gave them the power to "push a button"—i.e., issue a magical command—and set in motion a chain of events. Someone within a British brotherhood had pushed just such a button to cause Franz Ferdinand's assassination. If one studies the events in Sarajevo that day—the botched plans, ineffective cyanide pills, one assassin's attempt to drown himself in a too-shallow river—it all seems more accident than design. One of seven Black Hand members who lined the route of the Archduke's automobile, Gavrilo Princip had abandoned the plan after one of his co-conspirators threw a hand grenade that blew up the car behind the Archduke's. Princip was in a café eating a sandwich when Franz Ferdinand's car drove by, having taken a wrong turn. When the driver realized his mistake and braked, the car stalled; Princip stepped forward and fired two shots into the car from just five feet away. One bullet pierced Franz Ferdinand's neck; the other entered his wife Sophie's abdomen. Both died within the hour.

The assassin's name holds an uncanny key to the entire affair. "Gavrilo Princip" means "Gabriel Principle," and thus reminds us that in the 354-year period from 1510 to 1879, Europe was under the regency of the Archangel Gabriel, whose impulse had been toward the formation of nations. Since 1879, the new rulership of Michael, nationalism was rightfully destined to wane, to be replaced by new cosmopolitan impulses, new forms of cooperation. The events of June 28, 1914, and all the catastrophic events that followed, showed clearly that the Gabriel Principle lingered on in Europe past its appointed time, with devastating results.

Stop and Smell the Milkweed

This morning I got up at 4 AM to work on this chapter, and around 9:30, as my housemate was leaving for work, she asked me where I was running, and pointed to my leg, which was bouncing up and down under my desk. "Time to take a run, don't you think?" she called as she went out the door. I usually begin my day with a run to Rock Point, a spectacular dolomite cliff above Lake Champlain, but for the last two weeks, anxious to finish this book, I have been skipping these morning runs, thinking it would give me extra time to write.

What a crazy thought! I have just returned from the run that my friend recommended, and I feel totally restored. While I have been inside wrestling with this chapter these last couple of weeks, the milkweed has come into bloom, and the field behind the St. Joseph's Orphanage is filled with migrating monarch butterflies who have stopped to feed on the milkweed blossoms. Think of it. These gossamer creatures, who, only a month ago were laid as tiny eggs on milkweed plants just like these, are now embarking on a 2000-mile journey, to fir forests in Michoacan, Mexico, to spend the winter before coming back north again. Such incredible effort!

The milkweed too is a small miracle, its sweet scent filling this whole meadow. The big globular cluster of blossoms are so heavy that they droop, and the monarchs hang upside down on the individual flowers and stick their long, threadlike tongue down in to sip the nectar. Take a look at these flowers; each is a perfect 5-pointed star, a tiny tracing in pink of the dance of Venus against the Zodiac...

Perhaps you would rather go for a walk on a beach and skip stones, or collect chanterelles or fiddleheads (there's a great spot for this just below Kent and Wilson Halls, on the floodplain of the Saranac River), or pick wild blackberries, or a bouquet of Queen Anne's lace (isn't that purple spot in the center amazing?) These and a thousand other outings are all great; *just don't forget to make some solitary excursion into Nature as often as your busy schedule will allow.* Writing this book, it is just such excursions that have kept me balanced, kept my senses alert, and my spirits high. These are dark chapters, about dark chapters in human history, and we need to apply homeopathic doses of sunshine as a healing tonic as we go.

If I forget to come up for air, and smell the milkweed, don't let that stop you! Just put this book to the side, head for the woods or the meadow, and stay there long enough that whatever massive conspiracy of secret brotherhoods that I have been speaking about (or whatever term paper or exam is coming due) seems like a passing cloud. Bring back a sprig of catnip from the meadow, or a yellow-shafted flicker feather you found in the woods, or a water-polished, thin piece of grey shale from that beach, and place it in this book, to remind you that Nature's wisdom is so magnanimous, so abundant, that even the dullest or most difficult textbook you'll hold in your hands—including this one—is no match for the beauty and intelligence of the milkweed or the monarch.

The Ghost of Kaspar Hauser

On the 6th of November 1917, Rudolf Steiner spoke of another assassination in the dynastic history of Austria-Hungary—the murder of Empress Elisabeth of Bavaria, consort of Austrian Emperor Franz Joseph. Empress "Sissi" was a European celebrity known for her beauty, fashion sense, and her eccentric diet and exercise regimens. While walking along the promenade of Lake Geneva on September 10, 1898, she was stabbed in the heart with a file by a young anarchist named Luigi Lucheni, in an act of "propaganda of the deed," an anarchist principle that saw violent action as an effective form of propaganda for anarchist causes.

At the time of the assassination Steiner was attending a play in Berlin, and during the intermission the news came of the Empress's murder. He had been standing next to a well-known literary critic who expressed his incomprehension for the act; the man's reaction was for Steiner a picture of how nearly everyone attempts to make sense of the world out exclusively of the physical senses, and thus is left baffled.

Sissi's assassination, Steiner explained, was instigated by occult brotherhoods in order to gain illicit spiritual knowledge of future events. In the spiritual world after death, all souls are given detailed pictures of their tasks in their next incarnation, and as part of those pictures, are shown a whole array of future events and situations. Individuals like the Empress were usually shown events of great social and political import, since their succeeding incarnation was often into karmic situations with important consequences for world history. Knowing this, the members of the black brotherhoods carried out assassinations to capture occult secrets for their own ends, employing mediums to make the necessary link to these souls in the spiritual world. In particular, the groups working at the time sought the secret of how to gain extensive control over the masses in Russia, where the next epoch of consciousness evolution was to take place. Steiner said that these same black or "grey" magicians sought through these assassinations knowledge of how to create inoculations that would immunize people against all spiritual ideas; in other words, children would be given shots that caused them to lose any urge toward the spirit.

According to Steiner, this was but one of many such techniques that the occult groups could use to bring about evil on Earth. Though always seemingly reluctant to speak of these things, he stressed that it was necessary for such knowledge to enter the Age of the Consciousness Soul, particularly since, after 1879, a host of adversary Angels had been cast out of the spiritual world into the earthly realm, where they worked to prevent the onset of the new clairvoyance. This was a necessary development that had to be met by humanity. The only way to guard against the influences of these beings was to recognize them. And the only way to keep the black magicians from monopolizing the secret wisdom was for individuals to cultivate the new etheric clairvoyance themselves.

Steiner constantly presented the simplest of exercises to begin on the path the new clairvoyance. He closed this lecture by suggesting that people simply pay closer attention to the incidents in their own lives which they took to be accidents, and examine them for indications of the spiritual forces of destiny playing through them.

Earlier in 1917, Steiner had written a "Memorandum" that outlined his ideas for a threefold ordering of Austrian and German society. Based on the human microcosmic triad of thinking, feeling, and willing, Steiner laid out a schema in which society was an "organism" comprised of three separate domains: the political or rights sphere (thinking); the spiritual-cultural sphere (feeling); and the economic sphere (willing). These ideas had been in the air at the time of the French Revolution, but went unrealized. The Revolution's slogan of "*liberté, égalité, fraternité*" concisely expressed the threefold social ideal of liberty in the spiritual sphere, equality in the rights sphere, and fraternity in the economic sphere. Applying any of these ideas to inappropriate realms led to immediate problems. Equality applied in the realm of thinking would lead to tyranny; think of the "mind control" agenda of totalitarian regimes.

In the rights sphere—the proper sphere of politics—no freedom other than universal suffrage was needed, to ensure a freely elected government. In economic life, humanity needed to cooperate like brothers to produce enough for all. Based on this foundational separation of spheres, Steiner elaborated a set of social and institutional changes in all three spheres. In the economic domain, he proposed replacing joint stock corporations with cooperative associations of producers, distributors, and consumers, thus putting an end to the pervasive power and influence of financiers and banks, and eliminating the need of state support or special privilege for individual sectors of the economy. The state, losing many of its traditional functions, would be reduced in power and authority, keeping its important task of maintaining and enforcing the rights of all citizens. Even with its highest promise of eliminating the causes of war, it is easy to see why politicians and bureaucrats sustained by the existing order would feel threatened by Steiner's proposal.

The Threefold Commonwealth initiative led by Rudolf Steiner was another deed to extend and redeem the impulses that were to have been brought by Kaspar Hauser to the Baden region, and then to all of Germany. Again, Steiner's task was enormously more difficult, given the spiritual vacuum that had been created by Kaspar Hauser's murder. Incredibly, Steiner's initiative depended for its success on the individual who had in a sense taken Kaspar's place. Through a friend, Steiner had managed to place his Memorandum into the hands of Prince Max of Baden, whose grandfather Leopold had ascended to the throne in 1830, during Kaspar's lifetime. Leopold's mother was the Countess von Hochberg, who had helped orchestrate the crime against Kaspar Hauser, in order to see her son gain the throne. The wise angels of history had made it possible for a descendant of Kaspar's enemies to make amends for the crime committed by his family. Though his acceptance and implementation of Steiner's Threefold Commonwealth, Prince Max would not only redeem the family's misdeed, but he would perform a karma-healing deed for the German folk and their destiny, which had been so derailed by the crime against Kaspar Hauser.

Prince Max actually knew of Kaspar Hauser's true identity, regarded him as the legitimate heir to the throne, and had even promised to bury the remains of Kaspar Hauser in the ducal tomb in Pforzheim as soon as he succeeded to the throne of Baden. Knowing of this, Rudolf Steiner was hopeful when, on the 20th of January, 1918, he met with Prince Max in Karlsruhe. Their conversation focused on the logistics of implementing the Threefold Social Order in Germany, but Prince Max also asked Steiner to give him a larger picture of the destinies of the other European nations; Steiner responded by sending to the Prince an annotated lecture cycle he had given in 1910 in Oslo, in which he explained how each nation was guided from the spiritual world by an archangel, the "folk spirit" of that nation. Much of Steiner's work through the war years had been directed at alerting Germany to their true mission, and in doing so he was building a bridge to the folk spirit.

Steiner met with Prince Max later in Berlin; by this time, it was clear that the Prince was the only possible candidate to become Chancellor, and Steiner, who foresaw the tremendous upheaval that would seize Germany if the Threefold Commonwealth were not brought into being. Steiner expected that as Imperial Chancellor, Max would proclaim the Threefold Commonwealth in his inaugural address to the German people, in so doing altering the nation's path away from war toward peace. Lecturing on the inaugural day, October 3, 1918, Steiner anxiously asked for a copy of the newspaper, and found that the new Chancellor had instead indicated that he subscribed to the ideas of American President Woodrow Wilson. Two days later, Chancellor von Baden announced his acceptance of Wilson's "Fourteen Points," which became the basis for the terms of the German surrender, as negotiated at the Paris Peace Conference in 1919 and formalized in the Treaty of Versailles.

On November 9, the Chancellor proclaimed the abdication of the Kaiser and thus the end of the monarchy. He resigned the following day. Eleven years to the day later, Max von Baden died, never having carried out his promise to bring Kaspar Hauser's body to its rightful royal resting place at Pforzheim. Thus he once again failed to fulfill a karmic obligation to the wronged "Child of Europe." In Germany the 9th of November is known as "Schicksalstag," which means "day of fate." Along with this crucial 1929 event, the 9th of November has been a significant date for Germany on other occasions: Adolf Hitler attempted his Munich putsch on 9th November

1923; *Kristallnacht*, the Nazis' attacks against the Jews took place on 9th November 1938; and the Berlin Wall came down on 9th November 1989. (Previous to 1929, the date had also seen in 1848 the execution of liberal leader Robert Blum, which was widely seen as the symbolic event for the ultimate failure of the Revolutions of 1848 in the German states).

The Beast of Bolshevism

So many rhythms! Remember how your head hurt way back at the beginning of the course, with that "Why 1414?" lecture, and the crazy story of the 25,920-year wobble of the Earth's axis? So many rhythms have followed that one, that you have likely lost track of them all. Why not take a moment and plot out below just two sets of rhythms—the 33-year rhythm from Kaspar Hauser's birth (1812) and death (1833), and the law of mirroring, with 1879 as the center point?

I will leave out all but the initial dates, so that you can surprise yourself by seeing how many you come up with. Plot the dates, and then draw arcs (for the 33-year rhythm on the first line) and straight lines (for the mirroring law timeline).

1833

1800   1812

The 33-year rhythms issuing from Kaspar Hauser's birth and death

----

1879

The Mirroring Rule in History: 1879 as Focal Point

For this second timeline, I'll give you a starting example:

1841

1879   1917

Remember that 1841 is the year that the Dragon began to battle the Archangel Michael in the spiritual world, 38 years before the beginning of Michael's regency began in the fall of 1879, at which time the Ahrimanic spirits were cast down to the earth. A spiritual event as momentous as the beginning of that battle would be mirrored on the physical plane in a significant way. The catastrophic events in Germany in 1917—and the effort by Rudolf Steiner to forestall them—would seem by themselves to fulfill the mirroring rule. But there is another, even more sobering, world historical event of 1917 that clearly has its origin in the Dragon's attack of 1841.

On November 7, 1917—the day after Steiner's lecture about the assassination of Empress Sissi and the brotherhoods' black magical theft of secrets about humanity's future destiny—Bolshevik leader Vladimir Lenin led leftist revolutionaries against Russia's provisional government, replacing it with *soviets*, local councils elected by workers and peasants. Even before the Bolsheviks came to power, Steiner had warned of the dangers this posed to the world. Steiner recognized that Karl Marx, by birth and education a Central European, had, in going to England (he wrote the *Communist Manifesto* in London), immersed himself in the one-sided form of the Consciousness Soul, that was directed solely to the "It Matters" view—the life of the physical senses. Steiner's many years of educational activity at the school for industrial workers in Berlin was his attempt to create a spiritual alternative to the Marxist vision of the proletariat.

As with the events of World War I, Steiner saw far beyond the outer political and social dimension of the Bolshevik Revolution to its demonic underpinnings. The "dictatorship of the proletariat" was a polite euphemism for the eruption of the deepest form of evil on to the plane of history, in an unprecedented way. In all of his years of exposing the machinations of the British brotherhoods, Steiner had identified the motivation—the crushing of Central Europe—for those brotherhoods' black magical manipulation of European politics, but he had said little about the ultimate source and "benefactor" of the simultaneous destruction of Central Europe and domination of the Slavic peoples by what was essentially British materialism.

Steiner knew that the Russian Revolution was ultimately an attack not by the British brotherhoods on the Age of the Consciousness Soul, but *an attack by the Earth's greatest adversary upon the whole of humanity.* "If things were to turn out the way they are developing in Russia at present," said Steiner in August 1919, "it would mean that the Earth would lose its task, would have its mission withdrawn, would be expelled from the universe and fall prey to Ahriman." These words of Steiner suggest that some being other than Ahriman was at work through Bolshevism. Steiner stated without hesitation that Lenin, Trotsky, and other Bolsheviks were "instruments of Ahrimanic powers," but he said that Bolshevism was actually a form of demonic initiation that "belonged to another world sphere from our own [with] the power to destroy everything on Earth that has arisen by way of human civilization." At first he merely hinted at the source of this initiation, but the events following the 1917 Bolshevik Revolution continued to draw forth more damning revelations. In 1908, he had revealed that in the 7th century AD a mighty spiritual being—the "Beast" of John's *Apocalypse*, i.e., Sorath, the "Sun Demon"—had around AD 666 entered the stream of Earth evolution through inspiring a small group of people (perhaps only a couple of hundred) connected to the Academy of Gondhi Shapur in the region that would become Baghdad. Through this great scholarly academy, Sorath sought to artificially "inoculate" 7th century humanity with certain powers of the Consciousness Soul, eight centuries before these powers should rightfully appear. Rudolf Steiner brought for the first time before the public the mystery knowledge of the name Sorath, which is composed from the Hebrew letters *samech—vau—resh—tau.* These letters have number equivalents: *samech* (60) + *vau* (6) + *resh* (200) + *tau* (400) = 666.

Sorath's second appearance was, in keeping with the "Number of the Beast," 666 years later, in AD 1332, when the Order of the Knights Templar was destroyed under Sorath's influence. The Templars' mission was to establish a Christian social order in Europe, and to help in this task, they were given knowledge of the spiritual powers of gold. The Knights were individually poor, but their gold and their growing political influence and moral authority around opposition by the French King Philip IV ("Philip the Fair"—called *le Bel* for his fair appearance, his cruelty earned him less flattering nicknames) in alliance with Roman Pope Clement V. Tortured by the Inquisition, the Templar Knights made false confessions that provided the official sanction for Philip and Clement to slaughter the Knights. Sorath's demonic influence upon these events was another devastating setback for the Grail.[1]

In the Grail legend, the Castle of the Grail at Monsalvaesche is opposed by another Castle— the *Château Merveil,* the home of Klingsor, the evil knight whose lance has wounded the Grail King Amfortas. Amfortas, the representative of the Intellectual Soul, is wounded by Klingsor, the bearer—like Lenin and the Bolsheviks—of an Ahrimanized, animalized Consciousness Soul. The wound keeps Amfortas from sustaining the life of his father Titurel, the representative of the Sentient Soul and ancestor of the guardians of the Holy Grail directly from the spiritual world, that is, from the Angels.

The *Parzival* tale gives a picture of humanity at the crossroads, where *all* peoples on earth— from the Sentient Soul traditional cultures of Africa, the Americas, and Asia to the Intellectual Soul peoples of Europe and Russia—can only survive by the mediation of a higher member of the human soul, the Consciousness Soul, embodied in the figure of Parzival. Only Parzival can overcome the power of Klingsor, the demonized Consciousness Soul, and thus bring healing to Amfortas and salvation to Titurel.

The Triumph of the Will

Just ten days after Max von Baden was named German Chancellor, and failed to redeem Kaspar Hauser's mission, Kaspar Hauser's black counterpart, Adolf Hitler, began his mission. On that night, Hitler suffered mustard gas poisoning at the Western Front, at Ypres. On the brink of death, and blinded for several weeks, this poisoning brought about a sinister change in Hitler, which made him the willing tool of an evil spiritual being. The identity of that being is hinted at

---

1. The story of the Templar "heresies" can only be understood from an esoteric, "It Spirits" perspective. In the Templar initiation, candidates had to undergo severe trials at the threshold of the spiritual world, where certain experiences could manifest as either grandly edifying, or terrifying, since each candidate was at that moment seized by his own darker side—his Double. Under the intense pain of torture, the Templars came to believe that they had committed the actions which they had overcome in their initiation trials. This was due to the influence of Sorath. From this episode of the Templar torture there is much to be learned about the recent condoning and encouragement of torture by the Bush administration.

by Hitler's thoughts (from *Mein Kampf*) during this period: "hate grew in me during these nights…" Hate is a powerful form of diminished consciousness, and whenever human consciousness is lowered, demonic spiritual beings are permitted entry into the human soul. Hate —which would become above all the central principle of National Socialism—allowed the Sun Demon to enter the body of Adolf Hitler.

What looked out into the world from Adolf Hitler's eyes from that night forward was the greatest embodiment of hate in the Cosmos, *Sorath*. On the same night as Hitler's near-death experience, Rudolf Steiner spoke of the Beast, by way of speaking of the Academy of Gondhi Shapur, and its master, an unnamed individual who "was the greatest opponent of Christ Jesus." In identifying this seventh century individual who provided a vessel for Sorath to inhabit, Steiner was bearing silent witness to the Sun Demon's return to the physical plane, at the very moment that the Beast took hold of another vessel, via the diminished consciousness of Adolf Hitler.

It is an occult law that a demon comes to power when the genius at the destined hour fails to take hold of his task in freedom. This law can alert us to just how astonishing were the deeds of Rudolf Steiner (and explain why I am spending such a great amount of time following his biography). At every single moment, given the magnitude of his tasks, Ahriman (and behind him Sorath) lurked close by, waiting for an opportunity to use Rudolf Steiner's great spiritual powers to their advantage. You may think it rather odd that I have highlighted Steiner's lecturing activity; how, given the grave events unfolding for the world between 1914 and 1918, can I justify such a detailed examination of one man's lectures? During every lecture, Rudolf Steiner was simultaneously doing battle with hosts of demons who constantly attacked him. One of Steiner's most radical teachings was that *every thought is a deed*; by bringing forth Sun-filled Grail thoughts at nearly every moment, Steiner was under continual attack by the Ahrimanic beings, the most destructive opponents of the Grail.

At the beginning of the course, we considered the great difference between today and a century ago in how Genghis Khan has gone from being seen by historians as the scourge of the Earth, to virtual silence about his deeds. Historians today are often timid about pronouncing moral judgments upon individuals or events. The greatest villains of history, like Hitler, continue to receive moral scrutiny, but no academic historians are writing books saying that Hitler was possessed by a demon. How can I do so?

For support, I turn once again to Rudolf Steiner, who revealed that a human being's physical body and soul-spirit can take separate paths of evolution, that is, an individual soul who is good may come to exist in a body that is destined for evil. At the time of the mustard gas attack, Hitler's astral body and ego separated from his physical and etheric bodies; at that moment, Sorath was able to enter the physical/etheric body that had previously been "home" to the individuality we know as Adolf Hitler. This split itself is a consequence of karma; it will be the task of future spiritually informed researchers to discover why this development occurred in Hitler. But one can even now examine the historical record of Hitler's earthly thoughts and deeds to track the presence of the Sun Demon within his body. The most common "magical" characteristic pointed out by historians is Hitler's spellbinding oratory. Dr. Karl Alexander von Mueller, a professor of modern history and political science at the University of Munich, an eyewitness to Hitler's Munich Beer Hall speech in 1923, said: "I cannot remember in my entire life such a change in the attitude of a crowd in a few minutes, almost a few seconds…Hitler had turned them inside out, as one turns a glove inside out, with a few sentences. It had almost something of hocus-pocus, or magic about it." Without realizing it, Mueller and the many others who have commented upon Hitler's "spell" fail to realize that within him were true powers of black magic.

Hatred is always a black magical force, since it feeds Sorath. In *Mein Kampf*, Hitler describes his reaction to the news of Germany's surrender: "Only fools—or liars and criminals—could hope for mercy from the enemy. Hate grew in me during those nights, hate against the perpetrators of this deed." With the assistance of General Erich Ludendorff, Hitler promulgated the *Dolchstoßlegende*, the "stab-in-the-back" social myth that attributed Germany's defeat to public failure to respond to its "patriotic calling." Ludendorff became Hitler's first political backer, and together they organized the Munich putsch of November 9, 1923, the failed coup d'état that sent Hitler to prison.

Mein Kampf ("My Struggle"), the Hitler's autobiography and political manifesto, is a lesson in hatred, and how hatred and lying feed each other. As the hatred within Hitler grows, he discovers new powers. As an Education officer shortly after his release from the hospital, he is stunned to find that he can lecture: "Many hundreds, rather thousands, of comrades have been led back to their country and Fatherland through my lecturing." Next, Hitler discovers his "electrical" effect: "After thirty minutes the people were electrified." This is the telltale of Ahriman, who lives in the electrical forces of Nature, including the human Double. Hitler's observation already alerts us to the fact that Sorath operates through the human will; in this "electrical" effect" there is essentially an eclipse of the will of both speaker and listener, allowing a demonic will to be exerted. By the 24th of February 1920, when Hitler first presented his National Socialist program, Sorath's will could radiate out to large numbers of people, and was in turn "fed" by the mass hypnosis affected. Hitler describes what took place at the Festival Hall of the Court Brewery in Munich that day: "When I finally put the twenty-five theses point by point to the mass of people and asked them to give their verdict about them, they were accepted one after another amid ever growing jubilation, unanimously again and again unanimously, and by the time the last thesis had found its way into the heart of the crowd, a room full of people stood before me bound together by a new conviction, a new belief, by a new will."

The Age of the Consciousness Soul is the age of the individual, free consciousness. In Hitler, the individual is erased, and the "mass," bound together by an electrical effect (thus the *fasces*, the tightly bound bundle of sticks, an ancient symbol of the Roman Empire, takes on new meaning under Nazism), dominates all. In Hitler, both Lucifer and Ahriman have free reign— the mad frenzy and blood lust are the mark of Lucifer; the calculated, mechanical working of the Nazi bureaucracy, which reaches its demonic apotheosis in the death camps, is the signature of Ahriman. The working together of these polar opposites within one individual and his ideology lays it open to the unearthly power of Sorath.

Hidden within the Sun Demon's Hebrew name is coded the plan of Sorath's attack upon the human being. *Samech* expresses the principle of the physical body; *vau* the etheric; *resh* the astral body; *tau* is the lower "I" that has not yet been raised to the higher "I." 666, as a numerical coding of these four principles, symbolizes the human being who denies and destroys his true inner nature. Knowing that the Sun Demon actually dwelled within Adolf Hitler, we can make sense of how it was that Hitler chose the swastika as the symbol for Nazism. In ancient cultures all around the world, the swastika (a Sanskrit word meaning "favored" or "good") symbolized the Sun, its fourfold limbs reaching out to simultaneously express life, movement, and all the forces of health and wholeness in the Universe. As the Sun Demon's symbol, the swastika expressed all of the counter-forces that were Nazism's hallmarks—death, destruction, chaos.

The theft of higher spiritual images, processes, and principles is the most characteristic gesture of the Sun Demon. Having no creative powers of his own, the Sun Demon relentlessly copies and corrupts those of the Sun Spirit, Christ. Hitler was 30 years old when Sorath took possession of his body; Jesus was 30 when the Christ being descended into Him at the baptism in the River Jordan. Hitler/Sorath lived for 26½ years; during the present Age of the Consciousness Soul, 26 to 27 years is the period that the physical body lends its forces to support soul-spiritual development. After age 27, spiritual progress can only be made through one's own inner impulses. In Hitler's body, Sorath created a caricature of this, imbuing the body—and the outer world—with hostility to the spirit. The night of October 13, 1918 was the "birth" of this antihuman demon.

Even Hitler's death can be seen as a caricature or inversion of the Grail principles. The Grail forces increase in the world through human deeds of sacrifice, whose archetype is the sacrifice on Golgotha by Christ. Hitler's suicide in the *Führerbunker*, the shelter beneath the Reich Chancellery in Berlin, came just one day after Hitler heard of the execution of Benito Mussolini, and was above all a cowardly escape from being captured. His final orders were for the arrest and execution of officers—including Heinrich Himmler and Hermann Göring—whom he heard were conducting surrender negotiations.

As history's highest Grail Knight, Rudolf Steiner, like Kaspar Hauser, was Sorath's sworn enemy after death, as well as in life. There is nothing coincidental about Hitler's refounding (after his release from jail) of the National Socialist German Workers' Party (NSDAP) in Munich on February 27, 1925; this was Rudolf Steiner's last birthday, and Munich is where Steiner had originally intended to build the "Johannes Building," which later became the Goetheanum. February 27th in 1933 was the day that Hitler chose for the burning of the Reichstag, the criminal act that gave him the excuse to issue the Enabling Act and seize total control of the German state.[1]

Knowing of Sorath's activity in history around the years AD 666 and AD 1332, perhaps you have already anticipated the third occurrence of this rhythm in 1998.[2] In 1998, you were likely in

---

1. Just as Rudolf Steiner—like Christ—frequently acted in harmony with cosmic configurations of the planets against the stars, Adolf Hitler/Sorath chose certain cosmic configurations as impulses to support evil deeds. More than just the calendar date needs to be considered. A great historical research project in the future—and a great deed for humanity—will be to map the cosmic background to Rudolf Steiner's many grail deeds, and to understand them against the events of Sorath's activity. A beginning in this direction has been made by Robert Powell; see his *Hermetic Astrology*.

2. Note that all three of these dates should not be seen as exact, but as approximate markers. In each case, Sorath's activity stretches to the decades before and after.

2nd or 3rd grade, and you certainly have no memory of any Beast raging outside your bedroom or in your backyard. Ask your parents; they surely didn't see the Beast either. In 666 and 1332, only a small handful of individuals were aware of the Sun Demon's activity, and our time is no different. *The Beast acts freely in the world through the deeds and thoughts of human beings.*

The study of history can put us on the Beast's trail. We have identified the two previous episodes—in the 7th and 14th centuries—of Sorath's activity, and these can be found as "echoes" in the 20th century. There is a universally known esoteric law that every time evolution prepares to rise to a higher stage, the previous stages repeat in metamorphosed form. Again, we find that the Sun Demon is compelled to follow this same law, for Bolshevism is the metamorphosed form of the Academy of Gondhi Shapur, Nazism the metamorphosis of Philip IV and Clement V's activity in the 14th century. In the 7th century, most human beings were at the stage of the Sentient Soul. Only a small number of educated people in Europe and Asia could read, write, or even think in a manner that would be familiar to us today. They were at the level of the Intellectual Soul. Into this situation, Sorath worked to inspire through Gondhi Shapur a demonized Consciousness Soul impulse, which would have acted like a poison.

This is exactly what Bolshevism brought upon Russia! The majority of Russians were still at the level of the Sentient Soul, untouched by European civilization. The Intellectual Soul was present in a small number of educated members of the aristocracy, and the Consciousness Soul was all but absent altogether. With the Bolshevik Revolution of 1917, the Sun Demon burst into history, attempting to tear Russia away from its task in the next cultural epoch. If one looks at Russia today, where a native mafia controls much of the economic life, and Bolshevism, Communism, and Fascism still hold sway in the rights sphere, it is clear that the Consciousness Soul was never permitted its proper period of development, and a premature, demonic substitute settled in instead.

Similarly, there are a host of ways in which one can see the mark of the 14th century Sorath-inspired events in the history of National Socialism. The Templars' mission centered upon the conquest for all the Christian world of the Holy Land, particularly Jerusalem, as the site of the Mystery of Golgotha. Within the Order there was the understanding that since Christ's resurrection, the Earth was His cosmic body, and so the whole Earth should be consecrated to Him. In Templar ritual, each Knight consecrated his blood to Christ; he vowed to sacrifice every drop of his blood to help manifest the Grail upon the Earth. In Nazi ideology, these high ideals were twisted into the demonic cry of *"Blut und Boden,"* ("Blood and Soil"), the foundation of Nazi racialism. The obsession of some Nazis with the Holy Grail, the Spear of Destiny, and other medieval Christian relics can be seen as a further recapitulation—in demonized form—of the Templars' quest.

While the Grail impulse through human history can be seen to progressively elevate human thinking, feeling, and willing, the anti-Grail impulse of the Sun Demon can be seen as a three-fold *attack* on these same aspects of man. Sorath's activity in the 7th century explicitly sought to demonize human *thinking*; the 14th century destruction of the Templars was an attack on human *feeling*; both Bolshevism and Nazism were demonic onslaughts against the human *will*.

That Old Mirror Trick

In the house in which I grew up, there was a tiny bathroom right next to the back door, just big enough that one could stand between the toilet and a small porcelain sink. It was my father's bathroom, where every morning he would shave, aided by a big medicine cabinet mirror over the sink. Perhaps his paternal presence gave us the sense that this bathroom was not to be used except in an emergency, so no one else in the family ever used it. One day when I was quite young—for I recall that I needed to step up on the toilet to see myself—I discovered that if I opened the medicine cabinet door slightly, its surface caught the reflected image of itself from a little mirror on the opposite wall, and at once threw me into a delicious state of vertigo, as my face was multiplied infinitely into the receding space. For years, I used to occasionally slip into that bathroom and close the door, then slowly swing the mirror and myself into Eternity.

I still like to think back on that mirror trick from time to time. I'm thinking about it right now, trying as best I can to imagine what it must be like for you to be reading this chapter. *What a lot I have asked from you, to lay before you this tale of the Sun Demon's appearance in the 20ᵗʰ century!* It's like I made you stand in front of that mirror, and then cast you into Eternity without ever asking your permission. Or maybe it's more like the time my friend put me on a * line and pushed me straight towards a huge white pine tree, without telling me anything about what he was doing. I was zooming along, ten feet above the ground, so I couldn't jump, and there was that tree coming right at me. The moment before I hit it, the pulley reached a big spring that sent me bouncing back, while my friend doubled over in laughter below.

This of course is not what I have intended for you at all. From the beginning of the semester and of this book, I have introduced you to one outrageous, outlandish story after another, and I am confident that except for those of you who have long ago written off this entire course as a loss, you have learned how to take these tales in stride. I can be confident that if I set you zooming down that * or tossed you out into that sea of mirror reflections, you wouldn't fall or sink.

You have been incredibly patient, taking in these stories. Perhaps the reason that you have been able to do it is just this—you've considered the history within these covers to be "just stories." But if one stands before these stories, and turns one's head at just the right angle, they begin to cascade forward and back just the way my mirrored face fell into Future and Past. And in this moment perhaps you too have caught a glimpse of some Eternal image that can and will speak to every age, every place, every human heart, if only that heart is open to receive its message. If this book, and the knowledge upon which it stands, is *true*, and you accept it as true, it means that your life won't be the same after this course.

That is my intention every time that I step into a classroom, and it is my intention on every page of this Book of Wonders. The stories here are meant to *change your thinking, feeling, and willing, and thus, to change your life.* Though trained as an intellectual historian, used to tracing the leisurely lemniscate of unfolding knowledge down through the centuries, my grasp of the Past is shallow. My mastery of empirical knowledge is constrained to an incredibly narrow slice of Time, but something in my training has given me a reliable sense of certainty for knowing just when I am standing in the face of Eternal Truth. There is a shudder that passes down from my crown to the soles of my feet, leaving me feeling as if a bolt of lightning has just struck. Believe it or not, most of the stories here, when I first heard them, I was skeptical, resistant. But eventually, I had that lightning feeling. I have come to realize that the hours spent in front of that mirror were a kind of training for this encounter with the pictures that I'm trying to give you in this course.

We're in the twentieth century now (in our course of study), and one of the hallmarks of that century is *acceleration*. The Wright Brothers get airborne just a few years after 1900, and off the century goes, with an appetite for speed and the technological know-how to realize it. Every single transportation and communication (which is essentially the transport of messages, and so was equally in a dead heat against the constraints of Time) innovation left some folks slack-jawed and senseless, yearning for the old rhythms. Of course social change followed the same up tempo course, and demanded even more of each generation of adults, as their children passed them by as if they were standing still. Bob Dylan put it best: "Your old road is rapidly agin'/ Please get out of the new one if you can't lend your hand/For the times they are a-changin.'"

The times they aren't enough changin' for me, in that instead of a culture in sync with the higher potentials of the Consciousness Soul, we are largely mired down in its beginnings, or slipping backwards even in this 21ˢᵗ century toward old patterns of the Sentient Soul and Intellectual Soul. Just think of this university, or of your entire schooling! And of course, the discipline of history is stuck in "It Matters" thinking of a century ago, with no new ideas, no new stories, and no new potentials to offer to your generation. That stinks if you ask me. I've stopped to tell you that mirror story because things are about to get even crazier, *faster*. Hang on.

The Resurrection Rhythm

So far I have presented Bolshevism and National Socialism as caused by rippling rhythms from *prior* events—of the 7ᵗʰ and 14ᵗʰ century. But a more critical cause for these developments in world history of the first two decades of the 19ᵗʰ century actually lay in the future. Indeed, this event could be seen as the cause of the key events of the 19ᵗʰ century too—from Kaspar Hauser's birth, to Rudolf Steiner's birth and mission, to the casting down of the Ahrimanic spirits in 1879. In October 1910, Steiner chose Karlsruhe to speak about this event; clearly he did so as a way of paying homage to Kaspar Hauser.

Reminding his audience that during the time of Christ's incarnation, only a small handful of people were aware of Christ's existence, he asked: "Might it not then also be possible today that something of infinite importance is taking place and that human beings are not taking it into their consciousness?" Steiner went on to say that since the end of the Kali Yuga in 1899, humanity would increasingly gain the ability to perceive the etheric world, and thus, to have the "Damascus experience" of St. Paul, that is, *to see Christ in the etheric realm*. Like Paul, people would become "eye-witnesses" of Christ, making documentary evidence superfluous, or at least supplementary. Steiner's clairvoyance was such that he could already perceive Christ's approach toward Earth's etheric; as the "John the Baptist" of the Etheric Christ, Steiner was alerting humanity to the possibility that they too could experience this event.

At the same time, Steiner warned that the materialist mind would expect an actual *physical* return of Christ instead of this etheric return, and that certain individuals would claim to be the reincarnated Christ. Then he pointed particularly to the timing of the new etheric clairvoyance:

The first signs of these new soul faculties will begin to appear relatively soon now in isolated souls. They will become more clear in the middle of the fourth decade of this century, sometime between 1930 and 1940. The years 1933, 1935, and 1937 will be especially significant. Faculties that now are quite unusual for human beings will then manifest themselves as natural abilities. At this time great changes will take place, and Biblical prophecies will be fulfilled. Everything will be transformed for the souls who are sojourning on earth and also for those who are no longer within the physical body. Regardless of where they are, souls are encountering entirely new faculties. Everything is changing, but the most significant event of our time is a deep, decisive transformation in the soul faculties of man.

"If humanity overlooked these events, it would be a great misfortune," Steiner added. "If no understanding is developed, if this particular faculty is stamped out, if those who speak about faculties of this kind are put away as if they were insane, disaster is inevitable, and humanity will sink into the morass of materialism."

This is the only time that Rudolf Steiner identified the year 1933 as the specific date of Christ's return in the etheric, but on one other occasion, in 1919, he mentioned the year 1933: "Before the etheric Christ will be able to be rightly understood, mankind will have to cope with the Beast who will rise from the abyss in 1933." By 1919, Steiner knew that Sorath would seek to distract humanity from the twentieth century's most important event—Christ's reappearance in the etheric realm.

On January 30, 1933, Adolf Hitler became Reichschancellor, and the world, instead of receiving the Sun Spirit into the etheric realm of the Earth, received the Sun Demon. Instead of hailing Christ, the German people shouted "*Heil Hitler!*" Instead of a gesture of "Thy will be done" spreading across the planet, there was Hitler's clenched, right-fisted command of "My will be done." The new age of etheric clairvoyance would have to wait, as the world descended into a twelve-year reign of chaos and terror. Those few individuals who were gifted with the new organs of etheric clairvoyance were overwhelmed by the events precipitated by Hitler/Sorath. The dark spiritual powers fully succeeded in creating a counter-image on Earth of what was meant to be an etheric event. The German people, their consciousness dimmed by their own materialism, and taken hold of by "*Der Führer*," gave up their own wills to the demonic will. Every sporting event, parade, festival, and political rally became a mass hypnotic orgy designed to further fog the consciousness of the leading people of the Consciousness Soul era. The failure of Kaspar Hauser's mission now seemed complete; the effect of Adolf Hitler upon Europe and upon the entire world was as destructive as the blessing would have been that the Child of Europe was meant to have brought.

Kaspar Hauser's death in 1833 had been a Grail deed, a free act of sacrifice that helped to bring about the return of Christ in the etheric, *3 x 33 years later*. The element of freedom in these deeds—both Kaspar Hauser's and Christ's—comes from their existing outside earthly authority. Lacking this authority, their significance can only be found by an individual spiritual search. The same is true for the etheric clairvoyance necessary to establish a link with the Sun Spirit; no Reichschancellor or President or King compels it, and so only a few find their way toward it. Thanks to Rudolf Steiner's efforts, the spiritual event of the 20th century—Christ's etheric return—was available to all, and did not have to pass by unnoticed. Like Christ, Steiner performed mystery deeds in public. In Christ's case, the Pharisees and Sadducees put Christ to death for openly presenting the Mysteries; Steiner was attacked by the black brotherhoods for doing the same. (And Kaspar Hauser was killed because of the fear that he would also reveal the Mysteries). All of these sacrificial deeds were executed so that the power of one person over another would come to an end.

But the principle of earthly power has not come to an end; indeed, it has only grown more dominant since 1933. This does not negate the truth of these deeds, all of which are the bearer of *resurrection forces*, made available by the event of Christ's return in 1933, and originally created by his sacrificial death in AD 33. Kaspar's biography shows him to have been the bearer of resurrection forces. We confronted the mystery of Kaspar's having lived for the many years of his imprisonment upon just bread and water, but it was left a mystery. *Kaspar Hauser survived those dozen years without food because he was nourished by the 'Body of Christ.'* His superhuman sensory abilities too can be seen as characteristic of the resurrection body. Even the wounds—to the heart, stomach, diaphragm and lungs—which Kaspar suffered on 14 December 1833 were partially overcome by the resurrection forces within him. After the stabbing, Kaspar walked back to the treacherous tutor Meyer's house, and lived for another three days. Resurrection forces sustained Rudolf Steiner for the three years after the burning of the Goetheanum.

From the beginning of the course, I have maintained that an "It Matters" view of history and life is outmoded; from the events of the early 20th century, we can see how it is also dangerous and deadly. The fact of the Resurrection, and of the historical examples of the working of the resurrection forces, is by itself a refutation of the "It Matters" view. For Sorath, Ahriman, and for those who do their bidding here on earth, nothing frightens them like the Resurrection and its echoes through time. This they fight at all costs. And even the Resurrection, the very transubstantiation of matter, they must corrupt and invert as their sole means of resisting the knowledge of its power becoming available to humanity in the Age of the Consciousness Soul.

In October 1911 at Karlsruhe, Steiner had announced the coming of the etheric Christ *and the secret working of the resurrection forces into history, in the form of the 33-year rhythm.* 33 years later, on July 16, 1945, the Sun Demon grinned as humanity brought forth the counter image of the Resurrection, at the "Trinity" site in the desert near Las Cruces, New Mexico.[1] The place had reminded the early Spanish travelers of Golgotha, for they christened the route *"Jornada del Muerto"*—journey to death—for the bleached bones and skulls that lined it. Watching the first

---

1. "Trinity" was the top-secret code name for the test site of the United States Army's atomic bomb development project—the "Manhattan Project"—at the Los Alamos Laboratory. The name is attributed to Manhattan Project director J. Robert Oppenheimer, who was fond of a John Donne sonnet that began: "Batter my heart, three person'd God."

atomic bomb explosion in history, Oppenheimer quoted the *Bhagavad Gita*: "I am become Death, the destroyer of worlds." Not only had World War II obliterated the recognition by humanity of Christ's etheric return, but with the atomic bomb, humanity had created a power of destruction equal to the Sun Spirit's power of creation.

The nuclear fission reaction that creates an atomic explosion is fundamentally the *turning of matter into light*. In its proper sphere, on the Sun, this transubstantiation process radiates down to Earth its life-giving power, where green plants then perform in each of their leaves the opposite process, turning light into matter. One of Rudolf Steiner's most mysterious teachings, known within the secret orders for centuries, but hitherto veiled to the wider world, was that the ultimate goal of humanity was to *turn the Earth into a Sun*. This far off deed of humanity, based on the slow, lawful progress of human soul-spiritual evolution, was in a sense pre-empted on that day in July 1945, when the artificial sun was created in the New Mexico desert. Within a month from the test, the "Little Boy" and "Fat Man" bombs would burst over Hiroshima and Nagasaki, ending World War II, but beginning a reign of fear unprecedented in human history.

The explosion of the atomic bomb revealed the Sun Demon's end game, the ultimate aim of the 12-year reign of terror between 1933 and 1945. Just as Germany would be divided into two in the aftermath of the war, the entire world would be divided into two—East and West; Russia and America. The middle—Central Europe—was obliterated yet again.

It is a cruel, universal irony of history that the opponents of the Grail always recognize and understand the Grail Knight most immediately, and most completely. Kaspar Hauser and Rudolf Steiner are surely spectacular proof of this. In 1910 and 1911, Steiner gave to the world all the Resurrection knowledge required to healthily navigate the stormy waters approaching.[1] A mere handful of humans listened; the rest whistled patriotic jingles, stayed asleep, and suffered the terrible pain of their inattentiveness through the "Thirty Year Crisis" of two world wars. "It should not have happened like this, but what happened was necessary," Rudolf Steiner once told a friend, as he reflected upon the events of World War I. The same can be said of Kaspar Hauser's tragic fate, of the burning of the Goetheanum, Hitler's reign of terror, the Sun Demon's victories at the Trinity test site, Hiroshima, and Nagasaki. Some mercurial power within the

---

In a letter to Manhattan Project military leader Gen. Leslie Groves, Oppenheimer seemed to suggest the idea had been inspired in him from someplace unknown. Amazingly, given the link with Golgotha of the Trinity site, Oppenheimer also quoted to Groves these lines from Donne's poem, "Hymn to God My God, in My Sicknesses": "As West and East / In all flatt Maps—and I am one—are on,/So death doth touch the Resurrection."

1. Steiner was fully aware of what he sometimes referred to as the "third force"—the force within matter that was to become the basis of the atomic bomb. In a lecture in Basel, in response to a question from an audience member, he spoke of this: "If one thrusts the body down lower even than the physical world, one comes into the sub-physical world, the lower astral world, the lower or evil Lower Devachan, and the lower or evil Higher Devachan. The evil astral world is the province of Ahriman and the evil Higher Devachan the province of the Asuras. If one drives chemical action down beneath the physical plane, into the evil Devachanic world, magnetism arises. If one thrusts light down into the sub-material—that is to say, a stage deeper than the material world—electricity arises. If what lives in the harmony of the spheres is thrust down farther still, into the province of the Asuras, an even more terrible force, which it will not be possible to keep hidden very much longer, is generated. One can only hope that when this force comes—a force we must conceive as being far, far stronger than the most violent electrical discharge—one can only hope that before some discoverer gives this force into the hands of humanity, human beings will no longer have anything immoral left in them."

human being strives ever after the good, almost imperceptibly setting a limit on the powers of evil, even when they take the form of a world-destroying mushroom cloud.

Look Up, Hannah!

"The Sun is inside us, let the weather be as it will," said the 66-year-old Richard Wagner on July 15, 1879, 2 x 33 years before the false Sun's advent at Trinity. Earlier that year, on Good Friday, he had finished his new opera *Parsifal*, begun 33 years earlier, on Good Friday in 1845. An invisible resurrection rhythm had led Wagner to Wolfram's *Parzival*, and that same resurrection rhythm carried him to the completion of the Grail tale set to music. The *Parsifal Grundthema*'s sublime trio of chords is ever available to us as a reminder of the resurrection rhythm.

Perhaps those three chords do not speak to you, so I offer another rhythm. It is the rhythm of a bow-legged, mustachioed tramp, in a derby hat, ambling down the lane as he leans back on the heels of his oversized shoes, swinging his cane. The Tramp's odd gait and manner constantly put him in awkward, compromising situations. He picks up a red flag that falls off a truck, waves it in hopes of returning it to the driver, and finds himself leading a band of striking workers, and is thrown into jail. Broke and homeless, the Tramp meets and falls in love with a blind girl who sells flowers, and after she mistakes him for a millionaire, he goes to great lengths to keep up the charade; finally he secures money for an operation to restore her sight, but then ends up in jail. The deeper he gets in trouble though, the more he comes up smelling like roses. In the first instance, while in jail the Tramp fights off a group of jail breakers, and saves the warden; in the second, after he is freed, the Tramp finds that his beloved flower girl is hunting for a rich man, but when she gives him a coin and feels his hand, she recognizes him as her benefactor. Throughout all of these escapades, the rhythm of the Tramp's movements and gestures fixes our attention and admiration.

Charlie Chaplin's "Tramp" film character was a clown for modern times, his movements accelerated like the tempo of modernity and the film projector itself, but somehow more graceful, more balletic, more *free*. As industrial capitalism took hold of more and more bodies, turning them into cogs in the Megamachine, the Tramp's balletic gestures were independent of productive work. His arms and legs and hands didn't actually produce anything, and that is what made them so compelling. They sometimes seemed to each have their own rhythm, accentuating their independence. The Tramp's freedom from industrial rhythms seemed to protect and bless him, so that his every mishap turned to gold.

Charlie Chaplin was the first Hollywood film star, and his Tramp character is what made him loved around the world; everywhere a projector could be run, people recognized the Tramp. The character had appeared by an act of grace; in 1914, while filming *Mabel's Strange Predicament,* he was told to put on some funny make-up, and grabbed a pair of baggy pants, a tight coat, a small derby hat, and large pair of shoes from the studio wardrobe. He pasted on a small mustache, and the Tramp was born. Chaplin's gifts as an actor, acrobat, dancer, and mime found a home in the Tramp, whose silence only enhanced the exquisite comic rhythms that Chaplin created. "Movement is near to nature—as a bird flying," Chaplin declared, "and it is the spoken word which is embarrassing. The voice is so revealing, it becomes an artificial thing, reducing everybody to certain glibness."

Mute in a modern world where speech was routinely profaned into propaganda, jingles, and slogans, the Tramp's gestures were unmistakably truthful, authentic. When, in the late 20s and early 30s, "talkies" replaced silent films, Chaplin retired the Tramp, after putting him through some of his most exacting paces ever in *Modern Times* (1936), the tale of an exploited assembly line worker. But he was resurrected four years later, in Chaplin's first talking picture, *The Great Dictator*. The idea for the film had come to Chaplin in 1937, when a friend pointed out to Chaplin the physical resemblance between Adolf Hitler and the Tramp. (In Germany, there was a rumor that Hitler had adopted a Chaplin mustache to capitalize on the Tramp's popularity!) Though not Jewish, Chaplin greatly admired Jewish culture and had many Jewish friends, and the hate directed against Jews in Germany inspired him to make the satirical film about Hitler.

In the film, Chaplin plays both a Jewish barber (a variation on the Tramp) and the "Fooey" (Führer) Adenoid Hynkel, the fanatical dictator of "Tomania." Though both characters speak in the film, the genius of their personalities lies in their gestures and movements. In one scene, two uniformed Stormtroopers are roughing the barber up, when a woman leans out the window and hits them—and the barber—on the head with a skillet. The dazed barber does a fractured waltz up and down the sidewalk. In another scene, the barber gives a customer a shave, exactly synchronized to Brahms' *Hungarian Dance #5*, which plays on the radio. Chaplin studied the newsreels and Leni Reifenstahl's *Triumph of the Will* to copy Hitler's gestures and oratory for a series of satirical speeches in the film. In one brilliant scene, "Hynkel" demonstrates his desire for world domination by dancing with a large, inflatable globe, to the tune of a theme from Richard Wagner's *Lohengrin*.

Certainly the rhythms that Charlie Chaplin mastered to create his unparalleled film art are of a different order and nature than the sort of historical rhythms that we have been considering for the titanic events of the first half of the twentieth century. Still, there is something noble— almost Grail-like—about Chaplin and his Tramp. Chaplin was born just four days before Hitler, and it is as if he incarnated at that time in order to bring the gift of laughter at a moment of great tragedy. Remember that gestures are the language of the Angels; Chaplin spoke that language with unprecedented wit and wisdom, putting his talents in the service of a world that desperately needed to laugh, even as it witnessed its own apocalyptic folly. When you watch the Tramp careening to and fro in a Chaplin film, you can almost hear the Angels laughing *with* us, not at us.

12: *It's the End of the World as We Know It*

Prelude: Water Upon Stone

ONCE I CAUGHT A LITTLE WAVE of the resurrection forces, in June 1999, while I was attending the Dibner Institute, a week-long gathering of biologists, historians, philosophers, and sociologists of the life sciences at the Marine Biological Laboratory in Woods Hole, Massachusetts. The seminar, designed to get scientists and non-scientists to share questions and ideas with each other, had as its focus the great nineteenth century German embryologist, marine biologist, and philosopher/educator Ernst Haeckel. Despite the fact that most of the participants were veteran teachers and scholars, they all had a chance to be humble students again, since every Dibner seminar included elementary lab and field exercises designed to acquaint scientist and science studier alike with the rudiments of the particular biological practice in question. For the "Why Haeckel?" session, the organizers felt it was critical that we all have a brief refresher course in elementary embryology, and so after an afternoon lab session doing microscopic examination of sea urchin eggs, we moved on to extracting and then examining a living chick embryo.

At the end of the lab session, in which we had been witness to the awesome beauty of the embryo's pulsing heart and lungs, one after another pair of lab partners took their petri dishes over to a trash barrel and unceremoniously dumped their embryo before heading for lunch. Without giving it any conscious thought, I found myself holding my plastic petri dish as I walked across campus to the dining hall, and at lunch I placed the embryo next to me at the table. I had a crazy notion that if I just imagined my own life forces extending like an umbilical cord to the chick, that I could sustain it. Every few minutes, I would look down to see if the little heart had stopped beating, for I had asked the laboratory instructor how long I could expect it to live. "Oh, another two or three hours at most." I carried the petri dish with me to the afternoon discussion section, where we debated about Ernst Haeckel's theory that ontogeny recapitulates phylogeny—that the unfolding embryo traces in miniature the grand evolutionary unfolding of its ancestral line.

My heart would leap each time when, just as I had conceded that the embryo had finally expired, I would notice a small and silent surge of blood that was the telltale of this being's life force. Having only placed a few drops of water in the dish to keep it from completely drying out,

I took it to bed with me that evening, and was amazed in the morning to find it still alive. Again the petri dish accompanied me to lab and lecture sessions, until finally, over 28 hours after I had first placed the embryonic disk onto a little doughnut of lab paper so it could go into the petri dish and onto the light microscope table, the embryo expired. I brought it down to a lovely sand beach next to the Laboratory, said a prayer, and buried it.

All the while that I had been in an intense mental act of focusing my attention and intentionality on that embryo, the other seminar participants seemed not to want to see it, to push it away mentally, especially this mystery of how it had come to stay alive. Instead of eliciting intense curiosity and reverence, the anomalous survival of the chick elicited a reaction not unlike the physical act of dumping the petri dishes unceremoniously after the lab—a sort of willful neglect. The seminar participants seem to have approached the embryo as if it were stone. And yet we all knew in our heart of hearts that the chick embryo was more of the nature of water—fluid, vital, and yet resistant to all of our scientific probing. The embryo was a wholly mysterious entity.

A year later I was eagerly anticipating the next Dibner Institute, which was to center on the science of ecology. This time we would be haunting the salt marshes and oak woods rather than the laboratory, as we sought to know more deeply the historical conditions that led to the founding of ecological science in the late nineteenth century. In early spring, I was in Florida on vacation, and chanced to meet a 77-years-young woman, who excitedly told me about a pilgrimage that she was soon to make, with a group called the Sophia Foundation of North America. The pilgrimage—entitled "The Dawn of A New Millennium: The Return of Christ and the Emergence of the Divine Feminine"—was to begin at Chartres Cathedral in France and end at Pentecost on the Island of Iona in Scotland's Inner Hebrides. The journey was explicitly timed to coincide not only with the 2000th return of the heavens to the configuration they were in around the time of the Divine Birth in Bethlehem, but more particularly with the Saturn-Jupiter conjunction. Such astrological auspices meant nothing to me; I thought astrology was bunk! Though a travel tour, the pilgrimage was to have a devotional nature, employing eurythmy, sacred dance, choral singing, and prayer to honor and welcome the earthly entrance of Sophia, the Feminine Face of God that had been so deeply forgotten by Western Christianity for well over a thousand years. The pilgrimage was conceived as sacred work that would resurrect and resuscitate Western culture's connection to Sophia.

My new friend, two days after we met, invited me to go as her guest on this pilgrimage, and I was about to accept the invitation, when I realized that it would conflict with the upcoming Dibner Institute seminar. Despite having looked forward to the Woods Hole gathering all year, some inner voice told me that I should not pass up the opportunity to learn something entirely new, so I sent my regrets to the Dibner organizers and made arrangements to join the Sophia pilgrims.

When our daily lives seem sometimes to turn to stone because of repetitive habits of thought and action, we instinctively create for ourselves pilgrimages of a sort—watery, wild, serendipitous, and if they are truly successful, ultimately mysterious adventures that take us places where we have never been before. For me surely there was plenty of mystery in and about the pilgrimage: traveling with 30 women and only 5 men, through lands I had never seen, and never really even thought about, preparing an invisible welcoming chalice to a spiritual being of whose existence I had only just become aware, and to whom I frankly found it nearly impossible to pray; singing unfamiliar hymns and making wholly unfamiliar movements with a group of complete strangers, led by an Englishman named Robert Powell, a former atheist mathematician who now spent his entire life in service to awakening humanity to Christ and Sophia, employing "astrosophy"—an esoteric form of astrology—as his principle tool, I felt surrounded by mystery, or at least mystification. Each day I experienced odd and inexplicable happenings, midst a daily regimen of contemplation and discussion of a grand sweep of cosmic events, in which our little group increasingly seemed to be active participants.

After a week studying the extraordinary apocalyptic pictures in stone carved around the portals of Chartres Cathedral, we took the Channel across to England, and headed to Wiltshire, and the land of King Arthur. The morning after we arrived at Tintagel and checked into the "Camelot Castle" hotel—a spooky, rambling 1920s hotel directly across from what were purported to be the ruins of King Arthur's castle—I pulled Robert aside and asked him: "Is this a sightseeing tour or a Mystery School?" "Oh, yes, Kevin," Robert said with an impish smile, "this is certainly a Mystery School." This book is in great part the result of having fallen "by accident" into that Mystery School eight years ago.

The Unity of Knowledge, 1954

One by one, on a Friday afternoon in late October 1954, dozens of limousines made the three-mile switchback climb from the gatehouse, pulled past the pair of huge lion statues into the circular drive before the massive stone mansion, and delivered their distinguished occupants. Among those representing Nature were: Marston Bates, professor of zoology at the University of Michigan; Niels Bohr, from the Institute of Theoretical Physics; Theodosius Dobzhansky, professor of zoology at Columbia University; Harold Urey, professor of chemistry at the University of Chicago; B. F. Skinner, Harvard University psychologist; director of research at the Menninger Foundation; and John von Neumann, of the Institute for Advanced Study in Princeton. Representing History were Harvard sociologist Talcott Parsons; University of California anthropologist Alfred Kroeber; Margaret Mead of the American Museum of Natural History; Columbia University historians Jacques Barzun, Richard Hofstadter and J. Bartlett Brebner; Harvard philosopher Willard Quine; and essayist Lionel Trilling.

Those who had never made the pilgrimage to the top of the Ramapo Mountains at Arden House—the former estate of Edward, then his son Averell, Harriman—were stunned by such sylvan beauty just 50 miles from Manhattan. After the Harrimans had donated the house and grounds to Columbia University in 1950, Columbia President Dwight Eisenhower had hosted a number of international summit meetings there. This 1954 summit, the "Unity of Knowledge" conference, was being held as part of Columbia's bicentennial. The "unity" that the participants sought was an alternative to the polarity of the two cultures—science vs. the humanities—that had grown further and further apart during the last few centuries. Despite the presence of a seemingly wide array of humanists, the deck was stacked in favor of the scientists, who, even in that decade of American skepticism about the limits of science, possessed tremendous self-confidence that any future unity of knowledge would surely issue from their midst, not from the ranks of philosophy or history—and certainly not from that medieval authority, the clergy.

In 1954, despite the recent triumphs of subatomic physics, chemistry, and molecular biology, scientists still looked to organismal biology as the realm where macrocosm and microcosm merged, and where such a unity might be found. Since the mid-19th century the biological sciences had offered the promise of a unity of Nature, and after some early 20th century setbacks, the "modern synthesis" in biology—the marriage of natural selection theory to genetics— seemed to renew that promise. As the most enthusiastic interpreter of the modern synthesis to a wide audience, and especially given his ardent quest for an "evolutionary humanism," Julian Huxley was Columbia's natural choice for the keynote speaker at the summit. A lifelong eugenicist, Huxley was a spectacular specimen of good breeding, representing both sides of the two-culture divide: eldest grandson of "Darwin's bulldog," Thomas Henry Huxley, he was also descended from the historian Thomas Arnold, and his uncle was the poet and essayist Matthew Arnold. Ever since his collaboration in 1929 with H.G. Wells on a popular book called *The Science of Life*, Huxley had reached a wide audience with his view of biology, and in the decade before the 1954 conference, as the first director-general of the United Nations Educational, Scientific, and Cultural Organization (UNESCO), Huxley had emerged as perhaps the 20th century's premier international statesman for science.

Huxley began his keynote address by noting that the present age was the first to have a reasonably comprehensive, scientifically based picture of humanity's place and role in nature since the Darwinian "upheaval" had first put human beings *in* nature rather than above it. Though the late 19th century faith in humankind's achievements moderated this sense of the human being as "just another animal," the catastrophes of the 20th century had shaken that faith. Huxley, however, was ever a believer in progress, whether biological or sociocultural, and looked forward to "future possibilities."

The possibilities foreseen by Huxley lay outside the biological realm. He conjectured that sometime in the Pliocene, between 2 to 5 million years ago, "the last possibilities of major improvement in the material and physiological properties of self-reproducing matter had been exhausted." Huxley maintained that humans had put a "cap" on evolution, that even if biological evolution had note effectively ended in the Pliocene, human beings now stood in the way of any major evolutionary developments. As the "only organism capable of further major transformation or evolutionary advance," humanity had taken on the role of creator, the "instrument" of evolutionary process. Borrowing from his friend and fellow conference member Teilhard de Chardin, Huxley acknowledged that evolution had passed out of the biosphere into the "noosphere."

In the French philosopher and Jesuit priest Teilhard de Chardin, the post-war West had found a rarity—a man of the cloth who was also a scientist. Trained as a paleontologist and geologist, Teilhard also had fashioned a philosophy of the evolution of consciousness that appealed to many non-Christian scientists. The Catholic Church had ordered him not to publish his writings, but he had formed friendships with a number of prominent scientists, who were admirers of his evolutionary philosophy.

Modern biology had labored long and hard to rid itself of any metaphysical crutches in its quest to explain the nature of life. There were many at the conference—like logical positivist Willard Quine—who saw the "emergent evolutionism" of Père Teilhard and Huxley as pure mysticism. But Huxley was as confident about the prospects for a unified knowledge of History as he was for a transcendental knowledge of Nature: "Our age is the first in history in which we have acquired a comprehensive knowledge of historical fact, from the present back to the Paleolithic, and therefore the first age in which it is possible to attempt a unified history." He pointed to his own UNESCO effort—the *Scientific and Cultural History of Mankind*—as an example.

No one at Arden House used the language of the "Consciousness Soul," but it was as if Huxley were claiming a kind of materialist version of it as having been achieved by modern humankind. The pride that he and the participants felt in this collective achievement was undoubtedly enhanced by the presence in the audience of Harold Urey, who just the year before, with fellow University of Chicago chemist Stanley Miller, had synthesized organic compounds from inorganic precursors, convincing a wide array of scientists and humanists that the mystery of the origin of life had been solved in the laboratory. The work of another guest at Arden House that October weekend—radical behaviorist B. F. Skinner—did away with the human being's divine origin with as much certainty as the Urey-Miller experiment. Skinner, whose stated goal was to prevent humanity from destroying itself, believed that an effective and humane technology of human behavior—employing such devices as Skinner boxes (a mechanical crib), teaching machines, and pigeon guided missiles—was the only solution for the problems that human technology had created, like the atomic bomb.

Cracks in the Wall

Despite the many philosophical and methodological differences that stood in the way of unification of the disciplines represented at Arden House, there was an overwhelming sense among the participants that they were headed in the right direction. If the scientists could just stay alert to the dangers of reductionism, if the humanists could watch their romanticism, all would eventually be well. But in 1954 there were small signs that a fissure or two marred the magnificent unified wall of modern wisdom. In the eyes of some unifiers, these cracks were temporary, easily reparable; more of them dismissed the cracks entirely, rationalizing them as hallucinations, illusions, atavistic reversion to obsolete noösystems.

Even at Arden House, at least a couple of individuals believed these cracks demanded serious consideration. Gardner Murphy had been a keen student of parapsychology for decades. Six weeks after the Arden conference, Murphy advocated research on extrasensory perception in a letter to *Science* magazine. Margaret Mead, who had encountered paranormal phenomena on a number of occasions in her anthropological fieldwork in traditional societies, was an outspoken defender of parapsychological research, who led an effort to get the American Association for the Advancement of Science to accept a parapsychology branch.

Julian Huxley was not unaware of the challenge to any "modern synthesis" posed by the violations of space and time represented by phenomena like precognition, retrocognition, telepathy, and other forms of clairvoyance. His brother Aldous in 1954 was coming face to face with the paranormal in his experiments with mescaline. Aldous Huxley's *Doors of Perception* was published in February, and in April he had attended a parapsychology conference with Eileen Garrett, one of the century's most renowned psychics and mediums. For his part, Julian Huxley believed that extrasensory perception might represent the "more ultimate state," the "Omega point" toward which the universe, including human consciousness, was evolving, as prophesied by Teilhard de Chardin.

Without realizing it, those gathered at the summit meeting at Arden House were wrestling with the same "divide" as we have confronted in this course—"It Matters" vs. "It Spirits." "It Matters"—the modern materialistic world conception—had the upper hand in 1954 as surely as it does today, but the "It Spirits" view hung on feebly, if only by virtue of the anomalous experiences of parapsychology. Both Huxley brothers were atheists; and whatever interest they expressed in the supersensible realm, neither looked to past spiritual traditions for help in understanding that realm. Teilhard's Omega point was essentially the Christian Logos, but the Huxleys and others in Teilhard's circle preferred Teilhard's terminology, shorn of the sectarian spiritual baggage of Christianity.

From a mountain summit one can see far, but often one easily misses details in the landscape just below. At the base of the Ramapo Mountains, less than twenty miles from Arden House, there was a community that had for 25 years been practicing a unity of knowledge in their thinking, feeling, and willing. Indeed, in honor of Rudolf Steiner's concept of the threefold human being, the community was called "Threefold Farm." Founded in 1926 by followers of Rudolf Steiner from Manhattan, the community was by 1954 home to a host of different initiatives—a biodynamic farm, a laboratory for studying the etheric forces, an auditorium for eurythmy performances, a summer conference on anthroposophy. At the first conference, in 1933, attendees heard Rudolf Steiner's student Ehrenfried Pfeiffer lecture about the etherization of the blood as a path toward effecting the respiritualization of the Earth, while each day the *New York Times* brought chilling reports of Nazi activity in Europe—storm troopers torturing trade unionists in Austria, swastikas being paraded menacingly throughout Germany, Jewish citizens beaten and harassed. Whatever antipathy the Threefold community may have felt for Hitler and the Nazis, they did not as yet know what they would unleash into the world, as a counterforce.

Most of the members of the Threefold Community were aware of Rudolf Steiner's having pointed to the year 1933 as the advent of Christ's etheric return, and of his prediction of an increase in the number of people who would have experiences of the supersensible world. The people gathered at Threefold Farm had a clear understanding of the role of the etheric body and the etheric formative forces, few as yet enjoyed the ability to perceive the etheric, so Ehrenfried Pfeiffer's lecture subject—"Making Visible the Formative-Forces in Nature"—attracted a great deal of notice. The possibility of somehow developing a technique to make the formative forces visible was tantalizing; to make the unseen seen gave hope to their own aspirations toward developing supersensible capacity. Pfeiffer himself was widely understood to possess clairvoyant abilities; many in the audience had heard of Pfeiffer's magic jackknife, that he could plunge into the soil, and then pronounce in great detail the land use history of the site. There were rumors that Pfeiffer could see the "nature spirits," the elemental beings of field and forest.

First in Dornach at the Goetheanum, but then, at Threefold Farm, after he moved there in 1940, Pfeiffer carried out a research program to demonstrate the etheric forces, and to use them as a diagnostic of etheric vitality. Working from an indication by Rudolf Steiner that he should observe the process of crystallization that would occur when plant substances and human blood were added to certain salts, Pfeiffer created a setup where copper chloride was placed in a glass Petri dish with extracts of water lily and chamomile. The first experiments produced grayish-blue patterns like frost on a windowpane. As his experiments continued, he found that healthy plant extracts or blood from healthy subjects produced radially symmetrical crystallizations, while chaotic patterns were characteristic of ill plants or people. Pfeiffer used the simple crystal patterns to diagnose the nature and location of inflammations, infections, even cancer. The key to this unorthodox diagnostics was proper mental preparation; Pfeiffer found that the best results came from pure observation combined with intensive meditation. He believed that any success he had was because he followed Rudolf Steiner's advice to make the laboratory a place where the elemental beings of nature would feel comfortable.

Pfeiffer often spoke of the elemental beings, and when out walking with people, would stop and describe his past experiences of elementals at particular sites. The Ramapos were a craggy region of glacially-eroded gneiss (metamorphosed granite) bedrock, where the elementals of earth—the gnomes—were most prominent. (The region was riddled with iron mines from the Revolutionary era, when they produced ore for Continental Army cannon and cannonballs; there was a rich local folklore of gnomes associated with these mines). Pfeiffer taught that gnomes in their outer work depended totally on the forces of nature, but in their inner development, they were influenced by the thought life of man. Especially sensitive to theoretical, abstract thoughts, Pfeiffer said they were confused by modern scientific theories. "Everything connected with materialism and intellectualism, the hunt for money, questions of physical power on earth (i.e., political questions), all thoughts and emotions of men regarding this sphere increase the disturbance in the elementary world…If there are one or more human beings devoting their thoughts to questions of eternity, the elemental beings feel a relief and lose more or less of their worries."

When human beings were wracked by materialistic, selfish, fearful thoughts, the elementary beings who were charged with maintaining the proper relations of the earth's body went wild, and the results ranged from cancer to insect and fungal infections to the disruption of regional and global climatic patterns. A close observer of local weather conditions and their influence on his biodynamic garden at Threefold Farm, Pfeiffer regularly reported that abnormal weather resulted from human action. The freak weather patterns in the spring and summer of 1941, he explained, were caused by a group of elemental beings who were charged with providing Europe and America with adequate moisture and warmth; he attributed their aberrant activity to the eruption of fascism and war in Europe during the 1930s.

On his very first trip to America in 1933, Pfeiffer had executed a comparative study of the elementals of Europe, the Atlantic Ocean, and America, making a series of drawings that he occasionally used to illustrate his lectures. His observations confirmed Rudolf Steiner's research, which posited that the elementary world of Europe—save remote regions like northern Scotland, Norway, and the Swiss Alps—was more "refined" than that of North America, which tended to be "rather uneducated and naughty." Though this sounded like unabashed German chauvinism, Pfeiffer explained that the difference was based upon fundamental variations in geological forces and upon the spiritual background of the two continents. American elementals were "younger" in both respects than their European counterparts. The relatively younger age of the North American landscape, particularly in its more extensive region of Pleistocene glaciation, was compounded by the relatively youthful age of human settlement upon the continent. In Europe, many millennia of human cultural achievements—from Greek art and architecture to the music of 19th century composers—had "educated" the elementals, refining and spiritualizing them.

From Asia to Western Europe, and particularly in any of the shrines connected with the mystery of Golgotha, those elemental beings associated with mystery centers were filled with energy, harmony, peace, balance and health. The "wildness" of North American elementals, on the other hand, was exacerbated by the cultic activity of some of the continent's aboriginal occupants. In particular, the Toltec and Aztec centers at Teotihuacan and Tenochtitlan and the Olmec and Mayan centers in the Yucatan Peninsula—had powerfully retarded any evolutionary development of the New World elementals. The dark magic and cruelty of those peoples had cast a shadow which Pfeiffer said "*penetrates every elemental being, every moral effort, every human being in the North American continent, even in our day.*" That "day" was 1948, but since then, new forms of materialism have only worsened the situation for the elemental beings. Throughout America, Pfeiffer had witnessed places where elementals had abandoned their former habitats, becoming "homeless." New York City, for example, had been deserted by legions of its original denizens.

A New Gospel of Nature

The community at Threefold Farm looked upon the attempt to perceive and communicate with the elemental beings as a uniquely rewarding, redemptive activity. They saw the human redemption of Nature by way of sensitive work with the elemental beings as one of contemporary humanity's most pressing tasks. Nature spirits received their nourishment from the right action and thoughts of their neighbor human beings, which included contemplation and cultivation of harmony with the elemental world. A preeminent act of reciprocity toward the elementals that humans could engage in was the creation of spiritualized art; the community at Threefold Farm pioneered such efforts in drama, movement, architecture, painting, and music. They longed for the day when America might build a new Mystery center, like the Goetheanum, where Americans might begin to repair the relationship with the nature beings of the continent.

But in postwar America, such a Mystery center was far from possible. Indeed, just ten miles from Ehrenfried Pfeiffer's laboratory, at the nation's premier "nature center," the Trailside Museum, the exact opposite curriculum was in full swing, attracting half a million visitors a year. Founded in 1927, the Trailside Museum took its original inspiration from American

Museum of Natural History (AMNH) entomologist Frank Lutz's invention in 1924 of the world's first "nature trail." In the wake of widespread urbanization, children growing up in the early 20th century industrial world had little primal experience of nature, and educators had developed a variety of new programs of "nature study" to remedy this. A Boy Scout leader as well as a gifted scientist, Lutz was keen to create a nature study curriculum that combined active scientific research with outdoor living. Under the auspices of the AMNH, he founded the Station for the Study of Insects, at the gateway to the Ramapo Mountains, near the New Jersey/ New York border. There he and a group of Boy Scouts cut a half-mile trail through the oak woods, and then proceeded to attach to trees, shrubs, and herbaceous plants small linen Dennison labels, with identification information written in waterproof ink. Along the trail Lutz also set up small screen-wire cages with living insects, and tables with glass jars holding aquatic insect larvae, all with accompanying informative labels. Lutz's teenage assistants maintained these trailside exhibits, checking the insects, putting fresh leaves in their cages, and cleaning out the insect excrement so that the cages would not appear dirty.

By the end of the first summer, dozens of other nature trails had sprung up at summer camps around New York City; overwhelmed by the response, Lutz write a short notice for *Science*, recommending the nature trail as a tool for natural scientific instruction. By the summer of 1926, Lutz estimated that more than 2000 nature trails had been created around the United States. The original popularity of the idea came from the visits to Lutz's trail by automobile tourists on their way to nearby Harriman State Park to picnic, swim, or hike. None seemed to realize that the automobile had inspired Lutz's idea in the first place.

In outlining an education plan for the AMNH, Lutz championed the possibilities for nature study that could be adapted from the latest advertising sensation—billboards. The 1920s were truly the golden age of billboards. The economic optimism that swept across America after the signing of the Treaty of Versailles in 1919 was nowhere so dramatically evident as in the new landscape of outdoor advertising that rose across the country in perfect sync with the explosion of the personal automobile. The propaganda campaigns sparked by military mobilization during World War I had provided outdoor advertisers and their artists and illustrators with a nationwide test of the effect of synthesizing newly perceived understandings of color, word, and image into persuasive, psychologically effective messages. In 1900 the total amount spent for regulated outdoor advertising in America was $2 million; by 1925 it was $60 million. Much of that 3000—percent increase occurred in the five years before Frank Lutz's experiment at the Station for the Study of Insects.

The most popular American billboards were the Burma-Shave Company's jaunty jingles spaced out at intervals on the American road. "Shave the modern way / No brush / No lather / No rub-in / Big tube 35 cents—Drug stores / Burma-Shave" read one of the first sets of consecutive signs. The signs got more and more inventive over the years, as motorists made a sort of sport out of reading them. "Keep well / To the right / Of the oncoming car / Get your close shaves / From the half pound jar / Burma-Shave"; "You've laughed / At our signs / For many a mile / Be a sport / Give us a trial / Burma-Shave." At a hundred paces apart, traveling at the era's usual motoring speed of 35-miles-per-hour, it took three seconds from one Burma-Shave sign to the next—18 seconds to read the whole series of six signs. Frank Lutz knew that he was up against the same time limit with his nature trail; he had to keep visitors' attention just long enough to impart a new fact.

Nature trails shared with billboards an aesthetic of realism. In the 1920s, American billboards' unfailingly conservative designs were immune to European abstract or surrealist influence; realism was the style understood by the mass of Americans. Dishing out nature lore to the five-second audience required staying close to nature's surface, to the visual representation so matter-of-factly before the trail walker's eyes. No consideration was given to the possibility of alternate representations, of other ways of seeing. The proof of the outdoor advertiser's representational prowess was in sales volume. Lutz put his skills to the test by creating a "Testing Trail" where visitors regurgitated back the facts that they had just been fed. The spread of the nature trail idea was proof of the twentieth century's positivist faith in the infallibility of its representations, mixed with the Progressive faith in the beneficent powers of "publicity."

A nature trail became the focal point of the Trailside Museum, which was located on a spectacular bluff overlooking the Hudson River, along the first section of the Appalachian Trail, which had been started in 1923. (And which was quickly transformed from the original democratic, communitarian dream of its creator, Benton MacKaye, into a plaything of the expanding urban consumer culture) By the 1950s, the "advertising" agenda of American nature study was in full bloom, its exhibits founded upon principles first worked out by B.F. Skinner's mentor, behavioral scientist turned advertising executive John B. Watson. "Cheerful," "agreeable," "attractive," "appealing" were the keywords of the radio age, and they played a key role in the pedagogical program at the Trailside Museum. Animal exhibits were planned to showcase the "personality" of the birds, snakes, frogs, turtles and other creatures on display. Museum staff referred to particularly popular animals as "stars".

The tendency of Trailside pedagogy to speak of visitor "actions" and "reactions" placed it within the web of collaboration between academic psychology and commercial advertising that was so pervasive in the 1920s. "City-bred" people—clerks, factory employees, and other metropolitan workers—who got off for a day's recreation at the Bear Mountain dock on the Hudson River below the Museum were subject to a kind of Arcadian Taylorism (the system of "scientific management" that had turned much of the industrial age workforce into addled automatons—as Charlie Chaplin had so accurately portrayed in *Modern Times*). Museum staff studied the visitors, and engineered the labels to "attract" and instruct them in the most "efficient" manner.

Re-enchantment and Redemption

Imagine what the elemental beings at the Trailside Museum were feeling, as tens of thousands of children were subjected to this strange pedagogical program! Children at Threefold Farm's nature study programs had an entirely different experience. Nature was above all met as a wisdom-filled arena of living beings, whose forms and behaviors could be intuited by close observation and artistic activity. While at state of the art nature centers like Trailside, geological exhibits were common, at Threefold all modern geological concepts were avoided, since they tended to build up in the child an inner picture of the Earth as a mineral entity rather than a living being. The "beingness" of Nature was imparted early and often through the telling of fairy stories that communicated the important creative role played by fairies within Nature. Children learned how each of the four elements—earth, air, water, and fire—had its respective fairy form in gnome, sylph, undine and salamander. Springtime awakening of plants was presented not as the result of inanimate forces of energy, but as the particularized task of animate beings. Gnomes awakened the seeds and rootlets out of their winter sleep and taught them how to grow and transform themselves into the variegated shapes of growing plants. Undines created just the right elixir of sap for each plant and collaborated with the gnomes to ensure that the right mixture of minerals was taken up. Then the undines handed the labor over to the sylphs, who had the task of "painting" the leaves and flowers and deciding on their proper perfume. Finally, Fire Spirits (salamanders) formed the fruit and seed.

The few American children that received this introduction to Nature were in a sense given a 14th or 15th century rural person's *enchanted* sense of the natural world. Only a few of the children were actually clairvoyant for the nature beings, but as they grew up, and encountered more abstract knowledge about Nature, they retained their intimate original experience of the living spiritual aspect standing behind all of nature's forms. Fairies had of course experienced an altogether different fate in the mainstream "It Matters" world of the 20th century West. Beginning with the phenomenal popularity of theatrical performances of J.M. Barrie's *Peter Pan* in the 1910s and 1920s, and culminating in Walt Disney's domestication of the fairy world in the animated films *Snow White and the Seven Dwarfs* (1937), *Fantasia* (1940), and his own rendering of *Peter Pan* (1953), fairies experienced a rapid process of "disenchantment" in the modern world. Although theosophical writers and romantics like William Butler Yeats and Walter Yeeling Evans-Wentz celebrated nature spirits as real, and folklorists continued to collect descriptions of fairies from traditional cultures around the globe, the Western imagination denied the existence of such beings while at the same time creating a sentimentalized caricature as a substitute.

By 1954, America's elementals were under siege. The cult of postwar consumerism meant the triumph of *things*—new cars, TVs, toys, appliances, clothing fashions—over *beings*, and the nature beings suffered accordingly. Radioactive contamination, pesticide poisoning, and industrial chemical pollution of earth, air and water threatened the fairies as acutely as they did the birds, butterflies, and humans. The 1950s saw the rise too of America's obsession for green, uniform lawns—an obsession maintained through copious doses of chemical fertilizer and herbicides. I can remember how my dad would send me and my brother out to kill dandelions with a three-foot-long plastic syringe filled with some form of what must have been 2,4,5-T, one of the chemicals that made Agent Orange so deadly to the jungle foliage of Vietnam. It was also deadly to the jungle's inhabitants; close to half a million people were killed or injured by the chemical, and over half a million Vietnamese children have been born with birth defects caused by the United States Army's use of Agent Orange as a defoliant during the Vietnam War.

Growing up in the 1960s in a house at the edge of the New York metropolis (I could see both the NYC skyline and the Ramapo Mountain front from the apple orchard at the top of our street), my childhood memories of relatively unrestricted outdoor exploration—catching cray-fish and baby snapping turtles in the nearby brook; bringing fish and frogs home to keep in the bathtub; even live-trapping the local garbage-raiding raccoon—are punctuated by some unsettling glimpses of the true state of my home environment. At least half a dozen times in my memory, we had major fish die-offs in that brook, caused no doubt by a car wash just upstream. My friends and I used to play with toy trucks in a great mound of fine earth at the end of our street; only as an adult did I realize that the fine earth was full of perchloroethylene, the solvent used by the dry cleaning company whose lot backed up to our street.

The Mission of America

If we could travel back to 1954, and sit at the long oak boardroom table (given by Wall Street financier J.P. Morgan to Mrs. E.H. Harriman) at Arden House, along with the members of the impressive brain trust assembled for the Unity of Knowledge conference, we would have heard stunning conversations full of unbridled enthusiasm for the miracles of technology that America was bringing to the rest of the world. Not a single person sitting around that table raised an alarm about any of the environmental issues just mentioned. Arden House was full of icons of America's natural environment. One room was home to an impressive array of trophy heads of American big game animals—buffalo; moose; elk; mountain lion. In an upstairs hallway there was a fresco of a group of Lenape Indians, standing before a dugout canoe on the bank of the Ramapo River, with the Ramapo Mountains in the background.

The Arcadian backdrop both inside and outside the building lent the summit meeting participants a strong sense of America's favored destiny, that it had reached the midpoint of the 20th century as the leading nation of the world, spared the devastating ravages that two world wars had visited upon Europe. They embraced a secular version of Massachusetts Bay Colony founder John Winthrop's sense of the Puritans as being a "city upon a hill"—divinely favored through their covenant with God. Three centuries of progress had delivered America into her destined position as a shining example—in her prodigious economy; her democratic institutions; and her leadership in scientific knowledge—for the rest of the world.

Down at the bottom of the hill, there were muffled murmurs of dissent. Between 1946 and 1961, Ehrenfried Pfeiffer gave an extraordinary set of lectures at Threefold Farm on the destiny of America, focusing on the role that America's "etheric geography" played in the unfolding of history. Pfeiffer frequently pointed out that wherever mountain ranges ran predominantly north and south, the forces of death, and the power of the etheric double, the *Doppelgänger*, were accentuated, and this had enormous consequences for the people living in these regions. North America was the place on the earth where this north-south axis was most pronounced; it was easy to see for the Threefold Farm community members, since their home sat almost astride the Ramapo Fault, from which the Ramapo Mountains rose up as part of the great Appalachian Chain.

At work in every human being, the Double does not have a heart, and so lives only in the head and in the will, not in the mediating realm of the rhythmic system. With its very strong connection to the forces that ascend from the earth—magnetism, electricity, and the "third force" of the atom—the double has the goal of binding human beings to the earth forces, so that their thinking and willing receive direction only from below, not above.

"Back to Nature," the slogan that conjured such positive associations for educated, progressive 20th century Americans, was a phrase that carried for the Threefold Farm folk a chilling picture of a possible future for the human being. If the work of the etheric double was not countered, humans would indeed go "back to nature," that is, become prisoners of the earth forces, and lose all consciousness of higher worlds. This was precisely the goal of Ahriman, devoid of the heart forces that kept man from becoming a mere material being—the very picture that the Unity of Knowledge conference—along with the entire American knowledge industry— was unabashedly embracing. In the anthroposophic view of history, supported by an esoteric reading of John's *Apocalypse*, earth evolution would come to a close at the end of the 7th post-Atlantean epoch, known as "Laodicea" in John's text, but known to the American anthroposophists as the "American" cultural epoch. Lasting from AD 5734 to AD 7894, that epoch would see America either fulfill or fail its mission in world history, just as Germany had in this century. At that future time, as described in the seventh and last letter of John's vision, mankind would split into two streams: one descending to a state between man and animal, the other ascending to become the Tenth Hierarchy and join the Angels, Archangels, and other spiritual beings in their task of guiding the earth on its proper evolutionary course, back toward its etheric origins.

Although this apocalyptic moment lay long millennia away, many of the members of the small gathering of "It Spirits" enthusiasts at Threefold Farm interpreted the signs of the times as indicating that the twentieth century was witnessing a foreshadowing of that Apocalypse. It seemed to them that in America, the Ahrimanic Double had seized hold of every domain of human life, thanks to materialist natural science. The pedagogical practice of nature study; the investigative apparatus of natural scientific research; and most diabolically, the application of Darwinian theory to the human social realm, via eugenics; were paths to the dark death of the living forces of the spiritual world.

The Rose of the World

I have focused on America because the twentieth century is truly the "American Century," the period—especially after World War II—when America assumes the status of the leading agent of change in the world. I have focused on this small and almost entirely unknown community of Threefold Farm as a way of giving us a picture from half a century ago, of the deep divide between the prevailing "It Matters" worldview in America and the dissenting "It Spirits" view, held by only a handful, if we now restrict this "It Spirits" rubric to anthroposophists, the followers of the teachings of Rudolf Steiner.

In portraying this divide in this way, I have unfairly left out all sorts of alternative cultural, intellectual, and social currents from all over the world. My only defense for doing so is that as a storyteller I am trying to follow this tale of world history where my nose leads me, to the places and times "where the action is." That action will become clearer I hope later in this chapter, but as a way of broadening out the parochial tale that I have just given, let us set ourselves down at some other place on the earth in the year 1954, and see what wonders we can find…

On the first day of 1954, the Soviet Union ceased its demand for war reparations from East Germany. Three weeks later, the first nuclear-powered submarine, the *USS Nautilus*, was launched from the shipyard of the Electric Boat Company in Groton, Connecticut. On March 25 the Soviet Union recognized East German sovereignty but left troops in the country. On April 7, President Dwight D. Eisenhower gave his "domino theory" speech during a news conference, arguing that if communism were allowed to develop in one country, the surrounding countries would follow. Eisenhower was thinking particularly of Vietnam at the time, but the domino theory became the operative ideology of succeeding US administrations to justify American intervention all over the world. In June the world's first atomic power station went online near Moscow; two months later, the Soviet Union tested a nuclear weapon.

In 1954, though the US was locked into a "Cold War" with the Soviet Union, and took every opportunity to demonize its enemy, it could say little about the "gulag archipelago" upon which the Soviet state was brutally founded. The murderous Soviet dictator Joseph Stalin had died the year before, and Soviet authorities were beginning to review prisoners' cases, but there were still tens of thousands of Russians incarcerated in Soviet gulags, including Aleksander Solzhenitsyn, whose masterpiece, *The Gulag Archipelago*, was published in the West in 1973. Though the existence of the Soviet *gulag* (an acronym for "Chief Administration of Corrective Labor Camps) system was known in the West since the 1930s, no one had any idea of how brutal and extensive it was. Solzhenitsyn showed that the Soviet economy depended completely on the productivity of the forced labor camps, and that the threat of imprisonment, torture, and execution was the entire basis of its rule. Western estimates of deaths in the gulags range from 15 to 30 million between 1918 and 1956. Alexander Solzhenitsyn estimated that as many as 66 million people had been killed—more than the death toll of all twentieth century wars.

About 100 miles northeast of Moscow was the Vladimir Prison, perhaps the most deadly in the Soviet system, where significant political prisoners were incarcerated. One of the prisoners was Daniel Andreev, a poet who had been arrested in 1947 and sentenced to 25 years in prison for the alleged crime of authoring anti-Soviet propaganda and planning to assassinate Joseph Stalin. In 1954, Andreev suffered a heart attack; conditions at the prison were so severe that prisoners often died before their release.

Upon his arrest, the KGB had destroyed all his writings, and in prison he restored his prose and verses from memory and wrote them down on tiny scraps of paper, which were invariably confiscated. After Stalin's death in 1953, Andreev was given paper and ink and allowed to write on a regular basis, completing the first draft of *Roza Mira—The Rose of the World*—which was a detailed description of the visions he had had of multiple planes of existence "above" and "below" the earth. In the beginning of the book he briefly describes a series of five mystical experiences he had between 1921 and 1943, and then finally on numerous occasions between 1949 and 1953, while he was in a communal cell in Vladimir Prison. He says nothing at all about the conditions of his imprisonment, but we know from later published accounts that in the late 1940s, 10 x 10 foot cells sometimes housed as many as 30 persons.

At night, while his cellmates slept, Andreev made vast "transphysical" (a word he used in place of "spiritual") journeys, and returned with perfectly clear pictures of the landscapes through which he had passed. Like Dante, who had Virgil as his guide on his journey through the 9 Circles of Hell, the 7 Terraces of Purgatory, and the 9 Spheres of Heaven, Andreev had guides to help him interpret what he was seeing. Sometimes they appeared to him during the day, and in the crowded cell, he would lie down on the bed with his face to the wall, to hide the tears of joy streaming down his cheeks, so overcome was he by the presence of beings whose names he would not speak. At such times Andreev would conduct long conversations with these guides, via lucid inner speech, in which he could work out the names of the places and beings that he had encountered, since they were in an odd language for which his Russian tongue had no equivalent sounds.

Being a man of words, a gifted and passionate poet, Andreev carefully chose the words for his breathtaking supersensible geography. To describe his entire experience, he chose the Greek word *apocalypse*, which he understood to mean a revelation of "the destinies of peoples, realms, churches, cultures, all humanity, and of those hierarchies that take part in these destinies in a most active and direct manner." Through his *apocalypse* experiences, Andreev came to a revelation of what he termed "metahistory," the entirety of processes on invisible planes of being, which are intertwined with history.

Andreev described three stages of how this metahistorical knowledge came to him: first, "enlightenment"—lightning-quick episodes in which entire era of huge historical change were instantly synthesized; second, "contemplation"—a chain of inner states running daily for weeks or months, where he could consciously manipulate the "images"—which were more than just visual—that came before his inner organs of perception; third, "formulation"—interpretation, which Andreev said was the most removed from suprapersonal powers, and thus most prone to error.

Though presenting *Roza Mira* as a work of metahistory, it was equally unique as a work about Nature. Andreev was extremely critical of both the Western scientific-utilitarian attitude toward Nature and the "Arcadian" attitude, which he called "an unconscious egoistic-bodily love of nature." He was hopeful instead for a love of Nature that was enriched with moral and religious meaning, and that entered into relationship with the *stikhiali*—the elemental beings of Nature. Andreev stressed that this relationship would be completely different from the way that ancient peoples approached the elementals through propitiation and praise.

> For our part, we will strive to actualize our link with them through a readiness to participate in their play and creative work, through encouragement of their beneficent participation in our lives . . . and last, through aid to elementals of Light and through work in enlightening dark elementals.

Andreev offered a primer on how one can make contact with the elemental beings. He recommended cultivating an inner attitude that recognized the natural world as fully alive, aware, and kindly disposed toward them. As a result, a feeling of calm and joy would grow stronger, and that at such times, in natural settings, the elementals would begin to appear. Andreev knew that his report would be dismissed: "To serve up such fairy tales in the middle of the 20th century!" He answered by saying that his description of the elementals did not contradict the scientific method at all.

His own encounters with the elemental world had begun when he was 23, lasted for a couple of years, and then stopped. He returned often to the place in the Bryansk Forest in the Ukraine to summon them, with no success. Then, 20 years later, in his Vladimir Prison cell, the elementals reappeared when his "journeys" began. They were part of the intricate matrix of the vast, multi-planed realm he called *Shadanakar*,—the *bramfatura* (a system of integrated planes of existence) of the planet Earth. The physical plane, which he called *Enrof*, was only one of more than 240 planes making up the Earth. Each plane had its own geography, history, and inhabitants, and differed from Enrof in having more than three spatial dimensions, and multiple dimensions of time, flowing at different rates and in different directions. The highest planes in Shadanakar have 236 time streams. Each planet has its own elaborate system of bramfaturas, which could be accessed through the bramfatura of the earth. Think of Tolkien's *Lord of the Rings*, Ursula LeGuin's *Earthsea* series, Neil Gaiman's *American Gods*, and J.K. Rowling's *Harry Potter* books all rolled into one, and you have an inkling of Daniel Andreev's account of the realms beyond the "It Matters" plane of Enrof.

As in fantasy literature, common to each and every bramfatura is a division into Good and Evil beings, the latter—from the lowest to the highest—all clinging to a dream to become Lord of the Universe. While the true original principle in the Universe is Love, and God always and everywhere gives of Himself, the powers that rejected God are eternally trying to absorb everything into themselves—to *take*. They exist in an immense hierarchy that mirrors the hierarchy of the benevolent Beings, and just as at the pinnacle of the Divine hierarchy there is a Triune Being, the demonic beings have at their head a being called *Gagtungr*, who is composed of three beings—*Gisturg*, the Great Torturer; *Fokerma*, the Great Harlot; and *Urparp*, the Principle of Form. These correspond to the three evil beings whom we have considered: Ahriman, Lucifer, and Sorath.

Before describing the "metageography" of Shadanakar, Andreev predicted that soon hundreds, and eventually millions, would need this map. He likened his era to the situation at the beginning of the era of exploration and discovery, when only a handful of mariners had any use for a map of the whole planet. His metageography takes us from Enrof to: *Darainna*, the land of the elementals that care for roots and seeds—the tiny beings there look like white caps with another cap on top, and have gentle limbs that are like a cross between arms and wings; *Arashamf*, the abode of the tree elementals, some of whom have lived for hundreds of thousands of years; *Vayita*, a plane of moving air; *Faltora*, the land of elementals of field and meadow; *Liurna*, where each of the Earth's rivers has its own unique female elemental; *Vlanmim*, a rhythmically rolling bright blue ocean of masculine elementals, whose influence is noticeable in the moral fiber and even physical appearance of fishermen and sailors; *Zunguf*, the blanket of atmospheric moisture, and *Irudrana*, the land of elementals whose activity manifests on Earth as thunderstorms and hurricanes, and is portrayed in myths of Indra, Perun, Thor, and the

"Thunderbirds" of Native America; *Nivenna*, the land of frost and snowflakes, whose elementals have a particular fondness for childlike innocence and play. These are all "lesser" elementals; the Greater Elementals are supremely good Beings of "inexpressible majesty," with dominion over the four elements—*Vayumn* over Air, *Ea* over Water, *Povourn* over Fire (the fourth Andreev did not name).

Myths and legends from around the world have always declared that the elemental world can be as dangerous as it is generous; Andreev concurs. Again, he takes a geographic approach to these beings, naming their transphysical abodes: *Shartemakhum*, whose terrifying elementals of magma shoot up to the earth's surface during volcanic activity and earthquakes; *Gannix*, the region of quagmires, swamps, and bogs, where faceless, guileful elementals sought to lure humans of earlier ages; *Svix*, sandy deserts whose elementals attack passing souls between incarnations; *Nugurt*, whose mind-numbing elementals are active on the open sea; and *Duggur*, an urbanized region whose elementals perpetually luxuriate in carnal excess.

Like Ehrenfried Pfeiffer and Rudolf Steiner, Andreev saw one of humanity's principal tasks in coming centuries to be the "taming" of these demonic elementals, and a renewed reciprocity with the benevolent ones. When would this come about? Andreev believed it was already beginning:

A mysterious event is taking place in the metahistory of contemporary times: new divine-creative energy is emanating into our bramfatura. Since ancient times the loftiest hearts and subtlest minds have anticipated this event that is now taking place

He pointed to the late 18th/early 19th century as a time when the Virgin Mary began to emanate into Enrof in the form of apparitions, and then noted his fellow Russian Vladimir Solovyov's visions of the Divine Sophia—whom Andreev calls *Zventa-Sventana*, meaning "Holiest of the Holy"—at the end of the century.

Zventa-Sventana was the great Being who had already begun to cultivate the Rose of the World, each of whose petals was one of the world's great religions and cultures. In the future She would bring about spiritual reunification of all peoples, as the great world religions found common ground. He ends his book looking toward this future:

Feminine power and its role in contemporary life is increasing everywhere. It is that circumstance above all that is giving rise to worldwide peace movements, an abhorrence of bloodshed, disillusion over coercive methods of change, an increase in woman's role in society proper, an ever-growing tenderness and concern for children, and a burning hunger for beauty and love. We are entering an age when the female soul will become ever purer and broader, when an ever greater number of women will become profound inspirers, sensitive mothers, wise counselors and far-sighted leaders. It will be an age when the feminine in humanity will manifest itself with unprecedented strength, striking a perfect balance with masculine impulses. See, you who have eyes.

The most striking promise of this new Sophianic culture, according to Andreev, would be an end to war and tyranny, and the establishment of a world federation of states.

Freed from the gulag in April 1957, Andreev was reunited with his wife Alla, who had been arrested at the same time as he had, and had served her sentence in a concentration camp in Mordovia. Although in poor health, Andreev completed *The Rose of the World* and a number of long poetic works within 23 months after his release from prison. His health deteriorated seriously and he died on March 30, 1959. Shortly before his death, he reread *The Rose of the World*, suddenly declaring to his wife Alla: "No, it was not a madman who wrote it."

Alla Andreev, knowing that Soviet authorities the book would destroy the book, at first kept the manuscript buried in a birch forest in the northern Caucasus Mountains. After Mikhail Gorbachev and *glasnost* came, she published excerpts in a Moscow magazine; when the full text was published in 1991, the first edition of 100,000 copies quickly sold out. The Russian peoples' desire for the Invisible City of Kitezh had survived the Communist Party's attempt to destroy all vestiges of spirituality.

From Elementals to ETs

Standing behind Daniel Andreev's brief taxonomy of demonic elemental beings is an extravagant elucidation of hierarchic cosmic evil that makes Dante's *Inferno* and the whole of Christian demonology pale in comparison. Given Russia's long history of suffering under the rule of human demons, it seems altogether fitting that a Russian should serve as the 20th century Dante in classifying the otherworldly demons.

On his journeys Andreev had encountered a frightening array of demonic planes and entities: seven divisions of *Egregores*, the psychic essence of great collectives (tribes, states, parties, communities); *Eiphos*, radiations from human lust; *Igvas*, a highly intelligent race of demonic beings who appear to be identical with the "greys" of contemporary UFO abduction lore; *Raruggs*, great predators of prehistoric times that continue incarnating on the demonic planes, these beings look and behave exactly like the "lizards" of David Icke and others; *Witzraors*, powerful, intelligent predatory beings that lay behind the accumulation of state power. The Witzraors have tremendous impact on human metahistory, for they radiate an enormous amount of psychic energy that manifests in nationalist, patriotic feelings—including chauvinism, tyranny, and xenophobia—towards one's state. The Witzraors of some previous empires—Babylon, Rome, Byzantine—have perished, but Russia's Witzraor, named Zhrugr, is alive and well.

Andreev's demonic nomenclature reminds one of Tolkien's Elvish word for a particular class of demons, the "Orcs." Tolkien took his word from the Old English word for demon, and the word has spread from *Lord of the Rings* to computer role-playing games like *Warhammer* and *Warcraft*, and fantasy card games like *Dungeons and Dragons* and *Magic: The Gathering*. The modern male rage for these role-playing fantasies comes partly from the disappearance of the traditions imparted ancient understandings of the elemental beings, and how humans were to behave toward them. The tales carried subtle instruction that for all their seeming power, the ogres and goblins dwelling in darkness could be brought into the light, *by human thoughts and deeds.* In his *Ring* books, Tolkien gave the last glimpse of that wisdom, in his portrayal of the Orcs as the adversaries of benevolent elementals, the elves. Now in the place of this motherwit, boys (and girls!) are given violent virtual reality caricatures, with no instruction on how to tame these demons.

Confronted as we are on a daily basis by ample *human* evil, it perhaps seems perverse to seriously consider the existence of otherworldly evil, *but we are living in a time when that otherworldly evil has erupted onto the physical plane—Andreev's "Enrof."* Given the modern world's continual allegiance to an "It Matters" outlook on events and phenomena, this eruption of the demonic goes almost entirely unrecognized. The "airship" hysteria that opened the 20ᵗʰ century grew apace, until 1947, when search and rescue pilot Kenneth Arnold encountered "flying saucers" while flying near Mt. Rainier, in Washington state. On the heels of widespread fascination with and fear of "UFOs," the acronym given by the US Air Force to what it termed "unidentified flying objects."

These objects continue to go unidentified because of our "It Matters" blinders! Nearly a century ago, Rudolf Steiner warned that if the elemental beings that are "bewitched" in matter and sub-matter (magnetism, electricity, and nuclear forces) were not recognized and approached in the right way, they would ally themselves with Ahriman, and work against the human being. This is the true meaning of the abduction phenomenon, and the continued explosion of UFO sightings in the modern world.

The impasse—between the millions of individuals who have personally witnessed "lights in the sky" or had abduction experiences, and the consensus reality that ignores, denies, ridicules, or explains away their reports—that characterizes contemporary thinking about UFOs is another indication of the limitations of "It Matters" thinking. "Aliens" have been living in our backyards since we first started making our homes on Earth. In fact, they are the reason we can make our homes here! The "etheric" in which the elementals have their existence is essentially what modern science calls the "biosphere." But while Joan of Arc and her inquisitors, John of Sponheim, and even the post-Enlightenment spiritual scientist Goethe realized that there were two distinct classes of elementals—those supporting humans through their work in Nature, and those who raged against both Nature and the human being—we grant empirical status to neither!

The 20ᵗʰ Century as Humanity's Encounter with Evil

In the early 19ᵗʰ century, when the Grimm brothers were gathering the folk wisdom of old Europe into their *Kinder- und Hausmärchen* (*Children's and Household Tales*, 1812), they heard plenty of tales of demonic elementals, but they were geographically circumscribed, and the tale tellers always understood the harmful elemental activity as a result of human misdeeds toward them. The 20th century saw the episodes of elemental outbursts become more general, affecting entire regions. It was as if *there were a widespread opening between their "bramfatura" and ours.* There were plenty of shocks to the biosphere to cause such an opening: airplanes, then jets, then rockets ripped through the formerly serene sanctuary of the sylphs; the undines saw their sacred watery element polluted, commodified, and desacralized; gnomes, who had co-existed for hundreds of thousands of years with miners all over the globe, felt all manner of disturbance from new mining technologies. All of the elementals, good or ill, were unsettled by the advent of industrialized warfare, culminating in the use of the atomic bomb. The most pronounced rise in UFO sightings came after the Trinity test, and sightings continue to be quite common around nuclear power plants.

The rise in activity of the evil elementals was but one symptom of a more universal characteristic of the 20th century, *the encounter with evil*. Though historians have chronicled in detail the horrors of Bolshevism and Nazism; the violence of the battles for decolonization in Africa, Asia, and the Americas; the proxy conflicts between the superpowers during the Cold War; the many genocidal campaigns of tyrannical rulers against their own people, they have not yet been able to make sense of them. And who can make sense of humanity's continued warfare not only against each other, but against Nature, in the form of genetic engineering, electromagnetic and nuclear technologies, and the epidemic of global industrial pollution? There is the smell of brimstone about our civilization, as surely as there was in the Valley of Mexico during Aztec rule.

In our journey through the last five centuries of wonders and mysteries, we have turned from time to time to myths and fables and legends—the City of Kitezh; the *Parzival* saga; Goethe's *Green Snake and the Lily* fairy tale—to help us make sense of things. The world's most wonderful stories are true for all time, because they carry within themselves universal archetypes, *from out of the spiritual world, brought down onto the plane of the physical*. Along with all the destruction that has been waged by humanity within the history of the 20th century, the very story that the modern human tells about that history is itself a force for evil, in that it has no connection to the Good, the True, and the Beautiful, which have their archetypes in the spiritual world. Let us turn to Western civilization's moldy old mythic text, the Bible, to see if we might find there any wisdom for our own challenging times.

The central event of the Bible, and the central event of earthly evolution, is the three-and-a-half year life of the cosmic Sun Being, Christ, in the human being, Jesus of Nazareth. Jesus Christ's life from the Baptism until the Mystery of Golgotha bore an archetype for the future evolution of humanity, and so we can find its signature written into significant historical events in every century since AD 33. There is a deep mystery lying behind this fact. Perhaps the best way to imagine this is to think of your birth horoscope; at the moment of your birth, the configuration of the entire cosmos was written into your being. For Christ, this was true at *every moment of his life on Earth*. We saw how the 33-year rhythm of Christ's etheric body became a living rhythm within earthly history; now imagine that each day, each hour, each instant of the last 3 years of Jesus' life as a rhythm within that rhythm, that can and does manifest at different places and times, according to the unfolding of human destiny.

We have seen how different world traditions have pointed to this time—the 20th century—as particularly significant for humanity. The Hindu Kali Yuga ending in 1899 is the most well known example; we could add to this the ending of the Mayan Long Count in 2012, and various other ancient calendrical systems which point to this time. Why and how is there such a convergence? The answer lies in the canonical New Testament gospel texts of Mark, Matthew and Luke, where it is described how, immediately after Christ's descent into Jesus of Nazareth at the Baptism in the Jordan, "At once the Spirit sent him out into the desert, and he was in the desert forty days, being tempted by Satan. . . ." (Mark 1:12–13) This archetype of the temptation in the wilderness has many dimensions; at a microcosmic level, it speaks to how Christ experienced successively an attack by Lucifer in his astral body (the first temptation, "on a high mountain"); by both Lucifer and Ahriman in his etheric body (the second temptation, upon the "wing of the temple"); and by Ahriman in his physical body (the third temptation finds Jesus "hungry," that is, the Christ being has now completely united with Jesus' physical body, and experiences hunger).

Christ's overcoming of these temptations is an image for all humanity as a path toward the future; at the present time, every human individual is aided by divine spiritual powers—the Angels, Archangels, and Archai—to overcome the influences of Lucifer and Ahriman within his own *body*, but the individual must wage a battle against them himself in his *soul* members— Lucifer in his Sentient Soul; Lucifer and Ahriman in his Intellectual/Mind Soul; and Ahriman in his Consciousness Soul. One can imagine that at any time in modern history, the form that this battle takes will be shaped by the soul-state of a particular people. Transferred to the stage of East European history in the 16th century, we find Lucifer's influence over the predominately Sentient Soul stage of the Russian people expressed in Ivan the Terrible's reign; nearly two centuries later, Peter the Great's Intellectual Soul became prey to the combination of extraordinary Luciferic cruelty and an abstract, legalistic thought and civic life characteristic of Ahriman; finally, the Bolsheviks, led by the Ahrimanically-possessed Lenin and Trotsky, attacked the Consciousness Soul of the Russian people as it emerged in the 20th century.

The United States of America, born at the end of the 18th century primarily out of the peoples—Great Britain—in whom the Consciousness Soul was most acutely developed, is of particular interest to Ahriman. We already found that the Americas provide Ahriman with a favorable environment due to the magnetic forces here being channeled north and south by the mountains; can one find the archetype of Christ's temptation in the wilderness in American history?

As the American century, the 20th century bears the unmistakable stamp of the three temptations in the wilderness.[1] In first temptation, while Jesus was praying and fating in a cave on Mt. Attarus, Satan appears and promises Him everything "if you will fall down and worship me." Forced to "fast" by the economic depredations of the Great Depression, Americans of all classes were in dire straits, and thus prey to the temptations offered by various voices promising relief through authoritarian measures. Founder of the fascist "Silver Shirts," William Dudley Pelley traveled throughout the US orchestrating mass rallies, lectures, and public speeches— whose main topics were anti-Communism, antisemitism, racism, extreme patriotism, and isolationism—in order to attract Americans to his organization. Publisher Seward Collins

---

1. Note that the sequence of temptations given here runs *opposite* the sequence given in Matthew's Gospel, which is: (1) "If you are the Son of God, tell these stones to become bread"; (2) "If you are the Son of God, throw yourself down"; (3) "All this I will give you, if you will bow down and worship me." This is because all of the gospels were read by the evangelists in the Akashic Record, which runs in reverse order to earthly time; the Evangelist Matthew did not in this instance render the events in the proper order.

seduced American intellectuals toward fascism. Throughout the 1930s, Father Charles Coughlin supported Hitler and Mussolini and denounced President Roosevelt in radio broadcasts that sometimes reached as much as one-third of the entire nation. White nationalists, the KKK, and a variety of other hate groups spread fear throughout the land, intimidating minorities as a way of bolstering their own authority.

Christ avoided Satan's temptation at Mt. Attarus with the reply "You shall worship the Lord your God and him only you shall serve"; despite the pressures to succumb to home-grown fascism, Americans in the 1930s resisted the temptation to bow before demagogues, the country re-elected Franklin Roosevelt and largely embraced the New Deal, which was a communitarian-spirited endeavor. Still, from widespread support for sexual sterilization laws and other eugenic measures; to widespread lynchings of African-Americans and other civil rights abuses; to American bankers, industrialists and publishers (William Randolph Hearst most conspicuously) who for their own financial interests aided, abetted, and championed European Fascism, America manifested multiple instances of succumbing to the temptation to fall down, worship, and execute Evil. Germany, the leading representative of the Consciousness Soul, succumbed totally to the temptation of the will to power, led by Adolf Hitler.

33⅓ years on from January 1933, when Hitler became Reichschancellor, takes us to May 1966. At that time the Etheric Christ was active in awakening a new spirit of love and community among humanity. I was ten in 1966, and I remember that in 6th grade, some friends and I dressed up in bell-bottoms and plastic love beads and paisley shirts, to perform "Where Have All the Flowers Gone?" Written by Pete Seeger shortly after he had been indicted by the House Un-American Activities Committee, the song became popular after Peter, Paul and Mary recorded it. We admired the communitarian impulse we saw in our older brothers and sisters who piled into Love Bugs and psychedelic-painted VW vans to head north to Max Yasgur's farm for three days of love and harmony in the mud of "Woodstock." Even more than in the impulse toward communes or the flourishing of the peace movement in opposition to the Vietnam War, one can see this impulse in the triumphs of the civil rights movement in America; the liberation movements in Latin America and Africa; the women's movement.

Once again, however, the impulse toward love was met by opposition. From the dark machinations that stood behind the assassinations of President John Kennedy, his brother Bobby, Malcolm X, and Martin Luther King, to the destructive hedonism and illusions fostered by drug culture, it was as if Lord Stanhope and the Countess von Hochberg were again afoot. Matthew describes Satan's second temptation of Jesus as "casting oneself down from the pinnacle of the Temple." Certainly the 1960s saw this in the hedonistic surrender to base instinctual urges, often with the help of the new intoxicant—LSD—which was introduced to the world by the CIA. Instead of striving toward the pinnacle of the temple—the clear light of conscience and reason—a generation cast itself down by abandoning ego consciousness in favor of subconscious drives and impulses.

The last temptation of Christ described by Matthew's Gospel is that of "turning stones into bread." This is the temptation to substitute lifeless matter—"stones"—in place of the living substance, or "bread." I think of the *New York Times* headline that I just saw the other day, announcing that digital technologies would be the hottest sellers in toys this holiday season—for toddlers!!! The silica-based virtual reality *looks* alive, but it ain't alive! It ain't bread, but stones! This temptation for humanity that arose particularly at last century's end is all too currently with us as humanity enters its 21st year. My job as a teacher of history is in many ways a struggle to present what I consider to be bread—living pictures *that you make inside your own head*—as an alternative to the stones—the relentless cascade of virtual images—that modern culture fills you with daily.

The Coming of the Beast From the Abyss

In the last chapter we contemplated two earlier rhythms of the Beast of the Apocalypse, Sorath, whose "number" is 666. Do we find the Beast active at the time of the third rhythm, in 1998? Terry Boardman, an astute observer of Anglo-American occult politics, has this cogent diagnosis:

The New World Order has been proclaimed; there is one almighty superpower whose social heart is mightily afflicted; from this superpower has come the all-encompassing World Trade Organisation, the World Bank, the IMF, the UN, even the EU, NAFTA and APEC; a world wide web has been spun around the globe by computer spiders and satellitic insects; the uniform cultural values, icons, and language of Americanism are spread throughout the world by media monarchs like Rupert Murdoch and Bill Gates; megacorporations like Glaxo-Smith-Kline-Beecham, Sony-Columbia-Microsoft emerge. Distracting us all from angels desperate to help us, Hollywood's UFO aliens fix us all in their X-Files. The all-affecting Millennium Computer Bug threatens socio-economic breakdown. In the victorious "democratic" West which won the Cold War, CCTV cameras are erected in even the smallest towns to spy on fear-ridden citizens in the name of security. The world-spanning Internet is controlled by a group of supercomputers in one country, whose paranoid government wishes to ban encryption codes so that it may know everyone's computer communications. Paralleling a new interest in reincarnation, genetic technology, the Human Genome Project, neo-Darwinian evolutionary biology, and the physicists' Holy Grail of the Grand Unified Theory of Everything, seek to reduce all life itself to new levels of matter. This neo-Darwinian philosophical development in the West claims to bravely accept a random meaningless evolution based on blind natural selection and adaptation. This in turn underpins the current economic model of post-Cold War, red-in-tooth-and-claw, free market capitalism. The neo-Darwinian world view is said to be "grander" and "more awe-inspiring than the old ontological superstitions of religions," and it is as the new self-evident and objectively true "scientific'" orthodox world view that it is being increasingly promoted from the top down by mainstream media. In parallel to this philosophical centralizing orthodoxy from the cardinals of science in our age, there is mushrooming up from below with an inexorable energy the people's enthusiasm for myriad forms of spirituality, be they ancient, Asiatic, New Age, neurotic, fundamentalist, or free-spirited. While the news media occasionally feel they need to acknowledge the existence of this popular spirituality, they mostly focus on death, party political games of division, sexual and gender-based divisions, materialistic technology, and ecological devastation. There are cultic mass suicides, massacres in Algeria, Rwanda, war in Iraq near Gondishapur, with Palestine threatened. In many of the events around 1998, we see Sorathic willing—false or misdirected willing.

As we saw, we need to consider a broader period of activity than a single year; what if we considered a period of 3 years on either side of 1998? The third temptation's theme of stones vs. bread (or the alternative: stones = bread, i.e., the power of gold over life) is again apparent, in that a major theme of the year is the triumph of the forces of money and greed. The year opened with the establishment of the World Trade Organization. A few days later began the 104th Congress, the first with Republicans in control of both houses since 1953; its "Contract with America" (better known as the "Contract *on* America"!), a set of legislation rolling back progressive social initiatives, began in earnest the era of Orwellian doublespeak (in such legislation as the "Fiscal Responsibility Act," the "Personal Responsibility Act," the "American Dream Restoration Act," and "National Security Restoration Act") that would become the true hallmark of the Bush administration. The Dow Jones average closed above 4,000 in February, and then hit 5000 in November, the first time the Dow ever hit two "millennium marks" in a single year. It was a clear signal that money was indeed triumphing over *manna*.

Three years out from 1998, we arrive at the year 2001, and the events of September 11. How curious that today, seven years after these events, they are known the world over by a name that is simply the date when they occurred, and even that is typically abbreviated to just the numbers, "9/11." It is as if once again Ahriman is showing off his love of cold calculation. Indeed, cold calculation of some mysterious consortium of individuals lies behind the attacks on the World Trade Center, the Pentagon, and Congress; cold calculation followed by the neocon-organized rush to war against Afghanistan and Iraq; and cold calculation has stymied citizens seeking answers to their questions about the actual events on that day. Clearly, this event will remain as mysterious to us as Kaspar Hauser's murder unless we escape "It Matters" logic for "It Spirits" penetration of the occult crime lying behind it.

Revelations continue to come out, and will no doubt continue to come out, that indicate that members of the Bush administration were instantly prepared to exploit the attack for their own ideological purposes; many believe that some of them even helped to orchestrate the attacks. Still, the most perceptive analyses of the "dynastic crime" will do little to highlight the occult crime that undoubtedly stands behind it.

The "Crime of the Century"—perhaps the crime of the millennium—that began with the September 11 attacks is in full swing. A friend of mine likes to refer to it as the PNAC, the "Plan for the New *Ahrimanic* Century," and indeed, that is the occult crime to which we need to awaken—the crime of Ahriman's impending incarnation, which is the counter-event to Christ's incarnation in the etheric realm that began in 1933.

Like Judas' scorpion kiss of betrayal; like the burning of Joan of Arc; the rise of Aztec black magical rites; the incarceration and killing of Kaspar Hauser, the tyranny of Ivan the Terrible, Peter the Great, Joseph Stalin; the assassination of Franz Ferdinand and World War I; even Hitler and the Holocaust, this incarnation *had to be*. What was it that Rudolf Steiner said? "It should not have happened like this, but what happened was necessary," or, as my Cajun friend Bobby Matherne likes to say: "EAT-O-TWIST!, which is an acronym for "Everything Always Turns Out The Way It's Supposed To!"

What is supposed to be happening to humanity now—and particularly in our upstart nation, the United States of America, the first country in history born without an actual *name*— is that we are meant to meet and overcome the powers of evil. The journey of the prodigal son that humanity has been taking for all these centuries has swung way out like a pendulum bob, away from our source in the Divine, in order to initiate us into a condition of *Freedom* and *Love*. The reason why we are all here *right now* is to turn this planet, this humanity, this cosmos, from being a mere cosmos of wisdom into a true *Cosmos of Love*. Take a look at that drawing of Ashley's again. No one can do this but us.

To do this, we have to be free to make a choice, and freedom requires opposition, determined, brutal, cunning opposition. That is where Lucifer, Ahriman, Sorath, and the hosts of demons come in. They've been honing their weapons through these 500 years and long before that, all for the showdown *in our time*. Now perhaps you can understand why I have taught this course in such an unorthodox manner. *The time is at hand!* The greatest weapon that the adversarial powers have over us is our own sleepiness, which they work round the clock to encourage. But without this opposition from them, *we could not wake up*. Parzival needed to encounter Klingsor and overcome him before he could return to the Grail Castle and "wake" Amfortas. Same goes for us.

And Behold, Angels Came and Ministered unto Him

"Then the devil left Him, and behold, angels came and ministered unto Him." So says Matthew at the conclusion to the three temptations by Satan. We have not as yet completely passed through the period of the temptations, but it is not too early to look for Angelic assistance. As you might have guessed, the Angels are here, standing ready to help, but our "It Matters" mindset blinds us to their presence.

"That's enough, Dr. Dann! For 12 chapters I have listened to your crap about fairies and angels and demons, and I have held my tongue. I want proof! Show me something, anything, that proves that angels and fairies are real."

OK. Follow me. *Wait, where are we going?! I have to get to my next class…*

As luck would have it, we touched down at Milk Field, outside the village of Alton Barnes, in Wiltshire, England, on August 8, 2008, the opening day of the Beijing Olympics. I spared pointing out to you that the games will begin at 8 minutes and 8 seconds past 8 PM, on this 8th day of the 8th month in the 8th year of the millennium, because the Chinese word for "eight" in Mandarin sounds similar to the word which means "prosper" or "wealth". I resist the temptation to connect this very present day magical thinking with some of the themes of the course. I'm through lecturing you. I've had enough. You have clearly had enough. It's time for show, not show & tell.

We get to the field just as the sun is setting, turning the chalk White Horse—a massive figure carved into a hillside—pink, then crimson. There are a dozen or so cars parked at the edge of the field, and we can see people following the tramlines out toward the crop circle. We follow them through the waist-high barley. When we get to the first circle, we kneel among the bent plants and pull one toward us. It is completely normal, except at the node, where the stem makes a sharp angle. Each and every one of the "fallen" plants has this same angle in the node, while all around them grow countless normal, erect stems.

It's as if some giant had focused his breath through a straw and blown down these plants, without killing them or even breaking them slightly.

Oh good, you are interested, I think. We walk on, greeting the other people in the circle. They are all grinning from ear to ear, and tell us that it appeared at dawn that morning. One particularly jolly fellow comes over and tells us: "I've seen the aerial shots. The formation shows the phases of the Moon leading up to the next lunar eclipse, on August 16th. Each of the circles is sized relative to the area of the moon visible at that phase. There are also little spikes between some of the circles, to indicate when the Moon will be visible above the horizon at sunset."

Our eyes are glazing over, but I am secretly delighted that the circlemakers picked an astronomical subject.

"It's all about rhythm, isn't it?" I volunteer.

"Definitely," he says. "And hey, there's a Celtic cross overlaid on the central Moon—the Full Moon. That's the symbol for Earth, and shows the day of the eclipse."

Dr. Dann, none of this makes any sense to me. I need to see this thing from the air. Can we charter a helicopter?

"I've got a better idea." As the man walked off toward another part of the field, I lead you up a small hill in the opposite direction, thinking that perhaps it was a high enough vantage to get some sense of the geometry of the figure in the field. At the top of the hill, it was still far too shallow an angle to discern any shape. A helicopter was circling the field.

"Lie down," I said. You do, and so do I.

"Close your eyes. Now picture yourself getting up out of your body, and running down the hill until you get full speed. Now, *jump!*"

Now we are up over the formation, over the helicopter.

Dr. Dann! It's a figure 8—what's the big deal?! It's just a figure 8.

"Lemniscate, a lemniscate," I say. "The Swiss mathematician Jacob Bernoulli first called that figure a *Lemniscus*—that's Latin for "ribbon"—in 1694, 40 years after English mathematician John Wallis used it as the sign for infinity."

Oh, c'mon Dr. Dann, lay off of it, will ya? We're not in class anymore. We're... Hey, what's that? It's us! There are our bodies, down there on the hill. What's with that, Dr. Dann?!

"Good question. Hey, you hear that music? Sounds like R.E.M. Yeah, that's 'It's the End of the World as We Know It.'"

Oh man, Dr. Dann. That's not the name of that song. It's 'I Feel Fine.'

"That's much better. Thanks."

Thank you, Dr. Dann. And, hey... PAKWANONZIAN!

Bibliographical Essay

Chapter 1

For the legend of the Invisible City of Kitezh, I have drawn upon Chapter 12 in Sergei Prokofieff, *The Spiritual Origins of Eastern Europe and the Future Mysteries of the Holy Grail* (Temple Lodge Publishing: 1993). I quote briefly from the popular world history textbook by Robert L Tignor et al., *Worlds Together, Worlds Apart: A History of the Modern World from the Mongol Empire to the Present*, (W.W. Norton: 2002). *Ghengis Khan*, by Jacob Abbott, (Harper & Brothers: 1902). The text can be found online at: *http://www.mainlesson.com/display.php? author=abbott&book =genghis&story=_contents.*

This text is offered through The Baldwin Project, which makes available online a wonderful collection of resources for parents and teachers of children. Many popular works of history from before 1923 (and thus in the public domain) are available at the site, which offers a wealth of literary material—Nursery Rhymes, Fables, Folk Tales, Myths, Legends and Hero Stories, Literary Fairy Tales, Bible Stories, Nature Stories, Biography, History, Fiction, Poetry, Storytelling, Games, and Craft Activities—that constitute an incredible resource for classroom teachers.

I used to assign Marco Polo's *Travels* (*Travels of Marco Polo*, Manuel Komroff, editor, W.W. Norton: 2003), even though they come before the time period of our course, because they are just downright charming. I now regularly hear in class from students that they have been told by other history teachers that "they think that Marco Polo never even went to China, and made it all up." Even his Venetian neighbors who knew his knack for storytelling would not go that far!

I also used to assign *Parzival*, for the pure pleasure of the story. If its appearance throughout this text has gotten your interest, a good translation is: Wolfram von Eschenbach, *Parzival* (trsl. Helen M. Mustard and Charles E. Passage; New York: Vintage Books, 1961).

You can find Jan Dlugosz's narration of the Battle of Legnica at: *http://www.impub.co.uk / dlug3.html.*

Chapter 2

Mark Twain's *Joan of Arc* has many editions; a recent one is from Ignatius Press, 1989. You might also enjoy the children's biography by Andrew Lang, *The Story of Joan of Arc*, (T.C. & E.C. Jack: 1906), which is available at the Baldwin Project site. In this chapter I quote briefly from Mary Gordon, *Joan of Arc* (Lipper/Viking: 2000). You can find Joan's Trial of Condemnation online at: *http://www.stjoan-center.com/Trials/sec14.html.*

Johannes Trithemius's *De Septum Secundeis* (*The Seven Secondary Intelligences*) can be found online at: *http://www.esotericarchives.com/tritheim/tritem.htm*.

Both of Noel L. Brann's books on Trithemius, *The Abbot Trithemius (1462–1516): The Renaissance of Monastic Humanism* (Brill: 1981) and *Trithemius and Magical Theology: A Chapter in the Controversy Over Occult Studies in Early Modern Europe* (SUNY Press: 1998), are full of wonderful detail, but lack an esoteric perspective on Trithemius's life. For an esoteric context, see Rudolf Steiner, *Mysticism at the Dawn of the Modern Age*, (Rudolf Steiner Publications: 1960); available online at: *http://wn.rsarchive.org/Books/GA007/English/GA007_index.html*.

Chapter 3

The general concepts of "perspectival" and the outlook on the magical and mythical forms of consciousness in this chapter are drawn from Jean Gebser's magisterial *The Ever-present Origin: Part One: Foundations of the Aperspectival World/ Part Two, Manifestations of the Aperspectival World*, (Ohio University Press: 1986). WOW! Before I ever met any esoteric writings, I found this book's evolution of consciousness framework the key for helping to make sense of world history. Gebser's book is also my source for the discussion of Petrarch.

Champlain's remarks are drawn from *The Works of Samuel de Champlain*, general editor H.P. Biggar, Publications of the Champlain Society, 6 volumes (1922–1936), reprinted facsimile (Toronto: University Press of Toronto, 1971), II:71. The recent 400th anniversary of the founding of Quebec has led to new scholarship on Champlain; see *Champlain: The Birth of French America*, edited by Raymonde Litalien and Denis Vaugeois; translated by Käthe Roth (Montreal: McGill-Queen's University Press, 2004).

Michael Ladwein's, *Leonardo da Vinci: The Last Supper: A Cosmic Drama and An Act of Redemption* (Temple Lodge: London, 2006) is a beautiful book, and a necessary antidote to current Dan Brown-inspired nonsense about Leonardo's *Last Supper*. The discussion of the gestures in this chapter draws also from conversations with Robert Powell, whose *Hermetic Astrology*, vol. II: *Astrological Biography* (San Rafael, California: Sophia Foundation Press, 2007), is the source for the final section of this chapter, on the relationship between the astrological and cultural ages, the precession of the equinoxes, and the Venus pentagram. See also his *History of the Zodiac* (San Rafael, California: Sophia Academic Press, 2007).

Chapter 4

My students are accustomed to long digressions from me about the origin, meaning, and history of words, and if I could, I would spend even more of our time together thinking about the words we use when we study history. Each word *is* a history, and there is no better way of studying that history for the English language than the *Oxford English Dictionary*. I wholeheartedly recommend you make its acquaintance; skip the online version and go hold the big heavy blue volumes in your hands instead. Your friendly reference librarian will point you toward it.

Gennadyi Bondarev's, *The Crisis of Civilization*: *Anthroposophy at the Crossroads of the*

Occult-Political Movements of the Present Time, (translated by Helga Schulte-Schröer, edited by Graham Rickett (Lochmann-Verlag: 1999) is a much more extensive look at some of the themes that I raise here about "deep politics."

Chapter 5

After many years of studying the large secondary literature on the Mexica, I recently read R.C. Padden's *The Hummingbird and the Hawk: Conquest and Sovereignty in the Valley of Mexico, 1503–1541* (Ohio State University Press: 1967). Along with being beautifully written, Padden is truly the only modern scholar of the Mexica whom I believe has fathomed the mythological "reversal" brought about by Tlacaellel. He makes excellent use of the standard primary works for the Conquest—Bernardino Sahagún, *Florentine Codex: History of the Things of New Spain*, translated and edited by Arthur J.O. Anderson and Charles Dibble (University of Utah Press, 1950–1982) and Diego Durán, *The History of the Indies of New Spain*, Doris Heyden, ed., *Civilization of the American Indian* series, #210, Norman: University of Oklahoma Press (1994). The chapter's perspective on the AD 33 events comes from the lectures of Rudolf Steiner in *Inner Impulses of Evolution: The Mexican Mysteries and the Knights Templar* (Hudson, NY: Anthroposophical Press, 1984).

My discussion of Mexica concepts of the subtle body comes from *The Natural History of the Soul in Ancient Mexico*, (Yale University Press: 1997), by Jill McKeever Furst.

D.A. Brading's *Mexican Phoenix: Our Lady of Guadalupe: Image and Tradition Across Five Centuries* (Cambridge University Press: 2002) is a perfect exemplar of what "It Matters" scholarship does with miracles. All of the excellent documentary research in the book is founded on the assumption that *there was never an apparition of the Virgin to Juan Diego*. This is true of *all* the scholarly books on this event; for a different view one must look at the devotional literature. An exception is the beautiful work of art by Carla Zarebska, *Guadalupe* (University of New Mexico Press: 2004). The power of both the original vision and its vital power down through the centuries are captured in this extraordinary book.

Chapter 6

I quote very briefly from Hendrik van Loon's *The Story of Mankind* (Harrap: 1922). It is very hard to only quote van Loon briefly, for his witty way of speaking about the past is irresistible. He is equally winning on geography, art, science, biography, literature, and I steal this moment to bring him to your attention. His books were extremely popular in their day, so you can pick up most any of his dozens of works (always whimsically illustrated by the author) in used bookshops for $5 or $10.

My understanding of the "symptomatology" (Rudolf Steiner's term) of Russian history, from the Mongols through Stalin, comes from Sergei Prokofieff's *The Spiritual Origins of Eastern Europe and the Future Mysteries of the Holy Grail*. For the discussion of the period from Ivan the Terrible, through the episode of the false Dmitri, to Peter the Great's rule, see Chapter 16;

much of the most interesting material is in Prokofieff's extensive footnotes. Ernest A. Zitser's *The Transfigured Kingdom: Sacred Parody and Charismatic Authority at the Court of Peter the Great* (Cornell University Press: 2004) is a brilliant discussion of the "All-Drunken Council," and its importance for an understanding of Peter's empire.

You can read Goethe's fairy tale, helpful esoteric commentary and interpretation, and a description of how it played a central role in Rudolf Steiner's teachings, in *The Time Is at Hand!: The Rosicrucian Nature of Goethe's Fairy Tale of the Green Snake and the Beautiful Lily and the Mystery Dramas of Rudolf Steiner* (SteinerBooks: 1995), by Paul Marshall Allen and Joan Deris Allen.

Chapter 7

This chapter is largely drawn from my own biography of Thoreau, *Expect Great Things: The Life of Henry David Thoreau* (in manuscript). My understanding of 19th century Spiritualism relies on a number of lecture cycles of Rudolf Steiner, which can be found in *The Occult Movement in the Nineteenth Century* (Rudolf Steiner Press: 1973) and *Spiritualism, Blavatsky, and Theosophy: An Eyewitness Account of Occult History* (Steiner Books: 2002). For a fascinating corroborating account by a member of the Berean Society, an English occult brotherhood, see C. G. Harrison, *The Transcendental Universe: Six Lectures on Occult Science, Theosophy, and the Catholic* (SteinerBooks: 1993).

Chapter 8

Though the translation from the original German is often awkward, there is no finer plumbing of the depths of the Kaspar Hauser story than Peter Tradowsky's *Kaspar Hauser: The Struggle for the Spirit: A Contribution Towards an Understanding of the Nineteenth and Twentieth Centuries* (Temple Lodge: 1997). Also see Terry Boardman, *Kaspar Hauser: Where Did He Come From?* (Wynstones Press: 2006), which goes even farther than Tradowsky's book in considering the historical rhythms emanating from Kaspar Hauser. Boardman's book also goes into detail about the occult brotherhoods behind Kaspar's abduction and murder.

Chapter 9

The karmic relationships of and reincarnation research on Wagner, Ludwig II, and Nietzsche are detailed in Robert Powell, *Hermetic Astrology*, volume II. David Tresemer's *Star Wisdom and Rudolf Steiner: A Life Seen through the Oracle of the Solar Cross* (Steiner Books: 2007) has additional insights on Friedrich Nietzsche.

Chapter 10

The principle source for this chapter is Sergei O. Prokofieff's Rudolf *Steiner and the Founding of the New Mysteries* (Temple Lodge Publishing: 1994). It also draws upon Tradowsky's *Kaspar*

Hauser and a variety of lecture cycles from Rudolf Steiner; many of these can be accessed online at: *http://www.rsarchive.org/Lectures/Dates.*

Chapter 11

Rudolf Steiner's lectures that reveal the workings of the secret brotherhoods in causing the war are collected in *The Karma of Untruthfulness: Secret Societies, the Media, and Preparations for the Great War* (Rudolf Steiner Press: 2005), 2 volumes; these include two exceptional introductions by Terry Boardman. The chapter's discussion of Bolshevism and Fascism is taken principally from, respectively, Prokofieff, *Spiritual Origins of Eastern Europe*, and Tradowsky, *Kaspar Hauser*. The understanding of the 33-year rhythm is drawn from Tradowsky and from Robert Powell, *Chronicle of the Living Christ* (Steiner Books: 1996).

Perhaps you were curious about this chapter's enigmatic final subhead: *Look Up, Hannah!* That is the commonly accepted title for the speech made by the barber, who is mistaken for "Hynkel," and thus gets a national audience for a speech that makes a fervent plea for peace and brotherhood. Like much of the rest of *The Great Dictator*, this has to be seen to be believed. You can see this speech, and other choice excerpts from the film (including Hynkel's globe dance), on YouTube.

Chapter 12

The descriptions of the 1954 "Unity of Knowledge" conference, and the activities at the Trailside Museum are drawn from my book, *Across the Great Border Fault: The Naturalist Myth in America* (Rutgers University Press: 2000).

There are very few sources in English that take up Daniel Andreev's *Rose of the World* (SteinerBooks: 1997). Mikhail Epstein, "Daniel Andreev and the Russian Mysticism of Femininity," in *The Occult in Russian and Soviet Culture*, ed. by Bernice Glatzer Rosenthal (Cornell University Press: 1997) is a brief but excellent scholarly analysis that puts the book in helpful cultural and historical context.

The presentation of the three temptations in the 20th century comes largely from Powell, *Chronicle of the Living Christ*. Other sources for this chapter include: Rudolf Steiner, *The Reappearance of Christ in the Etheric* (London: Rudolf Steiner Press, 1972); Sergei Prokofieff, *The Encounter with Evil and Its Overcoming Through Spiritual Science: With Essays on the Foundation Stone* (Temple Lodge Publishing: 2000); and Terry Boardman, "Aspects of the Occult Significance of the Year 1998," at: *http://www.monju.pwp.blueyonder.co.uk/OccSig1998.htm.*

Printed in the United States
209329BV00004B/1-132/P

9 781597 311656